The Journey West

CALIFORNIA PIONEER SERIES

The Journey West

ELAINE SCHULTE

Guideposts®

CARMEL • NEW YORK 10512

This Guideposts edition is published by special arrangement with
LifeJourney Books, an imprint of Chariot Family Publishing.

THE JOURNEY WEST
© 1989 by Elaine Shulte

(Another version of this book was previously published under the title
Westward, My Love.)

Edited by LoraBeth Norton

Illustration by Kathy Kulin

Printed in the United States of America

Schulte, Elaine L.
        The Journey West
        (California pioneer series; bk. 1)
        I. Title. II. Series: Schulte, Elaine L. California pioneer series; bk. 1
PS3569.C5395J68   1989   813'.54   89-23954
ISBN 1-55513-986-8

*In memory of our
sisters and brothers
who brought His love
by covered wagon*

Prologue

Benjamin Talbot gazed out the open carriage window as the horses clip-clopped up the cobbled drive to Miss Sheffield's School for Young Ladies. The soft evening air held a scent of lilacs and distant pines, and birds twittered across the estate garden, flitting from the trees to the splendid statues that surrounded the massive gray stone edifice. "Another French chateau transplanted to the state of New York," he observed.

His young companion, Daniel Wainwright, nodded as he peered out the carriage window.

Benjamin asked, "How could a girl possibly leave such luxurious surroundings to go to the frontier?"

"If she goes," Daniel answered. "It may be she will marry the banker in the city."

"Perhaps. She wouldn't be the first young woman to marry for position and money," Benjamin said, "though I should not like to think of my niece married to him."

"But to move from such a wealthy life to Missouri . . . and then to a foreign place like California—" Daniel objected.

Benjamin smoothed down his thatch of graying hair. "Perhaps she is meant to be part of the journey. I hadn't

1

considered that possibility, but now that I reflect on it, why else would all of this have happened to her?"

"I have a curious feeling," Daniel said, "almost a premonition. . . ."

Benjamin turned to him. "Yes?"

Daniel shook his head, then his blue eyes filled with amusement and he smiled through his dark beard. "Only a curious feeling, nothing else. . . ."

"Ofttimes it behooves us to give credence to curious feelings," Benjamin replied as the carriage drew to a halt.

1

Abby Windsor Talbot lifted her sapphire-blue evening dress decorously as she descended the grand staircase of Miss Sheffield's School for Young Ladies. *Take heed*, she reminded herself. The numerous petticoats under the bouffant bell skirt made the marble steps more treacherous than usual, and it was precisely here that one was apt to be caught for lack of grace and propriety. Ever since supper, she had harbored a vague premonition that something might go amiss, and this was no time for complications, not with her Class of 1845 graduation only weeks hence.

"Wait for me, Abby!" her roommate, Rose Wilmington, whispered insistently from the upper hallway.

No one else was about, and Abby lingered on the landing, enjoying the early evening sunshine that streamed through the open French windows. Spring had burst with splendor over the estate grounds, and a fine black carriage had just halted at the front door.

Rose arrived on the landing, breathless. "Abby—do you know that you look like a painting for the Louvre? Yes, you do! *Blonde Beauty on a Marble Staircase!*"

"Oh, Rose! I only look nice because you dressed my chignon and I'm not wearing a wretched uniform."

3

After wearing the gray school garb day after day, month after month, she had scarcely recognized herself in the mirror: silk evening dress and sapphire pendant as blue as her eyes, golden hair wound into a French chignon, long white gloves. She would be seventeen years old tomorrow, and finally she was beginning to give every appearance of her new maturity.

She glanced at her roommate and best friend, who wore a pale green silk gown that set off her black hair and brown eyes. "You're a painting yourself. I would title it *Raven-Haired Beauty Descending a Marble Staircase!*"

Rose laughed. "It is being free of those uniforms. We should have a class burning of them in the drawing room fireplace!"

They laughed together at the very notion of such an event.

Starting down the lower flight of stairs, Abby took pleasure in the luxurious entrance hall, especially the exquisite Persian rug and magnificent portrait of the school's founder. She was scarcely conscious of a maid's opening the ornately carved double doors, but at the sight of two men visitors, Abby paused for an instant. The men were well dressed in black broadcloth suits and vests, and white linen shirts with high stocks around their necks. "*Two Gentlemen Calling,*" she whispered to Rose, continuing their pastime of bestowing titles upon people and scenes as if they were paintings.

"Perfect!" Rose barely suppressed her smile as they proceeded to the marble entrance where the men now stood.

Abby glanced at them again. They looked familiar. Had she seen them before? The younger man, perhaps thirty, was tall and bearded, darkly handsome with intense blue eyes. The gray-haired gentleman was clean-shaven and rather avuncular; for a moment she had the impression that he might step toward her, but he apparently reconsidered.

Passing by them, Abby and Rose entered the adjacent ballroom. "How I shall miss this," Abby murmured as she admired the frescoed ceiling, potted palms, and graceful French furniture. The ballroom was especially charming this evening, for its entire west wall of French doors was open to capture the soft spring breezes, and most of their classmates had assembled to practice for the mid-May reception and musicale that would take place on Saturday.

"Who are the men?" Rose inquired.

"I don't know."

Rose blinked in surprise. "I thought perhaps you did. The older one seemed to recognize you. The younger one is so handsome . . . and romantic with that dark beard. And those blue eyes! Like the sea at Marblehead!"

"Oh, really, Rose!" Abby replied with amusement. She turned to see the maid escort the men out of their line of vision. "They did appear familiar at first, but I can't place them."

She forgot all about the visitors at the sight of her classmates in their bright flounced and ruffled gowns instead of their usual gray uniforms. Someone played a lively air on the piano and voices bubbled with excitement. "If only I had my sketching pad and watercolors, I could capture this scene forever."

"Always the artist," Rose said, smiling with pride at her friend. "Perhaps you'll be a great one someday."

"A woman artist? I'd surely have to change my name to—Abner!" Abby returned, and they both laughed again.

She noticed Rose's perfume. "Fleur-de-lis?"

Rose smiled impishly. "Fleur-de-lis."

"What if Miss Sheffield notices?" Their headmistress was

adamant about her young ladies not using artifices such as face colors and scents, which she termed "nothing but common."

"I don't care," Rose returned with daring. "William gave it to me, and I feel closer to him when I wear it."

"You are hopeless!"

"And you're too sensible, Abby. Wait until you fall in love!" Rose beamed at her, then said with joyous anticipation, "Just three more days until William arrives!"

Abby gave a laugh. "I may be sensible, but I'm afraid you're far beyond curing!"

"I hope someday you'll be smitten, too," Rose replied with her usual good humor. "Love is wonderful. I never understood until I fell into love myself." Rose, like many of their classmates, was eighteen and engaged to be married this summer.

"I wouldn't know," Abby admitted.

"Would you wear Cornelius Adams's perfume if perchance he presented some to you?"

"It's difficult to imagine him giving me something so personal," Abby answered. The only romance between Cornelius and herself, she sometimes thought, was at their families' insistence.

"Ladies, please!" Miss Page clapped her hands, and her charges quieted, only to be interrupted by Miss Sheffield's assistant hurrying into the ballroom. The two women spoke quietly, their eyes darting momentarily to Abby, then the adviser said, "Miss Talbot, you may be excused to go to Miss Sheffield's drawing room."

Me? Abby almost asked, but stopped the impulse. "Yes, Miss Page," she said and started for the hallway. Why would the headmistress want to see her? Did her summons have something to do with the two men?

At Miss Sheffield's drawing room door, Abby nervously smoothed her skirt, tidied her chignon, and knocked.

After a moment Miss Sheffield opened the door, her expression as severe as her dyed black hair which was skinned back into a perfect bun. "Won't you please come in, Miss Talbot?" she invited. She held her chin high, accentuating her long neck.

The gracious drawing room and its beautiful European furniture were an inappropriate setting for the headmistress's severity, Abby thought as she stepped in.

It was a moment before she noticed the two men she'd seen at the front door. As they rose from their chairs, Abby suddenly recognized the older. "Why, you're . . . you're my father's brother—Uncle Benjamin from Missouri!"

He smiled warmly, his brown eyes shining. "I'm pleased that you remember, Abigail." He stepped forward to take her hand in his. "It's been ten years since I called at your home in New York City."

"I thought you looked familiar when I saw you at the door, but you wore a beard ten years ago!"

"And my hair wasn't graying," he added with a chuckle, "and you weren't yet such a beautiful young woman. I was almost certain it must be you . . . and your Grandmother Talbot's sapphire pendant, which suits you so perfectly."

Abby's hand went to the pendant at the modestly scooped neckline of her blue gown. "Thank you." Noticing the laughter lines around his eyes and mouth, she guessed her uncle was a convivial person, though his expression was now growing quite somber.

He turned to introduce the young man beside him. "Perhaps you also remember Mr. Daniel Wainwright."

She extended her hand to him, aware of his intense blue eyes upon her. "You visited my family together. You were a student . . . at Harvard, I think, Mr. Wainwright."

Daniel Wainwright's hand engulfed hers. "Exactly. I'm surprised that you remember. I was the beardless one then."

She smiled. "Yes, of course. It's a pleasure to see you again, too." Ordinarily she did not care for bearded men, but his wavy dark beard suited his manner and arresting face. How she'd love to attempt his portrait. And she did remember him! In fact, he'd made such a strong impression that she'd fantasized about him for weeks after his departure.

"Won't you all be seated?" Miss Sheffield suggested. "I regret there is unpleasant news for you, Miss Talbot."

"Unpleasant news?" Abby repeated as she sat down on the rose-colored settee beside her uncle.

"Mr. Talbot, if you would please proceed," Miss Sheffield suggested.

Benjamin Talbot cleared his throat. "I'm afraid it concerns your parents, Abigail. It seems there was a boating accident in the Mediterranean, a most unfortunate accident—"

"Yes?" Abby asked with a stab of fear. When he didn't reply immediately, she quickly put in, "Were they . . . were they injured?"

He shook his head. "I'm sorry that's not all it is. The fact is that . . . that they have both passed on. Fortunately they did not suffer, which is a blessing—"

"You mean they are d—dead?" Abby asked, stunned.

"Yes, child," her uncle replied. His strong but kind face filled with sympathy. "They have gone on to the next life."

Tears burst to her eyes. "But they are on their return voyage from France now! They promised to be here for graduation!" Her mouth trembled and she pressed her lips together.

Miss Sheffield said stiffly, "Compose yourself, Miss

Talbot. There is a great deal to be accomplished at times like this. You must not lose control of your emotions."

Despite the turmoil spinning in her head, Abby managed a tremulous, "Yes, Miss Sheffield."

"Abigail, my dear," her uncle began, "I know this comes as a dreadful shock to you." He spoke on, but the words merely floated about her . . . something about her resembling her Grandmother Talbot, who was so wonderfully strong . . . something about clinging to that kind of strength.

Miss Sheffield spoke up. "You have my deepest sympathies, Miss Talbot. I, too, had to summon up the courage to endure the deaths of my parents, and I assure you that you will come through such a tragedy all the stronger."

Abby stared at her blindly. "But they were to be here for my graduation—"

"Your graduation appears to be another problem, Abigail," her uncle said. "I am now your legal guardian, and I've had to make numerous decisions. Your Aunt Jessica and I are your only living older relations, and we invite you most wholeheartedly to live with us in Missouri. We have a pleasant house in Independence—not as grand as your parents' mansion on Union Square, of course."

"In Missouri!" she echoed. Her parents had said that Uncle Benjamin, despite his fine Boston education, had moved to the frontier, to the wilderness, next to Indian Territory. "Thank you, but I don't know—"

"We don't expect your answer yet. I only wanted you to know that you have another place to go," her uncle explained.

"But I was born and reared in New York City before coming to school here," she began. The house on Union Square was her home; she had assumed she would live there until she married and perhaps even then for what she'd expected to be a pleasant, unruffled life.

Her uncle's kindly voice spoke on, and <u>Abby</u> could only understand that she must leave with them tomorrow morning, that they would have a week to deal with affairs at her parents' house on Union Square . . . including a memorial service—a rite without even a last glimpse of Mother and Father!—and then they would leave for Missouri. It was inconceivable!

"But I must graduate!" she protested. "It was so important to Mother and Father! No other school than this would do—"

Uncle Benjamin reassured her, "I am certain you will be given your diploma since there are only a few weeks until graduation. I understand that you are a fine student—"

"I beg your pardon," Miss Sheffield said, "but we do not graduate young ladies who depart early. We have policies, and we are forced to uphold them, or this school would lose its reputation."

Uncle Benjamin's color rose. "Not receive her diploma when school is nearly finished? Under the circumstances, I find that unbelievable."

Miss Sheffield sat even more erectly in her chair. "Unfortunately, Miss Talbot's tuition for the semester remains unpaid. I expected it would be settled upon her parents' return from Europe . . . before the graduation ceremony of course."

Uncle Benjamin inhaled deeply. "Then I am afraid, madam, you would have been in for an unpleasant surprise." He looked regretfully at Abby. "I had hoped to break this all to you rather differently, but now I have little choice. The fact is that your father lost more and more money over the past years. If he had lived, he might have extricated himself from his financial difficulties since, after all, he was vice president of one of our country's largest banks."

"I don't understand . . ." Abby said, incredulous.

Her uncle replied sadly, "The estate is bankrupt."

"Bankrupt? That's impossible!" They'd always had money for anything they wanted. What could have happened? Father gambled, of course, and Mother called him improvident, but to be bankrupt—"Surely someone has made an error!"

"Unfortunately not," her uncle replied. "I know this must be shocking on top of your other news, but I will show you the books. It's clear that you must move West with us . . . unless, of course, you have other prospects."

Other prospects? He meant prospects for marriage! Did he know of her parents' hopes for her and Cornelius? If he'd been in New York and at the bank, he might have heard—

Her uncle interrupted her thoughts as he turned to the headmistress. "You have two options, Miss Sheffield. Either I can pay Abigail's tuition from my own funds and you give her the diploma . . . or I will pay nothing. I require your decision now."

Indignant, Miss Sheffield said, "Very well. You will have the diploma tomorrow morning upon receipt of the funds. I trust you will keep that as confidential as I intend to keep your financial affairs." She stood up in dismissal. "Please call for Abigail tomorrow morning promptly at ten o'clock. If there is nothing further, I shall see that her trunks are sent to her room now."

Abby swallowed with difficulty as they left Miss Sheffield's drawing room. In the hallway, she could only think that her parents were dead—dead!—and it seemed she was expected to act as if nothing upsetting had happened while her emotions flew about wildly.

At the foot of the staircase, she turned and met Daniel

Wainwright's gaze. "Courage," he said, his voice deep and vibrant. "Courage in trouble is half the battle."

"Yes," she replied. "I—I'll try to remember." Oddly, she did not resent his advice, perhaps because he gave off an aura of great inner strength.

Her uncle said, "We shall call for you then tomorrow morning. I deeply regret that we had to meet again under such unhappy circumstances. We are prepared to help you in any way possible."

She nodded wordlessly and hurriedly bid the men a more tremulous good evening than she wished.

Courage in trouble is half the battle, she reminded herself and clung to the thought.

Upstairs, she blindly pulled her clothing from the chiffonier and armoire until everything was piled and folded on her bed. Her mind roiled with straining passions, but she fought to bring reason through the turmoil. Fortunately most of her paintings, sketchbooks, brushes, colors, pencils, and other art supplies were already stored in boxes.

Courage, she warned herself the instant her emotions threatened to overwhelm her.

Through a gray blur, she thought to set aside a favorite watercolor of the school garden as a parting gift for Rose, and, sorting through her work to find it, discovered an early attempt at a self-portrait. She had drawn herself with golden hair curling like a child's below her shoulders, great blue trusting eyes, an ordinary straight nose, sweet smiling lips, and a serene expression that had never known grief or fear of the future. *Happiness* seemed an apt title for it. How differently she would depict herself now. Tonight her self-portrait would be of a young woman torn with anguish.

Finally her two trunks were delivered, and she stuffed her possessions into them, even her despised gray school uniforms—wool for winter and starched linen for spring and fall. After all, her father had purchased them, and if there was no more money she might be forced to wear them. As it was, she would have to wear one home. Her recently acquired womanly shape caused her russet traveling dress to be too tight. She was a late bloomer, like Mother . . .

At the thought of her mother, hot tears burst to her eyes and rolled down her cheeks. Oh, Mother! And Father gone too! He'd been such a handsome and dashing man—full of love for her, bursting with pride at her every accomplishment. "Your every wish is my command, princess," he had said since her childhood. And he had truly given her everything she desired.

A sob escaped her, then another and another until she threw herself on the bed and wept.

She was still sobbing disconsolately when Rose returned to the room and asked in shock, "Abby—what is it? What's happened?"

"My parents—" Abby began and, between sobs, the heartbreaking words were finally spoken, even Uncle Benjamin's offer to take her to live on the frontier.

Rose caught her in her arms. "Oh, Abby . . . my poor, dear Abby . . . what will you do?"

Abby shook her head. "I don't know! I don't know! I don't want to live on the frontier with savages!"

At length she quieted and they sat on Rose's bed in bewilderment. "We must try to think clearly, to consider the options," Rose suggested. "Maybe Cornelius will propose immediately now and, under the circumstances, you could marry right away. You could stay with me in Georgetown and we . . . we could have a double wedding! That would solve everything! It would be so lovely . . . not perfect now, of course."

Abby wiped away her tears and blew her nose. "I'm not sure that . . . Cornelius loves me. We've always only been . . . well, I suppose one would call us friends. Our families have thrown us together, but now that the money is gone—"

"Oh, bother!" Rose replied. "Any man in his right mind would be happy to have you just for yourself. Why, you've turned into one of the most beautiful girls in the class. Moreover, Cornelius's family has enough money to last for centuries. What does it matter if you have none?"

Abby's spirits lifted, only slightly.

"You'll see, Abby. It will all turn out fine. Place it in God's hands. Place it in His hands and you can have a good night's sleep."

"I don't know," Abby said. She lacked her roommate's faith, although Grandfather Talbot had been an eminent clergyman in Boston years ago. Her father, the middle son, had been . . . well, she supposed the word was rebellious. Lately her parents had turned to Emerson; his transcendentalism was the current rage, though her mother did take her to a nearby church on Christmas and Easter. As for Miss Sheffield's School for Young Ladies, it was progressive and had no chapel; a minister called twice a week to teach religion, but the class was not required, and Abby had taken advanced art courses instead.

Despite Rose's optimism, Abby endured the worst night's sleep of her life. Toward morning she lay quietly in the warmth of her covers, not wanting to disturb Rose, drifting between wakeful agony and troubled sleep, watching the sky turn from black to pale gray and then take on a pinkish glow. Ordinarily she loved to watch the changing light, but this morning she watched it with dread. At length she heard Rose's stirring.

"Abby?" Rose whispered from her bed, sounding less

groggy than she did most mornings. "Are you awake?"

"Yes," Abby replied wretchedly.

"I—I hope you will always be my friend."

"Oh, Rose!" After last night's bout of weeping, Abby had thought she was cried out, but hot tears rolled down her cheeks again. Even Rose had lost last night's optimism, doubtless realizing the impossibility of her suggestions. Abby gave another sob before quieting. She answered, "I want always to be your friend, too."

Rose leaned up on an elbow. "If you decide not to marry Cornelius . . . if—well, no matter what you decide to do, promise that you'll write."

Abby retrieved the soggy handkerchief she had placed under her pillow last night. "I promise. I—I promise I'll write wherever I go." She turned to the window again.

After a long while her roommate asked, "What are you thinking about so quietly, Abby?"

"That I'll never wake up in this room again, that I'll never see another sunrise from this window. . . ."

Rose said thoughtfully, "I imagine your life will change a lot, especially if you live on the frontier."

"Yes, I imagine it will," Abby responded sadly.

The wake-up bell sounded through the hallway, and Abby heard Rose climb out of bed.

"Aren't you getting up?" Rose asked.

"Not yet. They can't call for me until ten o'clock." Abby inhaled deeply. "When the girls ask about me, please tell them that I—that I can't bear saying good-bye this morning."

"Miss Sheffield says we must confront reality and carry on—"

"I don't care. I'm going to try to sleep now." She pulled the covers over her head, trying to blot out everything. Much to her amazement, she slept, not even hearing as Rose left the room, not hearing anything until the breakfast bell rang at eight o'clock.

Upon rising, she reminded herself of Daniel Wainwright's words: Courage in trouble is half the battle. Clinging to that, she placed the watercolor she had selected for Rose on her friend's desk. Moments later, she discovered a note tucked behind the frame of her mirror and a small package wrapped in white tissue nearby on her own desk. *I'm not going to wish you a happy seventeenth birthday,* Rose had written. *I only pray that something wonderful will happen to you today, and that you have a happy year. God bless you. Your dear friend, Rose.*

Her seventeenth birthday—she had forgotten all about it! With a catch in her throat, Abby folded the note and tucked it into her gray linen uniform's pocket, wondering what Rose might have given her. It was nearly impossible to shop here in the countryside. Tearing the tissue off the small package, she was overwhelmed. Fleur-de-lis . . . the treasured bottle of perfume that William had given to Rose. Abby steeled herself against more tears at the generous gesture made by her best friend.

2

At ten o'clock, Benjamin Talbot presented Miss Sheffield with the funds for his niece's tuition, and the headmistress handed over the impressive diploma.

Stiff as ever, she said, "I instructed our porter to place Miss Talbot's trunks in your carriage." She glanced toward the drawing room window. "He is outside now with your coachman fulfilling his duty."

"As you have fulfilled yours," Benjamin said in as kindly a tone of voice as he could manage.

She gave him a curt nod.

"I have already sent up a maid for Miss Talbot. And now, if you gentlemen will excuse me, I have other duties to attend to. Good day."

"Good day," Benjamin and Daniel replied in near unison.

She closed her door behind them and they started down the hallway, Benjamin muttering, "I hope the esteemed headmistress has not turned out a school full of young ladies quite that stiff and duty-bound."

"She may have tried, but she must not have succeeded entirely with your niece," Daniel remarked with a wry expression. "She looked quite charming last night as she came down the stairs with her friend, and then again in the headmistress's drawing room—until you told her the sad news."

"Yes, she did," Benjamin recalled. He cast a quizzical glance at his adopted son as they stepped into the entry. Daniel had taken little interest in women since his engagement to a Philadelphia beauty had culminated in disillusionment two years ago. He did not appear quite so disillusioned now.

Daniel gazed up the staircase and murmured, "Here she comes now."

This morning Abigail had only her gray starched linen uniform to lift carefully as she stepped down the marble staircase, and its one attractive feature was the lace edging on its white pointed collar. She wore a black cloak and a black cabriolet bonnet, both most likely of school issue, Benjamin guessed. He thought she might look quite mournful if her golden curls weren't spilling so rebelliously from under her bonnet. Doubtless she'd let down her hair as an act of defiance, for proper young ladies of sixteen and older were not seen in public—particularly not by men—with their hair down. He saw her glance toward the headmistress's drawing room and look disappointed.

He smiled up at her encouragingly, and they all exchanged polite but solemn greetings. As she joined them in the entry, he handed her the envelope. "Your diploma. You can always use it if you wish to teach school. Your Aunt Jessica has hers, and she sets great store by it."

Abby's blue eyes shone with gratitude. "Thank you." It was a moment before she added, "I—I hope that someday I can repay you for this."

"Nonsense," he replied. "We are a family, even if we do not yet know each other well. What sort of an uncle would I be if I didn't try to help?"

At that, she managed the hint of a smile and did not appear quite as upset.

"Come along," Benjamin said as he ushered her out the door. "We have a small suprise for you."

Outside in the sunlight, he noticed that she had the red eyes of a girl who had cried during the night, but the look of a young woman determined to be courageous. One of Daniel's innumerable sayings came to mind: Courage is fear that has said its prayers. Benjamin fervently hoped that would prove to be the case for his niece.

"You've brought Joseph and the carriage!" she said, brightening as she saw it.

"Yes," Benjamin answered, "a small touch of home."

She blinked, her blue eyes far too shiny, and he hoped she would not give way to her emotions; he was hopeless with young women who dissolved into tears.

Old Joseph, smart in his black livery, stepped forward and tipped his cap. "Mornin', Miss Abigail," the coachman said. "Ye have my . . . sympathy, miss. Mine and Molly's, who's at home waiting to hold ye in her arms."

She nodded, then managed to say, "Thank you, Joseph."

Benjamin saw her bite down on her mouth, and Daniel stepped forward quickly. "May I assist you into the carriage?" he offered.

"Yes, thank you, Mr. Wainwright," she answered without looking at any of them.

As he helped her into the carriage, she let out a quiet half-sob and it looked as if something passed between them. Perhaps it was the awareness of Daniel wishing to lend her more than physical strength as he held his hand under her elbow, just as Benjamin wished he could help her more himself.

While he settled beside her, she blew her nose, her lace-edged handkerchief giving off the scent of a flowery perfume. Likely the young banker, Cornelius, had given it to her, he thought.

Old Joseph glanced at her soothingly as he closed the carriage doors, and they sat in an uneasy silence while he climbed to the driver's seat. Finally he urged on the horses, flicking the reins lightly over them before their hoofs clopped against the worn cobbles of the circular drive.

Benjamin watched his niece turn toward the stone mansion, and he glanced back himself. Sunshine beamed through the towering elms and oaks that framed Miss Sheffield's School for Young Ladies, reflecting off its windows; lilacs bloomed here and there and, near the entry, urns of daffodils lent brilliant color. "It's a beautiful place," he said into the silence. "I hope you don't feel resentful about your early departure."

"No, not at that," she replied without turning to him. "I only wish Miss Sheffield hadn't been so . . . severe with you." Her words were soft, difficult to hear. "I am grateful for . . . for having painted the school and the gardens so often. I'll have the paintings for memories."

"A good attitude," Benjamin said, swallowing harder than he wished. "I firmly believe in counting one's blessings. I've had to do it often enough myself, as has Daniel."

The carriage rattled out onto the main road, but she continued to look back until the school was out of sight. When she turned forward, her young face was set with determination, as if that phase of her life had ended and it was time to move on. She even tucked her handkerchief into a pocket of her black cloak as if she had finished with tears.

Daniel, who sat across from them, eyed her as if awaiting a propitious moment. At length he inquired, "Did you study painting at school?"

"A little," she replied, smoothing her gray skirt.

"Watercolors or oils?" Daniel asked with interest.

"Both," she replied, giving him a fast glance. "Our art instructress said I have not discovered my best medium yet."

"So you are continuing in all of them?" he asked.

"Yes," she replied, sitting erect and staring at her tightly clasped hands.

"What do you paint?" Daniel continued. "Landscapes, still lifes, portraits . . . ?"

"All of them," she answered, her voice still quiet and brittle.

Daniel gave her a small smile. "Does your art instructress tell you that you haven't discovered your special branch of painting yet?"

With the hint of a smile, she replied, "Yes, not yet." She settled back a trifle and seemed somewhat more at ease.

Daniel said, "I don't know a great deal about art, only that I know what I like when I see it. Perhaps the art I like best is that which touches both my intellect and my emotions."

"Yes," she said, "when it touches both, it is said to be a great success."

That appeared to exhaust the subject of art, Benjamin thought. The long day's drive to New York City could be difficult. What might one say to a sensitive young woman whose entire life must seem a wreckage? He had dealt with young women's heartaches before, particularly his daughters', but every time was so different and each girl's reactions had varied with age as well.

He tried to recall what people had said to him when his wife, Elizabeth, had died and his own life had seemed a wreckage. Ofttimes it had been best when they'd spoken of other matters entirely.

"Daniel has traveled over much of the world," Benjamin ventured. "He is involved with our firm's shipping and trade. He's had a most interesting life for such a young man."

Abby asked in a polite but restrained tone, "Where have you been most recently, Mr. Wainwright?"

"Daniel," he suggested.

She managed a small smile at him, then at Benjamin. "Miss Sheffield would probably not approve of such immediate familiarity, but very well, if you like. And, while we are on the subject of names, the girls at school called me Abby. I much prefer it to Abigail."

"Then Abby it is," Daniel said. "And, to answer your question, I've most recently been to California. Do you know of it?"

"Yes, from my geography lessons," she replied. "California was Spanish, but now it belongs to the country of Mexico."

"Exactly," Daniel said. "And did your geography instructress tell how it came to be named California?"

"Not that I remember."

Daniel turned to Benjamin. "You tell it, Father. You're the one who told me, in any case, and I don't wish to damage the details."

"If you insist," Benjamin replied, pleased as always when his adopted son called him Father and deferred to him.

"As I recall," he began, "the discovery of the New World by Columbus gave a strong momentum to that age-old search for an earthly paradise . . . a place without work, of course, and with gold and beautiful women. It was said that Spanish sailors found a rich island of California inhabited by handsome black women like Amazons and a queen named Califa. Their arms were of gold and so were the harnesses of the wild beasts they rode. In fact, their land held no other metal than gold."

Abby turned to Daniel with disbelief. "Did you find that true?"

"Unfortunately not," he answered with a wry expression. "The tale seems to belong with those of El Dorado, the Seven Cities of Cibola, and other such earthly realms sought by the Spanish conquerors."

"Oh," she said. "I see." After a moment she asked, "What is California like?"

"It's an interesting place," Daniel replied. "For the most part, the people who live there are Spanish or native Indians. The Spaniards, many of whom have become Mexicans since their war of independence, are called Californios, and they live on vast ranchos given to them by the king of Spain. They make their livelihood by trading horses as well as tallow, steer horns, otter and beaver skins, and, of course, the hides of thousands of cattle. One might say the coin of their realm is cattle hides instead of gold. Indeed, accounts are usually kept in hides. Instead of cash boxes, one often finds hides piled high on the verandas of the few shops there."

"What a sight that would be to paint," she remarked as though she were trying to picture it. "And what do your ships take there?"

"Teas, coffee, spices, raisins, molasses, hardware, clothing, calicos and cottons . . . everything from Chinese fireworks to English cartwheels. We have ship stores with shelves and counters that resemble a country variety shop. In good weather, some of the wares are displayed on the deck."

"The Californios actually come aboard ship to buy?"

"With great delight," he replied. "The ranchero might concentrate on the quality of the rice, sugar, liquor, and tobacco. His senora's first interest is usually the prints, silks, and satins; and their daughters like bows and ribbons. Their young men especially admire the Wilson cook knives."

"It would certainly be different from shopping in New York City," Abby observed.

Benjamin was heartened to see her inquisitiveness rise to the fore. Last night when they'd arrived at the school, Miss Sheffield had mentioned Abby's lively curiosity, but he was glad to witness it himself. He sat back and listened to her and Daniel discuss shipping the cattle hides to New England, where they were made into shoes, many of which were ironically returned to California in trade for more hides. Richard Henry Dana had written that the Californios could make nothing for themselves, but then he'd been extremely critical of them and their endless horse racing, dancing, and fiestas.

During a lull in the conversation, Benjamin remarked with humor, "It's said that California's salubrious climate makes sickness so rare that people from all over would come to view a sick person. There are even tales of people living over two hundred and fifty years."

Abby's blue eyes widened with disbelief, and she turned to Daniel. "Is that so?"

"I doubt it," he replied with a smile. "You can't give credence to some of the tales told about California."

Benjamin smiled with them. "The one story I give credence to is that Jedediah Smith, the old mountain man called 'Bible-toter Jed,' opened the trail to California in '26 for good reason—for us to overspread the continent with the knowledge of Christ's saving power and love."

"I give that credence myself," Daniel said. "I, too, am an admirer of 'old Jed.'"

Abby eyed them strangely, as though such talk were entirely out of her experience, and they lapsed into silence.

As the carriage rattled along, Benjamin gazed out at the yellow buttercups blooming across the fields and pastures. Across the way, a village lay by the river. From this distance you could see its church steeple, and there among the trees were an inn, a smithy, and an icehouse. Even here in New York State's countryside, life was more civilized than on the Missouri frontier—and the frontier was far more civilized than life would be in California, despite the occasional trading ships that sailed into its few widely separated ports.

Perhaps Abby should marry the banker, fop or not, Benjamin thought. If her parents hadn't died, she'd doubtless have made her debut this year, and most of the New York's eligible young men would have thronged about her. But a social season was no longer a choice. Indeed, Abby had very little choice, and time was of the essence.

They stopped for lunch at a pleasant roadside inn. "Try to eat," Benjamin told Abby. "You'll need your strength."

How could she eat lunch? Abby wondered as she pushed the food around her plate with her fork.

"Try, Abby," Daniel urged. "It's quite good."

She nodded, remembering his words again. Courage in trouble is half the battle.

Finally she forced down a few bites of chicken breast, mashed potatoes, and peas. The gravy spread over it made her feel queasy.

After they'd finished, Uncle Benjamin paid the bill, then it was onward again. I must remain composed, Abby reminded herself as she climbed into the carriage. She had wept more than enough last night. She must hold up through this day. Courage in trouble is half the battle.

Once the carriage was rolling along again, her uncle said, "Our time is so limited that it behooves us to discuss matters even if they are difficult, Abby."

She inhaled sharply. "Yes, I expect so."

After a moment he said, "I am sorry to tell you that all of the bank stock has been liquidated over the past years. The house on Union Square and its furnishings have been sold to satisfy the creditors."

Abby closed her eyes, then nodded for him to continue. Doubtless he thought the kindest way to explain everything was to be straight to the point.

"I'm afraid I've already had to dismiss most of the staff at the house," he said. "I did retain Joseph and Molly until the end of the month since we need them and the carriage, of course. Molly is still the housekeeper, and she has also agreed to cook. I've had to make many decisions in a hurry. I truly have done my best."

"I—I'm sure that you have," she forced herself to say. "It couldn't have been easy for you to come across the country to New York so unexpectedly. I do appreciate . . . all that you have undertaken in my behalf."

Benjamin nodded unhappily. "Don't be too grateful until you see what we've accomplished, child. Daniel knows most of the bankers and merchants in the city. Without him, affairs would not have gone as smoothly as they have. He will stay here on the Eastern seaboard to deal with your family's matters as well as other affairs after we leave."

She turned to Daniel. "Thank you." She recalled that he had been an orphan taken into her uncle's family. An orphan . . . as she was now. At the thought of it she had to fight off a new threat of tears.

"It's my pleasure to repay your uncle in a small way for his help when I needed it," Daniel responded. "I'm sure that someday you will have such an opportunity, too. If not with him, then with helping someone else."

Her uncle explained, "Daniel and I have listed all of the matters still under consideration, and we will go through them with you in thorough detail later if you wish."

She nodded. Her father had not cared overly much for his family, whom he'd considered unsophisticated, but she felt certain in her heart that she could trust Benjamin Talbot—and Daniel Wainwright, too, for that matter.

The sun was setting when the carriage finally entered Union Square. The splashing fountain in the park sparkled reddish-gold in the sunset, and neighborhood children rolled their hoops home under the trees; ladies and gentlemen strolled along the gravel walks. As the horses turned into the circular driveway in front of the brown sandstone Talbot mansion, she saw that the pink rhododendron was in bloom. She looked at her beloved home sadly as Joseph brought the horses to a stop at the front steps.

"Who purchased the house?" she asked.

"A banker from Philadelphia," her uncle replied, helping her out of the carriage.

"It doesn't seem possible that it would be sold so soon," she remarked, resisting the impulse to add that it didn't seem fair!

Daniel replied, "Houses on Union Square are always in demand. It's an excellent location."

Abby felt powerless. "Yes, I daresay it is."

Molly opened the front door, dressed in her ample black dress, her round face framed by gray curls escaping the bun at the nape of her neck. "Welcome home, Miss Abigail," she said with her Irish lilt, tears in her eyes. "Oh, my dear . . . my dear little one!"

Abby flew into her arms. "Thank you, Molly! I'm so grateful that you and Joseph are still here!"

"We're pleased to help what we can. I'm only sad that

things don't look like they should."

Abby blinked at the wetness in her eyes and glanced around at the white marble-floored entry. The Persian rug was missing, as were the French chandelier and the ancestral oil paintings that had lined the walls, even her favorite painting of Grandmother Talbot.

She walked about, heartsick at the barrenness. Everything was gone—furniture, china, crystal, silverware, even the harp and old harpsichord that had come from her mother's family in Boston. In the library she said, half to herself, "I didn't expect it to be like this . . . that they would take even the books." None of the leather-bound volumes in the library remained, only worn copies of *Graham's Magazine, Godey's Ladies' Book*, inexpensive pamphlets, and the family Bible. It seemed a wonder that they'd left the Bible since it was like new, having seldom been used.

"*Barrenness*," she said, disconsolate.

"I beg your pardon?" Daniel said.

"It's only a—a game that my roommate and I played, entitling people and scenes as if they were paintings."

He surveyed the rooms with her. "Yes, *Barrenness* is unfortunately appropriate."

Her uncle appeared distraught, too. He explained, "I had the servants' table and chairs brought into the dining room for now, and their serving plates and dishes as well. I've tried to be practical. We do have to eat, and there are provisions in the house."

"And upstairs?" Abby asked, though she was unsure she wanted to know. "Is the furniture missing there, too?"

"I retained some of the armoires and beds for now, and the furnishings for Molly and Joseph above the carriage house."

"I see," she replied, her voice quavering.

"I am so very sorry," her uncle said.

Abby nodded, sure that he was. "Would you—would you mind if I go to bed now? I'm sure there is still much to accomplish—"

"Nothing that we can't accomplish tomorrow," her uncle said. "The best thing for you is sleep, child."

"Yes." She reached up and kissed his cheek as she might have her own father's. "Good night then, Uncle Benjamin." She turned to Daniel. "Good night."

As she ascended the stairs, she noticed the pale ovals, squares, and rectangles on the white walls that marked places where family portraits had once hung. The portraits had ranged from the Windsors—her mother's side that had immigrated from England and claimed royal descent—to Charles Talbot on her father's side, Duke of Shrewsbury, who was Prime Minister of England in 1714. Her father had told her, "Your lineage goes back to the Talbot who fought with William the Conqueror at Hastings. You have illustrious relations on both sides. Do nothing to shame the family name, my dear."

How heartbroken Father would have been by all of this! she thought, benumbed.

Upstairs in her room she tried to ignore the disappearance of most of the Venetian furniture she had loved. At least she had a bed. She undressed, hanging her gray linen uniform on a door peg. Noticing a bit of stiffness in the pocket, she slipped in her hand and discovered Rose's note.

Abby stood in her petticoats and read the words again. *I'm not going to wish you a happy birthday, only that something wonderful will happen to you today, and that you have a happy year. God bless you. Your loving friend, Rose.*

Tears burst to her eyes. She'd forgotten since this

morning that it was her seventeenth birthday—and what a miserable day it had been. She had never in all of her life been so unhappy. As for something wonderful happening today, there had been nothing but Rose's gift of her treasured perfume—and, she decided, Uncle Benjamin's and Daniel Wainwright's thoughtfulness.

She tried to remember about courage being half the battle, but such a feeling of desperation washed over her that it was useless. Where was she supposed to find such courage? Where? As memories of her mother and father returned, Abby lay down on her childhood bed and wept.

3

A new wave of despair washed over Abby when she awoke the next morning. Refusing to succumb to it, she flung off her covers and padded to the window. She pulled aside the heavy draperies and was heartened to see sunshine beaming over the bright spring greenery in Union Square Park. She must concentrate on enduring, she told herself, enduring this day, then another and another.

At her armoire, she rummaged through the dresses and felt a stab of panic. Nothing suitable for mourning would fit. She'd have to send Molly out shopping for black dresses. . . but there was no money.

A thought struck her. Her mother's rich wardrobe included a number of black dresses, and she certainly would not have taken all of them to Europe. But what a gruesome thought! Still, there was no money. . . .

In any case, she had no choice. She opened one of the trunks that Joseph had carried up to her room last night and took out another of her gray linen school frocks.

Later, when she opened her door, she half expected to see her parents down the hallway and steeled herself against reality.

"Good morning, Abby," Daniel said, just leaving his

bedroom. "I trust you feel improved this morning."

"Yes, thank you."

She tried not to notice the missing portraits as the two of them descended the staircase, and she made a special effort to concentrate on Daniel's idle conversation about the sunny May weather. Was it possible to discuss anything so banal as the weather now? Had he heard her weeping into the night?

The aroma of breakfast had already lured Uncle Benjamin to the stately dining room, where he sat drinking coffee and reading this morning's *New York Herald*. He rose to greet her. "Molly hoped you might sleep late, but here you are ready for breakfast quite early."

"Yes."

Someone had cut fresh lilacs from the garden for a centerpiece, and their heady fragrance filled the room. Lilacs did not, however, change the appearance of the old oak kitchen table and chairs that formerly seated eight servants. The sturdy furniture looked incongruous with the marble floor, rose damask wall coverings, and heavy draperies. The place settings were at the far end of the table, and her uncle had properly appropriated the chair at the head.

Uncle Benjamin folded up the newspaper and set it aside. "Did you sleep well, child?"

She bristled again at the word child, although this morning she must look it in her school dress and with her hair pulled back into a simple knot atop her head. "I'm almost ashamed. . . . I slept eleven hours."

"You must have needed it," Daniel said, pulling out a chair for her.

"It didn't seem right for me to sleep soundly . . . under the circumstances," she replied with embarrassment.

Her uncle said, "Sleep rarely hurts anyone."

Daniel settled in the chair across the table, the

drowsiness around his blue eyes bestowing a boyish appeal to his bearded face. "Now how does that go?" he asked himself. "Ah . . . 'Blessings on him who first invented sleep. It covers a man all over, thoughts and all, like a cloak. It is meat for the hungry, drink for the thirsty, heat for the cold, and cold for the hot. It makes the shepherd equal to the monarch and the fool to the wise.' "

Benjamin Talbot chuckled. "Isn't it a bit early for Cervantes, even for you?"

"My regrets," Daniel returned, though he did not look too regretful with his small grin.

Abby realized he was trying to lift her spirits, to take her mind off the difficult tasks ahead. "It is astonishing for anyone to quote Cervantes so early in the morning," she said. Her parents had rarely spoken at all on those few occasions they'd breakfasted together in this room. Usually Molly had served Mother breakfast in her sitting room.

"Don't tempt him, Abby, or we'll unleash a monster. He can quote until one's brains reel. Daniel has a memory for quotations like—like—"

"Like an elephant?" Daniel suggested with amusement.

"More like a caged poet," Uncle Benjamin responded, then smiled. "And now shall we say grace?"

Surprised to hear prayer at this table, Abby sat blinking while her uncle and Daniel bowed their heads; Molly, taken unaware as well, set the coffeepot down. Abby bowed her head quickly and her uncle prayed:

"Father in Heaven, from above,
Look down upon this home with love.
Keep us in health and strength this day,
Give us our daily bread, we pray,
And for Thy gifts so full and free,
We would return our thanks to Thee."

"Amen," he added, and Daniel echoed a firm "Amen."

Molly darted a questioning glance at Abby, then poured the steaming coffee, and Daniel remarked, "I haven't heard that prayer in a long time."

"It seemed most suitable," Benjamin Talbot replied.

Abby, unsettled by the prayer yet thankful for the quiet interlude, spread a worn white napkin across her lap. She helped herself to several spoonfuls of hot porridge and poured maple syrup on it.

It wasn't until Molly removed the dishes that Uncle Benjamin said in a regretful tone, "If you like, Abby, I'll make the memorial service arrangements for your parents. I have delayed in the matter so I might know your preferences."

"I—I don't know how to plan a memorial service," she confessed unhappily. "I have only attended Grandmother Talbot's funeral in Boston, but I was so young." Mainly she recalled the coffin being lowered into the grave and how she'd refused to throw a handful of dirt on it. She couldn't bear to think of it any more than she could consider her parents' bodies awash somewhere in the Mediterranean Sea. She swallowed with difficulty. "I would appreciate your assistance."

"The service could be held here at the house if your parents were not members of a church," her uncle suggested. "I am not aware of how they stood, spiritually speaking."

Abby quailed at the thought. Both of her parents had been brought up in Christian homes, but since leaving them, had rarely attended church. Her mother had spoken of Christian virtues and had contributed to Christian charities, and her father, despite his enthusiasm over transcendentalism, had allowed Mother to take her to church on Christmas and Easter. He had even accompanied them when she was very young. But in truth, she didn't know where they had stood "spiritually speaking," as Uncle Benjamin put it. Social events had meant everything to them—dinner parties, theater, concerts, balls.

She realized that her uncle awaited a reply. "I don't think we can hold a service in this—this empty house. Perhaps if you could contact the church—"

"I'll attend to it the first thing this morning," her uncle said. "Also, your parents' friends, Mr. and Mrs. Adams, have offered to hold the wake—a reception, they called it—at their home after the service. Would that seem right?"

"Yes," Abby responded with relief. "They and my parents were best friends. The Adams family lives just on the other side of Union Square, and they had always hoped that Cornelius and I—" She stopped in horror at her near gaffe. "Yes," she amended, "their having the reception would be very nice."

Her uncle inquired, "Do you have suitable mourning clothes? I doubt that school uniforms will do in public."

"I—I thought that Molly and I might be able to alter some of Mother's black dresses—" her voice faltered—"and there might be some black fabric upstairs in the sewing room."

Her uncle asked Molly, who was carrying out the last of the dishes, "Will you have time to help Abby with mourning attire?"

"Yes, Mr. Talbot, sir. We'll be doin' it somehow."

"Thank you," he said and turned again to Abby. "I understand you are not betrothed, but that there is a young man."

Abby's lower lip began to tremble and she bit down on it, aware that Daniel was watching her, too. His interest in the question made her feel oddly perverse. "Everyone said we were too young to consider any arrangement."

"I see," her uncle replied. "Unfortunately, time is running out now. Will your friend—Cornelius, as I recall—will he call on you soon?"

She decided that Mr. Adams must have told her uncle about both families' expectations. "Yes, I think Cornelius might call today. I should let him know not to come to the school musicale Saturday on my account." She shrank at the prospect of marrying him, if he asked her. He had not even hinted at it; in fact, he had never so much as given her a romantic glance when they went horseback riding, nor held her hand when they attended plays or concerts.

"There is another matter to discuss this morning," Uncle Benjamin said, his brown eyes clouding with concern. "My family and I expect to emigrate to California by covered wagon next spring to expand our trading and shipping interests. If you decide to come with us to Missouri—"

"Emigrate to California!" she exclaimed.

He nodded. "Judging by our discussion of California yesterday, I assume that you have studied a bit about it."

"We learned about Fremont's recent explorations in school. There are mountains to cross. . . ."

Daniel put in dryly. "Merely the Rocky Mountain chain and then the California Mountains."

She glanced at him. "Will you be going too?"

His blue eyes shone. "I sincerely hope so. One might not live to two hundred and fifty years there, but it is a magnificent place."

Uncle Benjamin said, "We would be heartsick without Daniel. He has been away from home far too much lately as it is."

They turned to her, and it began to come clear: she must either go West or marry Cornelius. Those were her choices . . . her only choices. She asked her uncle, "And when must I give you my decision?"

He took a final sip of coffee. "We must know in the next few days. We'll have to make travel arrangements to Missouri on Monday afternoon at the latest. We leave Wednesday morning."

That soon! The entire situation seemed unreal. At length she said, "I see." As if her parents' deaths weren't bad enough, now she must leave her home, perhaps even move to the frontier and then to a foreign land! How could she endure it?

"And now if I may be excused," her uncle said, "I'll be on my way to the church. We have no time to lose."

"Thank you. I am truly grateful, though I daresay I must not seem to be to you."

Uncle Benjamin replied, "You are handling this far more bravely than most young women might."

Only because I am so numb! Abby thought. *Because I can't believe it is all happening.*

As her uncle left the dining room, Daniel smiled warmly at her, arousing a vague contrariness again. After a moment she asked, "Do you think that Uncle Benjamin wants me to be married immediately? Do you think he wants me to . . . to encourage Cornelius?"

Daniel shook his head. "I doubt that very much. Your uncle is as fine a man as God ever placed on this earth. I'm sure he is only concerned with your welfare and happiness." He raised an inquisitive eyebrow and ventured, "Would you know how to encourage a man, Abby?"

His tone sounded innocent, but she could feel blood rush to her cheeks. "Why, I don't believe that is a proper question, Mr. Wainwright!" As for the answer, the girls at school had discussed ploys to bring recalcitrant suitors to their knees, but she could not imagine using any of them. They seemed dishonest—and often ludicrous.

Daniel's color had risen as well. "Forgive me. I didn't mean the question quite the way it sounded." His tone was sincere, his blue eyes regretful. "Will you forgive me?"

"Yes, of course, you are forgiven."

"Thank you." He gave her a slight smile before excusing himself from the table to go to the library. "And, please—not Mr. Wainwright again."

She nodded and returned a small smile.

As he departed from sight, her mind turned back to his question: *Would you know how to encourage a man, Abby?*

When Daniel left for the banking district, she discussed the mourning clothes dilemma with Molly, who agreed to drop her other duties and work on the clothing immediately. It was after nine o'clock before Abby sat down again at the dining room table to write a note to Cornelius. Perhaps she should encourage him a bit, but how?

Dear Cornelius wouldn't do for a greeting, she decided. She wrote line after line, then scratched them out. Finally she was satisfied with what appeared to be a hastily scrawled message: *Cornelius—*

I am home and will not be at the musicale at Miss Sheffield's Saturday night. As you must know from what you have heard at the bank, I have a great many difficult decisions to make and would appreciate your assistance. May I look forward to seeing you this afternoon for tea?

> *Sincerely,*
> *Abigail Talbot*

She rang for Joseph to carry the note to the bank, and then she had no alternative but to join Molly in her parents' bedroom suite.

Never having spent much time in it, Abby was uncertain

of what to expect. It took but a glance to see that the rooms were nearly empty. She started toward her mother's armoires, noting an appraisal firm's tags hanging from the hinges.

Molly remarked sadly as she opened an armoire, "There's things in life that got to be done if we like to or not, an' this be one of 'em."

Abby nodded, her heart constricting as she touched the beautiful morning, afternoon, and evening dresses her mother had worn. Special gowns evoked fond memories of Mother fashionably dressed for balls, parties, and musicales, and of Father in his formal attire. They had looked so magnificent, so immortal with their brilliant smiles. She could remember them as though in an oil painting, her father placing the ermine wrap around her mother's shoulders. *In Society*, Abby titled it, and the tears in her eyes did not distort the vision.

"Sure an' it's all right to cry," Molly allowed.

"No, I will not," Abby said as much to herself as anyone.

Her emotions, however, threatened to undermine her again as she tried on her mother's black dresses. There were two crepes, one bombazine, and a fine lawn—all too tight and too short, their necklines too revealing.

"They got wide seams an' good hems," Molly observed, "an' we'll fill in the low necks with insets. I know a bit about sewin'. We'll remake 'em ourselves."

"We have no other choice," Abby replied. "Show me what to do. If others can sew, perhaps I can, too."

At eleven o'clock Joseph returned from his errands. He brought an answering note from Cornelius upstairs.

Abby quickly tore open the envelope.

Abigail—

I shall be pleased to assist you and will call for tea this afternoon.

Sincerely,
Cornelius Adams III

Abby sighed hopelessly. He had struck the same noncommittal tone she had used. If only he'd given some hint of what he thought of her situation or how he felt about her. If only she had some notion, it might help her know what to say and do this afternoon.

At length she and Molly carried the black dresses downstairs to the dining room table, and Abby began to rip stitches from the seams and hemlines. It was a shame that at Miss Sheffield's she had not learned anything useful. At the moment, Latin, French, literature, elocution, art, and music seemed of small benefit . . . unless, of course, they impressed Cornelius.

She was still ripping stitches when Uncle Benjamin returned. "The minister has agreed to a memorial service at the church on Monday afternoon at one o'clock. Does that appeal to you, Abby?"

She was growing accustomed to the constant gnaw of anguish. "Yes, that sounds fine." She wondered if her uncle had made a point of Grandfather Talbot's ministry in Boston. Perhaps that was why they were being allowed the memorial service even though they were not members of this church. Perhaps Uncle Benjamin had even made a contribution. He had already paid her tuition to get her diploma, and she did not want him to pay for her parents' memorial service, too. Indeed, she did not want him to spend his money for any of their affairs. If only she had funds of her own!

At teatime Molly announced from the entry, "Mr. Cornelius Adams is callin'."

Abby hurried to the entrance hall, then hesitated as she saw Cornelius staring at the emptiness of the place with apparent regret. He'd especially admired the portraits of her ancestors on the stairwell. Indeed, he'd once said, "I often think that I must be descended from royalty as well."

As usual he was dressed in the height of fashion in a gray coat with short tails, white high-collared shirt, black cravat, and black trousers. He held a black top hat in hand. Cornelius always wore the latest styles, and she thought that if he had lived in the last century, he would have been at ease in velvet coats and breeches. Her father had once called him "a bit of a dandy."

Cornelius had grown a pointed mustache since she had seen him at Christmas, she noticed, though his flaxen hair kept it from being too obvious. He looked as if he would prefer to be almost anywhere else at the moment, so she said, "How kind of you to come, Cornelius."

He gave a start. "Oh . . . I didn't hear you, Abigail!" Recovering, he added, "May I convey my deepest sympathies to you? We . . . that is, my family and I are distressed about the entire matter. If there is anything we might do to assist you, please don't hesitate to ask."

Abby's eyes closed as a wave of anguish descended. "Thank you. I appreciate your parents' kindness, having the reception at your house."

"Yes . . . well, it was the very least we could do."

She hardly knew what to say into the silence that fell between them. Finally she ventured, "You've grown a mustache."

"Yes. Do you like it?"

"I'm not sure yet that I do. You look so different." From an artistic viewpoint, the mustache provided a horizontal break for his overlong face, dividing the aristocratic nose from his jutting chin. If the mustache were darker, perhaps it would be an improvement, but it was not unsightly, only a bit absurd. "Yes, I think I do like it, Cornelius," she said, stretching the truth. "It makes you look quite mature."

He gave her his careful smile, then his eyes traveled down her form. "And you've grown very beautiful, if I may say so, Abigail. You have indeed grown up."

She was uncertain how to respond. Several girls at Miss Sheffield's had heard that Cornelius had made quite a reputation for himself as a rake since Christmas, but that was difficult to believe. Probably she should flutter her eyelashes at him or give him a coy smile. Instead she decided to be her usually sensible self and said, "Shall we go out into the garden? I haven't seen it since I came home yesterday."

Outside, they strolled along the gravel path toward the wicker furniture that overlooked the garden, where white alyssum, pink rhododendrons, and lilacs bloomed. As they seated themselves on a settee, Cornelius remarked, "It's very nice, but I do prefer a formal garden, with everything precisely in place."

Everything precisely in place! her mind echoed. For the first time it struck to her that Cornelius would be the type who'd always expect everything "precisely in place," including his wife. She said, "I have always preferred the informality of an English garden like this."

He shot a glance at her. "Indeed?"

She nodded.

They both gazed at the garden again, and a hallowed aphorism of New York society occurred to her: It takes three generations to make a gentleman. Cornelius was the third generation of his branch of the Adams family in New York. Was it possible that he was taking this distinction too literally?

From behind them Molly said, "Beggin' your pardon, I'm bringin' the tea and cake."

Abby said, "Thank you, Molly."

The housekeeper nodded and turned an inquisitive glance at Cornelius before arranging the tea things on the table. She said in a pointed tone of voice, "I didn't bring out the good silver for here in the garden."

"Thank you, Molly," Abby said again. Probably all of the silver was sold, but Molly was trying to put a good face on matters.

When the housekeeper left, Abby poured the tea from a plain pewter pot and served a piece of jelly-filled cake to Cornelius.

His fingers brushed hers as he took his plate, and he looked at her curiously as though to judge what affect it might have on her.

What was he thinking? Abby wondered, not liking the hooded look in his gray eyes. Perhaps it was only his new mustache that made him suddenly seem a stranger.

He placed the plate with its cup of tea and cake carefully on the table, then reached for both of her hands. "Abigail," he began, "under the circumstances, what are you going to do?"

She felt uncomfortable in their awkward position, wishing to extricate her hands from his clammy grip. "I don't know."

Something in his eyes bespoke a special interest in her. Perhaps he meant to ask for her hand, yet he seemed uncertain. Suddenly she had no idea of how she might respond if he proposed marriage . . . though being wed to Cornelius would settle the question of her future. It was not as though their marrying were a sudden fancy; all four of their parents had encouraged it; even Rose had suggested marriage to him as a perfect solution.

He dropped his gaze and shook his head. "If only it

weren't such a scandal."

"A scandal? What do you mean, Cornelius—the bankruptcy?"

"That, too, of course."

"I don't understand," she said, her hands still held awkwardly in his.

His face turned quite red. "Surely you know about Roxanna Murray. It's all just come out because of her court appeal."

"Roxanna Murray? Who is she?"

"I shouldn't have spoken," Cornelius said with consternation. "Please forget my indiscretion."

A reason for his strange comment struck her. It must have to do with his rumored change of character. "Cornelius, are you trying to tell me that you are betrothed?"

His face grew redder yet. "Not at all. Where should you get such an idea?"

"Well, the girls at school said—" She stopped. "I thought that's what you were trying to tell me, that you were in a scandal and—" Words failed her. What then was he trying to say? And why did he continue to hold her hands so gracelessly?

He blinked in bewilderment, then finally said, "I am told that your uncle intends to take you with him to live in Missouri."

"Only for a year. Next spring they are emigrating to California—"

"To California!" he interrupted.

"Yes!"

"What a preposterous notion! Why would anyone want to go to such a vast, worthless place? It's full of savages, wild beasts, deserts, and cactus! I heartily agree with Daniel Webster's assessment that not one cent of the public treasury should be spent to place the Pacific Coast one inch nearer to Boston—or New York—than it is now."

Abby said nothing.

"And they plan to take you there?"

She nodded.

"Why, your father would be livid at the thought of it—"

Someone cleared his throat just inside the house, and Abby saw Daniel start through the garden toward them.

Cornelius dropped her hands at last. "Who is that?"

"Daniel Wainwright. He and my uncle are both staying here." She found herself babbling, "Daniel is a great one for quotations—"

Cornelius asked, appalled, "You mean to say he is staying here in your house? That you are unchaperoned?"

"Why, Uncle Benjamin is here . . . and Molly—"

"You know quite well that Molly and Joseph live over the carriage house."

She responded in the well-modulated voice Miss Sheffield's young ladies were taught to use when provoked. "Yes, I do, Cornelius." She turned away and smiled politely at their visitor.

"Good afternoon," Daniel said, his smile white and dazzling through his dark beard. "Molly sent me out for tea."

Cornelius stood up with barely concealed irritation, and Abby introduced the men. They shook hands, Daniel with genuine enthusiasm. "I hope I am not intruding."

Cornelius must have remembered her remark about Daniel being a great one for quotations, for he responded, "The more, the merrier, as the Bard said."

Daniel smiled and said, "I understand you were out of the city when I visited the bank last week with Benjamin Talbot."

"Yes, though I did meet him earlier," Cornelius replied.

"The bank often sends me out on important matters."

Abby busied herself with serving tea to Daniel. It was impossible not to compare the two men as they sat nearby making an effort at pleasant conversation. Cornelius appeared pale and indoorish as befitted a banker, whereas Daniel's face was brown and his well-trimmed dark beard and muscular physique presented an outdoorsman impression despite his urbane dark blue suit.

Why had Molly sent Daniel out? Had she seen through the kitchen window how matters were progressing? Whatever the reason, Abby felt as though she had gained a reprieve.

At supper, Benjamin Talbot said, "It's unfortunate that your friend, Cornelius, had plans for the evening. I would like to make his acquaintance. What did you think of him, Daniel?"

Daniel answered, "An old family friend . . . a young gentleman who seems rather fond of Abby."

"I had guessed as much," Benjamin said, wishing he'd seen Abby and Cornelius together. From what he had observed of them separately, they made an incongruous pair.

"He will call for me tomorrow afternoon and take me out for an early supper," Abby said somewhat defensively.

"I see," Benjamin replied.

Abby sat quietly, her eyes on her bowl of stew.

Benjamin Talbot suspected she must resent her predicament. It couldn't be easy to be a woman at times, particularly when one had reached a marriageable age and there was no proper suitor in sight. He fervently hoped his niece would not force herself to marry Cornelius.

As supper ended he said, "After Molly clears the table, it might be a good time to review the financial affairs of the estate. If you'll excuse me, I'll bring out the records."

Abby had already brought back one of the black dresses and begun to rip out stitches. She was not accomplished at it, Benjamin noted, but she was willing, which was perhaps just as important.

Returning from the library a few minutes later, he stopped when he heard Daniel asking, "Do you love Cornelius, Abby?"

Her voice sounded resigned. "Does it truly matter?"

Benjamin was glad to hear Daniel reply, "I am sure that it does. You promise to marry for life . . . for better or for worse, though sickness and health. Forever can be a long time if one is miserable."

She sounded chagrined. "Is that why you've never married? You've never been sufficiently in love?"

Daniel said, "I presume that is the reason."

Benjamin was surprised to hear it. Perhaps Daniel's beautiful Philadelphia fiancée had sensed that, too, just as he had in the end. She had not wanted to leave Philadelphia, nor was she as committed a Christian as Daniel.

He heard Abby say, "Perhaps it's not necessary to be in love."

"You mean it might only be expedient to marry someone?" Daniel asked.

"I understand that it happens," Abby said.

"Oh, I am sure that it does . . . and all too often," Daniel agreed.

Feeling guilty as an eavesdropper, Benjamin started back to the library.

"But it won't happen to you?" Abby asked.

"No," Daniel said, "I am waiting to steal fire from heaven." He gave a deep chuckle, perhaps at her reaction. "You see, I think God has chosen one special person for each of us. The difficulty is that most of us pursue love blindly instead of waiting to find the intended person, and that is precisely why so many marriages are far less than perfect."

He paused, then added, "I only say this to protect you, Abby. I don't want you to rush into marriage with Cornelius or anyone else you don't love because of your circumstances."

"I see!" she replied, sounding a bit angry.

Benjamin cleared his throat loudly and started back to the dining room. At least Daniel had told her the truth. Young people usually did not care to hear what their elders had learned by hard experience, so perhaps Daniel's words, coming from a younger man, might bear more weight.

"I have the books," Benjamin said and set them down on the table. "They are fairly well organized now, the lists of debits and credits, and the names of the creditors who have already appealed to the bankruptcy court."

Abby continued to rip stitches as he and Daniel organized the papers and books.

Benjamin suggested, "I think it behooves you to study it a bit, Abby."

She put down her work and began to look at the pages of names and figures herself. After a while she asked, "Who is this woman, this Roxanna Murray? Look at these huge monthly payments, and now she is appealing to the court for a large settlement, too . . . as if there is money left."

Benjamin felt the blood rush to his face. "There are some matters that are better left alone. I will say this, my dear, I am given to understand that it is a legitimate claim."

Abby raised her chin. "You are treating me as a child, and I have finished at one of the most progressive schools for young ladies in the entire country! What's more, Cornelius has already mentioned this Roxanna Murray and something about a scandal. Since I am apparently losing everything, I believe it is my right to know about this!"

Before Benjamin could speak, Daniel said, "You do not want to know about this, Abby."

She turned to Benjamin and said heatedly, "If you don't tell me who this woman is, I shall find out through the bank or the court or somehow. I am sure that, at the very least, I can find out from Cornelius!"

Benjamin drew a deep breath. "I had hoped to avoid this, Abby, but since you are determined to find out, it's better that you find out from me." He paused, trying to think how best to couch the abominable truth. "The fact is that your father . . . had two families."

"My father had two families?" she repeated. She frowned as though she were searching her mind for the sense of it, then looked appalled. "You mean he was a polygamist?"

Benjamin sat back, surprised at her suggestion. Now was the time to put it straight, to tell her that her father was a rebel, an out-and-out rebel against God and his family nearly all of his life, but he couldn't do it. "No, Abby, not a polygamist," he said. "Your father did not marry Roxanna Murray."

"Not marry her?" Her eyes filled with disbelief. "Then he was an adulterer!"

He nodded. "Unfortunately, that is the truth of it."

After a moment she asked in a small voice, "Did they—did they have children?"

Benjamin replied with reluctance. "Yes, they did. Five children."

"Five children!" She rose from her chair, her face pale. "But . . . what of Mother's situation in all of this?"

Benjamin shook his head hopelessly. "According to your father, your mother dared not have any more children after you were born. She . . . she simply accepted the arrangement." He hesitated. "When I visited here ten years ago it was about this matter. Just before she died, your Grandmother Talbot requested that I attempt to persuade your father to terminate the affair, but our suggestions were not well taken. My interference led to a rift between your father and me. Your father suggested that I not visit again. I was, in a word, unwelcome."

Abby exclaimed, "I can't believe it! This is a hoax of some kind. This woman is trying to extort money!" She fled from the dining room, Daniel behind her.

"Abby—" Daniel said.

Benjamin followed after them and couldn't help witness the scene in the front hallway. Daniel had caught her by the arm and turned her to face him.

"You must face the truth, Abby," Daniel told her. "And you must forgive them—your father, your mother, the woman."

"I will never forgive any of them!"

"Abby—"

"Leave me alone!" she said and pulled free.

Benjamin's heart went out to her as she ran up the steps, but if there was one thing he'd learned from having daughters, it was the pointlessness in trying to make them see reason when they were distraught. It was far better to hope and pray she'd see matters with new eyes in the morning. As for her father, Benjamin had forgiven him numerous times himself since their childhood, particularly for upsetting their parents' right to their deathbeds.

Benjamin returned to the dining room and the unfortunate financial and legal tangle. If nothing else, he and Daniel would get those affairs straight, he decided. God help them to accomplish that much at least.

4

When Abby awoke the next morning, the first thing to come to mind were Daniel's words about courage being half the battle. She recalled last night when she'd run up the steps, aware of the ghostly marks on the wall where paintings of her illustrious family had once hung.

Next came her father's words: You must never do anything to shame the family name. How dared he say that? she thought, anger filling her again. How dared he speak of shaming the family name?

Last, she recalled her mother's constant refrain of "What will people think?"

Likely the news of their scandal was all over the city since the court appeal. Perhaps with such news out, there was no sense in her staying here, she suddenly thought. She'd heard of families trying to live down such a disgrace for years to no avail. New York was still a young city, and gossip followed one everywhere.

Last night she'd been so amazed that she'd been unable to think. But now, in the clear light, perhaps it would be best to leave New York as soon as possible. If Cornelius did perchance propose—despite this scandal—at the very least, she would not care to live in this house. As for Daniel's insistence that she forgive them . . . they had ruined her life! No matter what Daniel Wainwright said, she would never ever forgive them.

She pulled herself out of bed, torn between her desire to flee the city and her dread of the frontier. It was all she could manage to wash and to dress. She seemed all thumbs and trembling fingers as she buttoned her shoes and the cuffs of her gray starched linen frock.

Downstairs, sunshine streamed through the dining room windows, and the fragrance of cut lilacs lingered about the table during breakfast. Abby picked at her breakfast, and neither her uncle nor Daniel mentioned the scandal, which she fervently hoped never to hear of again.

It was a subdued meal and the men occasionally eyed her with concern. Well, they need not worry about her breaking down; if nothing else, her fury lent her strength and determination. And, if that weren't enough, Cornelius had invited her out this afternoon, and she intended to make it a turning point in her problems.

After breakfast, Daniel adjourned to the library and Uncle Benjamin departed for downtown. She'd have to speak with Daniel alone, she thought as she set about finishing her job of addressing the memorial service announcements. By eleven o'clock they were done and she handed them over to Joseph for delivery to her parents' friends.

She settled again at the dining room table to rework her mother's black lawn gown. If only everything would work out as reasonably as her mourning attire solution. Now, however, she needed money, a great deal of it, whether she married Cornelius or not. In either case, she could not borrow from him or her uncle, who had already paid her tuition and was probably purchasing the household provisions with his own funds.

The library door opened, and she heard Daniel's approaching footsteps. This was the moment she had hoped for, the reason why she'd worn the pendant under her gray school frock, where it felt warmer than usual against her chest.

"Do you mind if I join you for a few minutes, Abby?" he asked, his voice low and resonant as always. He had removed his suit coat and cravat, and appeared at ease in his white linen shirtsleeves, fawn broadcloth vest, and dark brown trousers.

"Please do," she said. "I had hoped to speak with you alone."

He sat down at the head of the table, and the sunshine slanting through the windows burnished the reddish highlights in his dark hair and beard. "I hope you don't intend to scold me about last night," he said uneasily. "I came to ask your forgiveness for being so adamant."

His apology was unexpected. "Yes, of course."

He smiled briefly, his blue eyes still serious. "Thank you. I was so insistent about forgiving others because I had to learn the hard way myself. I hoped it would be unnecessary for you to endure what I had to."

"I appreciate your concern." She hesitated, uncertain how to approach the matter of selling the pendant. Finally she asked, "What is it like in Independence, Missouri?"

He raised his dark brows thoughtfully. "You might think it primitive after New York, but I find it exciting. The wagon trains gather there for trading expeditions on the Santa Fe Trail, as do emigrants traveling to Oregon . . . and to California now, too. The roads are full of oxen and covered wagons, mules, horses, dogs, and an amazing variety of people. The best word to describe it might be colorful."

"You find it more exciting than New York?" she asked.

He smiled at her astonishment. "Yes, I enjoy a great deal about the frontier. It's full of adventure. As an artist, you'd be interested in knowing that west of the Kansas River, the land is a vast prairie abloom with wildflowers, and the prairie sky is open and magnificent. I've only been along the trail partway into the Indian Territory, but I think the vistas would interest you. As for New York, it's culturally edifying, but there's a crowded, stultifying feeling about it after the frontier. I take it, however, that you don't care for change."

"No," Abby replied. "No, I daresay I don't."

He glanced about the spacious dining room. "After a life like yours in a fine school and living in a mansion, change cannot seem very appealing."

She shrugged noncommittally. The more she considered the West, the less appealing it seemed. After a moment's silence she asked, "I wonder if I might ask you for a favor . . . something confidential."

Daniel straightened in his chair. "I would be pleased to help in any way possible."

Abby reached behind her neck for the gold chain hidden under her dress, then carefully bared the sapphire pendant. "I hoped you might sell this for me."

His eyes widened at the sapphire surrounded by gold scrollwork. "It's a beautiful piece of jewelry. Are you certain you wish to sell it?"

"Quite simply, I must."

She feared she might have to endure a lecture on the responsibility of keeping family heirlooms, but at last he said, "If you must, I shall try to obtain the best price. It's Saturday, so there's no possibility of my finding a buyer until Monday."

Her hands trembled as she unfastened the clasp behind her neck. For an instant she recalled how the stone had matched her grandmother's eyes in the old portrait, and how it had matched her dress that evening when she'd descended the staircase at Miss Sheffield's and seen him. Her vision blurred, and she quickly thrust the pendant at him.

"I shall do my best," he promised.

"Thank you very much," she replied with a tremor in her voice. Before matters could grow worse, she got up and fled.

Abby picked at her midday meal in the privacy of her room before slipping into the altered black crepe dress. It was still fashionable with its tight, long sleeves and full bell skirt; stylishness would be important to Cornelius. Molly had not yet stitched in the neckline insert, the lack of which suddenly suited Abby's purpose; she must forget how she disliked looking—wanton. Besides, her mother had often worn low necklines. Fashionable women did, and one must not make too much of it. As it was, her mother had always told her that she was overly sensitive.

She studied her reflection in the mirror. If what she'd heard about Cornelius was true, he should be pleased at her womanly figure, which the dress showed off to advantage. Moreover, he must be made aware that she was no longer the girl he had been coerced by his parents into taking horseback riding and to suitable plays and musicales. She swept back her golden hair into a chignon. With her fair complexion and blue eyes she looked better than expected in the black dress. She only hoped that Cornelius would think so, too. She had made her decision: despite the scandal, she intended to remain in New York and, therefore, she must marry him.

She felt a twinge of embarrassment as she recalled Daniel's words: Would you know how to encourage a man? She was somewhat unsure, but she'd use whatever ploys necessary to bring Cornelius around to the idea of marriage.

Abby sprayed herself liberally with Fleur-de-lis, pinched

the pallor from her cheeks, and practiced fluttering her lashes demurely at her reflection in the mirror. She would manage it as well as she could, she promised herself, keeping an eye on the window.

Molly was out marketing and could not announce guests. At the first glimpse of Cornelius, Abby caught up her black parasol and hurried down the staircase. To her consternation, she encountered Daniel ascending the steps.

"How very . . . nice you look, Abby," he said, though he appeared surprised at her low neckline.

"Thank you," she said, lowering her eyes in embarrassment. "When Uncle Benjamin returns, please tell him I'll not be here for supper." It was fortunate that she and Cornelius would not have to see her uncle, for he might inquire too bluntly about Cornelius's intentions and frighten him off. She opened the door before Cornelius could knock.

"Good afternoon, Cornelius," she said, trying to appear inordinately pleased to see him.

"Well . . . Abigail!" Cornelius said, his eyes fastening upon her decolletage. "How very different you look."

"As do you with that handsome mustache, Cornelius," she replied smoothly. "But I am growing accustomed to your mustache . . . and to your being a man now."

His fingers went to the flaxen pointed mustache, and he gave his toothy smile. "Why, thank you, Abigail."

Stepping out the door, she added, "I do hope that you approve of . . . my growing up."

"And why shouldn't I?" he asked. His gray eyes brimmed with pleasure as he appraised her. "What a charming upstairs maid you would make in your black gown, if I may say so."

She was taken aback, then quickly rallied to tap his arm playfully with her parasol before opening it. "You may, but only you! And now, my dear sir, if you'll lend me an arm."

His toothy smile flashed again. "At your service, Abigail."

She took his arm, beaming at him. He did look rather attractive when he was pleased, and he wore a handsome suit, brocaded vest, and white linen shirt with the fashionable high stock around his neck. "Please call me Abby," she suggested, giving his arm a companionable squeeze.

He blinked in astonishment. "Yes, of course . . . Abby." Belatedly, he remembered to close the door behind them. "I—I thought we might stroll through the park, and then hire a carriage. I didn't think you would want to undertake anything too strenuous since you are in mourning."

"How thoughtful, Cornelius, but then you always have been. I think, however, that exercise is good for me just now. At Miss Sheffield's, they have begun to encourage strenuous exercise for ladies to combat distress."

"Well, then . . . we shall walk for as long as you like."

Abby suspected that Daniel might be watching them from his window as they crossed the street toward the park, but she refused to let the thought deter her. She carried on as if this were her first outing ever with Cornelius, as if they hadn't already walked through Union Square Park scores of times over the years. To her astonishment, her conversation issued forth as though she were an accomplished actress. Her mother had mentioned that a certain amount of illusion was required between the two sexes, a kind of haze through which men and women should not see each other too plainly. Despite her early misgivings, Abby now felt exhilarated by the success of her efforts.

After strolling through the sprawling park, they made their way to the roar and clatter of Broadway, discussing the latest concerts and plays. Later, they crossed over to Chambers Street and admired elegant shop windows that displayed cut glass, silver, and fine silks and gauzes in the stores of fashion. After she married Cornelius, she would shop here at the great store of Mr. Alexander Steward—that is, when she wasn't shopping in Paris. Marrying Cornelius would provide a number of advantages, particularly the one of remaining in New York instead of living on the wild Missouri frontier.

Cornelius suggested an early supper at Astor House, the finest hotel in America, which was also an incredible five stories high. Abby felt a trifle uncertain about dining in public while in mourning, but she felt famished and accepted.

Inside, Cornelius selected lobster pie and a French wine for both of them. Later, while they dined, she noticed several of her parents' friends passing by the table. They acknowledged her with a hint of disapproval. Her half glass of wine, however, cushioned their glances, and she smiled dolefully in return.

"They think I am awful, already dining out," she said to Cornelius, remembering to flutter her lashes tearfully. "Do you think I am awful, too?"

His nose had reddened slightly from drinking the wine, and he blinked at her coquettishness. "Not at all. It is none of their affair and I am willing to tell them as much."

"Thank you for being so understanding," she said, "and so wonderful." She gazed at him soulfully, trying not to despise herself for it.

His gray eyes began to fill with adoration and his mustache twitched. "You are the one who is wonderful. I had no idea you could be so brave. It appears that I truly never knew you."

"Oh, Cornelius!" she protested prettily, marveling at the ardor she could arouse so easily by a bit of acting. She had thought him an old stick, but perhaps she had been mistaken. Very likely her poor impression of him had been her own fault for giving him insufficient attention. In any event, he appeared enthralled with her now. *Young Couple Dining at Astor House*, she entitled the opulent scene and planned someday to sketch it.

As they left the dining room, she was thrilled at the admiration she received from the waiters and other diners. Quite suddenly, across the room, she saw Daniel dining with two other gentlemen. Perhaps he would take the opportunity to sell her pendant necklace, she hoped. He had undoubtedly been watching her for some time, for he was giving her a rather perplexed smile. She nodded slightly, delighted to have him witness her success.

She and Cornelius made their way out into the warm May air, Abby holding his arm as they walked through the stately columns and then descended the steps of Astor House. Horse-drawn carriages clattered along the street, the drivers and passengers gazing with awe at the hotel and its well-dressed guests. Abby basked in their approbation, noticing that Cornelius appeared as pleased as she felt.

The liveried doorman hired a carriage from among those waiting, and Cornelius tipped the man generously. At length, Abby was being helped into the cab of a fine carriage, and they rode away in elegance to the sound of the horses clip-clopping smartly through the city.

"May I?" Cornelius asked in a move to hold her hand, and, when she nodded her approval, he took it in his.

"It's not as though we haven't known each other for years," she replied, though she wished his hands were not quite so damp. "I don't know when I've had a finer or more interesting time, Cornelius, despite the sad circumstances." That at least was the truth. Their outing was most interesting, and she'd never before engaged in the rites of courtship.

He hesitated, then said huskily, "Abby, you know that our parents had always hoped we might be more than friends."

"Yes?" she encouraged, drawing closer to him.

His gray eyes darted toward the driver's back, then out the windows. With a look of wildness he slipped his arm around her, gathering her up to him. "I don't like the idea of your going West . . . or of leaving New York. I should like to discuss it further with my family," he said, "but—"

"Yes, my dear Cornelius?" she asked, lifting her face to his.

"Oh, Abby, I care a great deal for you!" His face tilted to hers, his mustache brushing her mouth, then his wet lips fastened greedily upon hers.

She dared not resist, though it was beyond her how Rose and the other girls at school enjoyed such a disgusting meeting of the lips. Perhaps with time improvement would come. When he finally backed away from her, it was all she could do not to wipe off her lips. In any case, the carriage had stopped in front of her house.

"I love you, Abby," Cornelius uttered. "I will not permit you to go West."

"Oh, Cornelius," she whispered with a flush of success.

The driver turned, leaving Abby no way to continue while Cornelius helped her out. Despite a twinge of apprehension, she bid him a coquettish farewell at the door.

Inside the house, she wiped her mouth and burst into tears again. What was wrong with her, she wondered as she sobbed. She had never in her entire life felt so miserable.

5

The next morning after breakfast, Uncle Benjamin said, "We should be getting ready for church now."

"We?" Abby asked uneasily.

"Certainly," he replied. "After all, they are giving the memorial service for your parents tomorrow, even though your parents were not regular members."

"Yes, of course, Uncle Benjamin," Abby said, not wishing to disappoint him.

"Molly tells me she has finished alterations on a suitable black dress for you," her uncle said.

Abby glanced at Daniel to see whether he had betrayed her about yesterday's dress, but his expression remained as unreadable as it had been all morning.

Later, she arrived downstairs in her black bonnet and the black lawn frock. Molly had snipped fabric from the full skirt to fill in the bodice and sewn jet buttons up to the neck.

"You look most presentable," her uncle said.

"Thank you, Uncle Benjamin," she replied, not daring to look at Daniel again. Today's black dress had a high stand-up collar lined with black rushing. Black on black.

Her uncle continued, "This morning we received an invitation for a quiet dinner after church from the Adams family. Since they are kind enough to have the reception tomorrow after the memorial service, I accepted the invitation for all of us."

"How kind of them," Abby said calmly, though her spirits rose. That meant Cornelius had already spoken to his family. Perhaps there might even be an announcement of their intentions this afternoon! She supposed that Cornelius would first have to ask her uncle for her hand in marriage. Under the circumstances, it could all be managed quickly.

Daniel opened the front door for her, smiling pleasantly. "After you."

Outside, the sky had clouded over, but even impending rain could not discourage her. As she stepped up into the carriage, it occurred to her that Cornelius sometimes had to accompany his mother to church, and that they might also be in attendance.

It was only a short ride to the brownstone Gothic church, which had stained-glass windows and a fine carillon tower. Daniel helped her down from the carriage and quietly inquired, "Did you have a pleasant dinner last evening?"

"Yes, I had a fine time, thank you. I trust that you did, too?"

He smiled ruefully, his hand still under her elbow. "Pleasant enough, but I suspect it wasn't as fine an evening as yours." He smelled clean, of soap, and pleasantly masculine, not of wine as Cornelius had last night.

She quickly moved away, trying to focus on his comment. He probably meant that he had been dining with men whereas she had been part of a couple. No appropriate reply came to mind, and she turned to look about as Joseph drove the carriage away across the cobblestones.

The church bells rang out, their deep tones drifting through the misty morning air as the worshipers converged upon the church. There was no time to reflect on Donne's famous line about for whom the bell tolled, for around them horses and carriages rattled away after letting out parishioners in their fine Sunday attire. A flurry of subdued greetings surrounded them, and Abby looked past them hopefully for Cornelius and his mother.

Inside, the nave of the church rose skyward in a great arc, and soft organ music wafted over the crowd filling the wooden pews. Abby followed an usher to a pew in the middle of the sanctuary, seeing no sign of Cornelius along the way. She sat down between Daniel and her uncle and, smoothing her black skirt, scrutinized the magnificent stained-glass windows.

The one nearest them depicted Christ, arms widespread with welcome; the words inscribed below it were: *I am the way, the truth, and the life.* She regarded His stained-glass eyes; it seemed that they peered into her soul.

She glanced quickly at her program and read, *Commit thy way unto the Lord; trust also in him; and he shall bring it to pass. Psalm 37:5.* She read the verse again. It sounded uplifting, but what did it mean? As always when she read Scripture and attended church, it seemed that she was at the edge of a vast mystery that was open to others, but never to her.

Hymnbook pages rustled as the organ began the prelude. Beside her, Daniel and Uncle Benjamin rose to their feet with the congregation, and she quickly put her ponderings aside and stood, too.

Daniel shared his hymnal with her, singing out with the others in his deep, resonant voice:

> "O worship the King, all glorious above,
> And gratefully sing His power and His love;
> Our Shield and Defender, the Ancient of Days,
> Pavilioned in splendor, and girded with praise."

A shiver coursed through her, and she sang along softly about His might and His grace. What did it mean—His robe is the Light? How peculiar that she, a minister's grand-daughter, did not even know or understand the songs of the church, except for Christmas carols, of course. And sometimes she didn't understand them. Why had her father turned from Christianity? To be fashionable? So that he might keep a—a mistress? What disgrace he had brought upon himself and upon the family name through his life! She tried to set her anger aside, to concentrate on the last verse.

> "Frail children of dust, and feeble as frail,
> In Thee do we trust, nor find Thee to fail;
> Thy mercies how tender, how firm to the end,
> Our Maker, Defender, Redeemer, and Friend."

Our friend? What did it mean, Christ as one's friend? It seemed a preposterous notion. She supposed that she vaguely believed in God, a faraway God who had made the universe. Her eyes went to the nearby stained-glass window of Christ, then quickly turned away. It was said that God sent Him, His Son, for them, but she still did not see the sense of it.

She sat down with the congregation again, glancing at Daniel, who appeared as intent upon the service as he had been fervent in song. His inner strength seemed to pervade the space around him. Did he receive that peculiar quality from his faith? She recalled the day he had spoken about his having to forgive; something dire must have happened to him.

Finally she forced her mind to the sermon, which bore the rather lengthy title of "Come unto me, all ye that labour and are heavy laden."

The minister repeated the title words, then he added with feeling, "and I will give you rest."

Abby's lips quivered at the idea of receiving rest from her current tribulations. She was heavily laden indeed with the death of her parents, the bankruptcy, the scandal, the problem of leaving her home and New York if she didn't marry Cornelius . . . not to mention being torn from Miss Sheffield's before graduation. She firmed her resolve. She would not leave New York! Tears clouded her eyes. Her parents would want her to remain here. She felt in her frock pocket for a handkerchief, but it was empty.

Beside her, Daniel handed her his neatly folded handkerchief, and she blinked gratefully at him before dabbing her eyes. If only she did not cry so readily now.

"My yoke is easy, and my burden is light," the minister said.

What did it mean? All she knew was that her burden was exceedingly heavy and that something within her yearned to understand more clearly about God. Yet it was too mysterious. Did the people here in this church understand? Did Daniel and her uncle comprehend what it was all about? From the look of them, they understood a great deal more than she.

At length the congregation sang a solemn hymn and then remained standing. The minister's hand reached powerfully out above the people as he blessed them and, though she could not explain it, Abby did feel as if her burdens were somewhat lessened.

There was still no sign of Cornelius when they left the church, and she could only think that tomorrow they would attend her parents' memorial service here. People all around looked at her with sympathy, and she bit down on her trembling lips. She did not want their pity! She did not want it!

Outside, Joseph awaited them with the carriage and, by

the time they had driven to Union Square Park, she had her emotions under control again. This dinner with Cornelius's parents and grandmother was important, indeed portentous, for it would help to determine the course of her life. She fervently hoped that his grandmother, who held the family purse strings, would not be as cold and formal as usual.

The Adams mansion on the opposite side of the park, though nearly twice the size of her own family's, was also of brownstone and equally plain on the exterior.

When the butler showed them into the entrance hall, however, the riches of the Adams family were evident in the fine old Italian paintings, French crystal chandelier, and Brussels carpets on the white marble floor. The butler escorted them into the equally sumptuous green drawing room, where Cornelius and his father rose from the Venetian antique furniture to greet them. His mother and corpulent grandmother nodded graciously as the introductions to Daniel and Benjamin were made.

Abby's eyes flew to Cornelius for reassurance, but his gaze studiously avoided hers. He was simply being careful, she told herself. Yes, that's all that it was. His aloofness was good manners for this somber occasion. She noted that he and his entire family wore black. Set against the drawing room's green opulence, she titled the scene *Society in Mourning*.

Cornelius's mother said, "How splendidly you are managing, Abigail. How proud of you your dear mother would be."

Abby caught a breath, then said, "Thank you. We appreciate your kindness in having the reception here tomorrow."

"It was the least we could do," her mother's friend replied gently.

Cornelius's father helped to seat Abby. His hooded gray

eyes, so similar to his son's, surveyed her figure quite openly, as if to discover what Cornelius might see in her.

Embarrassed, Abby turned to Cornelius's grandmother, whose late husband had been president of the bank. Abby's spirits sank even lower. The enormously fat woman, whose black crepe gown covered her like a great tent, scrutinized her icily.

Abby reminded herself that the older woman was a great arbiter in New York society, and finally managed, "It is a pleasure to see you again, Mrs. Adams."

The old dowager's gray eyes flashed like silver. "Indeed!" she replied with disbelief.

The butler stood by to take orders for refreshments, and the woman's attention turned to him. Beside them, the men had struck up a conversation. After a decent interval, Abby excused herself to freshen up. Cornelius's mother departed from the drawing room with her, chatting about the weather as if everything were quite normal.

However, in the dressing room Mrs. Adams said, "Cornelius has told us about your mutual feelings, my dear. You must notice that he is being circumspect. The fact is that his grandmother feels the two of you are quite young . . . too young to be serious."

"But he is twenty-two, and I am seventeen now," Abby protested in dismay. "It is not at all too young—"

"Yes, dear, perhaps I should have mentioned that there is something more to it. Cornelius will probably not have an opportunity to tell you of his grandmother's wishes. She would prefer that he . . . that eventually he marry someone else."

"Someone else! But then I must go on to Missouri!"

The auburn curls around his mother's ears bobbed slightly as she nodded, and her brown eyes filled with dismay. "You know I would like to help my best friend's daughter . . . if only there were a way."

Heartsick, Abby turned toward the mirror and pretended to smooth her chignon. Her voice faltered. "It is the scandal about that—that woman then, isn't it?"

"No," Beatrice Adams said, "although it is the excuse likely to be used." A trace of bitterness entered her voice. "A good many husbands in New York society have a 'friend' like your father's. When all is said and done, the problem is your family's finances. In the mind of most people, losing one's money is the real sin, although they would never say it. They can't bear to consider such a possibility for themselves."

"I see," Abby replied bleakly.

Later, in the ornate dining room, she was seated between Daniel and her uncle, leaving no opportunity for a private word with Cornelius. Perhaps he would elope with her! Yes, perhaps that was why he was being so careful now to be distant. She managed to catch his eye from across the table, and he nodded with what was surely more than mere politeness. Recently, more and more couples in society had eloped. The girls at school said it took considerable daring, and some thought it would be exciting beyond words to flee so romantically from one's parents.

The dinner courses dragged on with dreary magnificence, and Abby held fast to her golden hope. Something would work out yet. Somehow she would be able to stay in the city. She and Cornelius would solve this dilemma!

Finally the dinner came to its elegant finale, and it was time to leave. In the entrance hall, Cornelius slipped her a note, which she quickly concealed in her pocket. She tried not to smile too broadly at the flash of passion in his eyes. He had worked something out for them after all!

All the way home in the carriage, she held her pocket

shut, and, when they arrived at the Talbot mansion, she excused herself immediately and rushed to her room.

Breathless, she closed her door behind her and read Cornelius's words:

Dearest Abby, he began, and her heart quickened at the endearment.

It is said that love will find the way. It is said too that the course of true love never did run smoothly. We are star-crossed lovers like Romeo and Juliet, but we were never meant to give up. Come out to your garden at nine o'clock tonight, my love.

> *Adoringly,*
> *Cornelius*

Her spirits soared. It was as though he had read her thoughts during dinner. He was a gentleman, and since he was inviting her out for a tryst tonight, he meant that they should elope! She must pack now, immediately, before Molly or Uncle Benjamin or Daniel found them out.

At nine o'clock, Abby tiptoed down the steps, her small traveling bag in hand. Her uncle and Daniel had retired to their rooms, if not to bed, and she worried that they might hear. It was not an easy matter to think of eloping on the eve of her parents' memorial service, but no one would expect it of them tonight—which made it an even more brilliant plan. She wended her way through the kitchen, hiding her traveling bag near the door. Molly and Joseph were certain to be in their quarters over the carriage house.

The kitchen door squeaked softly as she opened it and stepped out into the moonlight. She closed the door quietly and, avoiding the pale flagstone path, stayed to the shadows, straining to hear his voice. Then there he was, stepping out of the darkness.

"Abby," he whispered and she ran to him, throwing herself into his arms.

"Oh, Abby!" he breathed warmly into her hair. "I knew you would come. If only you knew my anguish at dinner. If only you knew how I yearned to have you in my arms."

His kisses were wetter than ever, but the enchantment of their moonlit tryst caused her to tremble, and the wine on his breath intermingling with the fragrance of the lilacs nearly made her swoon.

"Abby, I love you," he murmured.

"Oh, Cornelius—" she whispered in reply, unable to vow that she truly loved him, too. Love would come after they were married; she'd heard the girls at school speak of that. She would do her best to be a perfect wife if he would only marry her and keep her in New York.

He kissed her again and whispered, "My dearest. . . ."

This, then was what it was like to be in love. This was what Rose and her friends at school had intimated was so wonderful. Abby felt a twinge of disappointment, but was determined to overcome it. She must love him, she must, she told herself. At the very least, she must pretend.

His arms were strong, and he whispered, "Abby, my dearest, how much do you love me?"

Abby leaned away at the calculating tone in his voice. How much did she love him? How much? "Why . . . enough to have packed my bag to elope with you."

His voice filled with astonishment. "To elope?"

"But isn't that why you meant me to meet you here?"

She suddenly remembered that the girls at school had called him a rake. Had she been wrong? Didn't he mean to elope? "Don't you mean to marry me?"

"You know that's impossible now," he whispered insistently. "You must see how my grandmother feels about it. It's simply a matter of waiting, of time to let the scandal die down. Let's not speak of it now."

He simply meant to take advantage of her situation! She was positive of it. His renewed hold on her seemed unbreakable, but she gathered her strength and, with a mighty effort, stamped her high-heeled slipper onto his shoe.

He howled, rearing back and loosening his grip on her, and Abby gathered up her skirts and ran.

"You are a cad, Cornelius!" she shouted behind her into the night, not caring in the least that Miss Sheffield's young ladies were to speak in well-modulated voices. "You are an unspeakable, unspeakable cad!"

Worst of all, she reflected as she let herself into the kitchen and locked the door, she had been just as bad in her own selfish way. She'd connived and led him on. If this was love, Rose and the girls at Miss Sheffield's could keep it. She wanted no further part of it.

In the midst of her anger and guilt, she knew with complete certainty that all possibility of remaining in New York was lost.

6

Benjamin Talbot waited uneasily in the front entry of his late brother's mansion for the carriage to carry him and Abby to the memorial service. Molly had taken breakfast up to Abby this morning, reporting that his niece was as well as could be expected.

He heard the swish of silk and glanced at the staircase again, and was relieved to see Abby slowly coming down the steps. She wore a sedate black dress and a long black mourning veil so heavy it hid her features, and she held onto the railing as if she hadn't slept well.

"Joseph should return for us shortly," he told her.

She nodded, but said nothing.

"Are you going to be all right, Abby?"

She replied so softly that he had to strain to hear. "Yes, thank you, Uncle Benjamin."

"I regret that I must inquire," he said, "but to make travel arrangements, we need to know today if you have made your decision about where to go."

She glanced about as if to see whether anyone might overhear them, so at least she could see through her veil.

"Daniel and Molly have gone on ahead of us to the church," he assured her. "They had matters to attend to."

Reassured, she murmured, "I would like to accompany you to Missouri if I am still welcome."

It was impossible to guess what she might be thinking behind the heavy black veil, but he must be certain that she knew what awaited one on the frontier. "You are most welcome and my family will be pleased, but I must warn you again that it's a far more rustic life there than we have here, and we shall set out for California by covered wagon next spring."

"I understand." Her voice remained quiet, the voice of one who had gone beyond anguish. "I hope I might have time during the year before I make a decision about the trip to California."

"Yes, of course. It strikes me as a good idea for you to make one such decision at a time. You have endured a bad shock, a number of bad shocks."

She must have felt she should explain herself, for she added, "I shall not be marrying Cornelius Adams."

"I see."

"We are not . . . we are not compatible," she explained.

"I tend to agree with your decision," he said, not surprised. Last night he'd been awakened by a noise down in the garden and had seen her flee up the moonlit path from Cornelius. Perhaps he should have gone down to comfort her, but before he was half dressed, he'd heard her lock herself into her room. He'd tapped at her door and called her name softly several times, but she'd made no response.

This morning Molly had told him she'd found Abby's traveling bag by the back door. Having viewed enough of the garden scene to guess what had transpired, he was grateful that she'd had the wisdom to flee. It couldn't be easy to be a young woman alone, but then it wasn't always so easy to be a young man, either—nor even an old one, for that matter.

He was tempted to say so, but he was in no mood for platitudes himself, and she'd doubtless hear plenty of them after the service.

At the sound of a carriage clattering to their door, Benjamin glanced out the peep window. "Here comes Joseph with the carriage now. Time to depart."

She gave a despondent nod under her heavy black veil.

It seemed to him that in less than a week she had been transformed from a vibrant young woman who had laughed her way down the staircase of Miss Sheffield's school in a beautiful gown to this black pillar stilled by grief. *Lord,* he prayed, *guide and comfort her.*

Wednesday morning, Abby's mood was as mournful as her black dress, cloak, and bonnet as she arrived with Daniel and her uncle at the North River. She scarcely noticed Daniel's dark brows knit with concern as he handed her down from the carriage onto the wharf at Pier Two. Indeed, she was scarcely aware of the early morning bustle about them, only that their trunks were being directed to the ferryboat and that she was leaving New York, perhaps forever. She must not cry, she told herself firmly. She had contained her grief all through the memorial service and the reception, even upon leaving her home that morning.

"It will be an adventurous journey, you'll see," Daniel said, his hand at her elbow as he and Uncle Benjamin escorted her toward the ferryboat.

People swarmed around them in the sunshine—stevedores shouldering trunks and rolling heavily laden barrows over the wooden planks of the pier, peddlers hawking their wares, passengers chattering excitedly on their way to and from nearby boats. The North River underscored the cacophony, steadily lapping against the sturdy pilings.

"Smell the salt air?" Daniel asked her.

She nodded. The tang of salt air mingled with the pungent aromas of hot pitch, sun-dried hemp ropes, bales of tobacco, and the pervasive smell of fish. She had been rigid with anguish since awakening, but now the sounds and the smells, the tootling of boats and excited voices and bustle began to pique her interest.

"You'll be feeling better soon," Daniel remarked as they strode up the ferryboat's gangplank.

She smiled, albeit wanly, for what must have been the first time in days. "Yes, I do feel . . . better."

Torment at the loss of her parents still gnawed at her heart, but not quite so achingly with Daniel nearby. He and her uncle had remained at her side throughout the memorial service and the dignified reception afterward at the Adams mansion. Even Cornelius had pretended that nothing unseemly had transpired between them the night before, and she almost wondered if it had been a dream. His grandmother's absence from the reception was blamed upon illness. Both Uncle Benjamin and Daniel had appeared pleased that she evidenced no further interest in marrying Cornelius.

Now Daniel remarked, "I would like to see you sketch a wharf scene like this, Abby, though it's doubtless rather raucous for a young lady of your upbringing." He arched a speculative brow at her. "Could you portray this?"

He had been genuinely impressed at how determinedly she'd sketched Union Square Park, her home, and the garden yesterday morning to add to her portfolio. She glanced out over the tumult around them. "I don't know. There is so much activity and excitement." She recalled his mentioning the spirit of adventure on the frontier, and despite her sorrows and fears, an unexpected twinge of adventure stirred in her. She quickly rejected it.

Once they were settled on a wooden bench on the deck of the ferryboat, Daniel placed upon her lap the large but narrow package he had insisted upon carrying aboard himself. "For you," he said.

When she hesitated, he urged, "Open it."

Still bewildered, she untied the string and removed the brown paper to discover a sturdy tan leather case. She unlatched the case and opened the hinged lid. "Why, it's a portable painting case! I've never seen anything quite like it." The case contained sketch pads, pencils, brushes, a good selection of colors, and even a collapsible easel. "I—I don't know how to thank you for this."

"Your using it will be thanks enough," he replied. "I thought you might like to draw your way to Missouri. The scenes cry out to be captured, sights that will disappear as surely as the wilderness will be gone someday. It would be a favor to everyone if you'd paint the scenes, especially to Aunt Jessica and the rest of the family in Missouri. Most of them may never have the privilege of traveling through the places you will see."

"Yes—I hadn't thought of that." *It would keep my mind occupied*, she mused, yet an instant later she objected, "I'm not sure I can do justice to such scenes."

Her uncle said, "No matter how you depict them, your drawings would be the finest gift you could ever bring to my family. They are unfailingly curious about the sights I see on my trade expeditions. Jessica, my sister, has traveled across the country, and Joshua, my second oldest, is our trader, so he travels a great deal. But the rest of my children—Adam, Martha, Rena, Jeremy, and Betsy—have not been East."

"Then I shall attempt it for them," she decided. "You have both been so good to me." Her mouth trembled, and she closed it firmly to regain her composure.

Daniel suggested, "Why don't you start now, Abby?"

At the concern in his eyes, she quickly turned her attention to the pencils. "Yes, perhaps I shall." She opened a sketchbook and took up a pencil. After a moment's deliberation, she began to lightly sketch the scene at Pier Two of the North River: the wharfside color and excitement, the ferries, skiffs, rafts, and elegant packets plying the swiftly flowing water. She would have to remember the precise colors and shadings to add later, perhaps when she arrived in Independence.

Daniel said, "You might call it *Tumult at North River*."

"Yes . . . *Tumult at North River*." The title fit her emotional state as well as the scene. Her eyes took in the sights and she began to sketch, at first tentatively, then with growing sureness. His title was even more apt as the sketch took shape before her; the ships moving through the river implied new beginnings, forward movement through tumult no matter what happened.

While the ferryboat steamed across the water and Daniel and her uncle strolled about the deck, she rapidly sketched the vistas up and down the North River and along its New York and New Jersey banks, everything she could see of the panorama in the clarity of the sun's radiance.

Later, on the other side of the river, Abby stepped with them into their railroad car with continued anticipation. Uncle Benjamin said, "You two take that empty seat together. I'll sit up there." He waved toward the other vacant seat near the middle.

Abby obediently headed for the empty double seat, scarcely noting Daniel's perplexed glance at her uncle. After they had settled themselves, he extracted the morning's *New York Herald* from his black leather valise. The two of them had spent little time alone except in brief discussion of the generous amount of money he had obtained for her sapphire pendant. She had insisted that some of the money be used for her fare to Independence; Daniel would accompany her to deposit the remainder in a bank when he joined them in Independence.

The locomotive blasted a throaty warning, emitting a cloud of steam, and the conductor called out, "All aboard! New Brunswick! Trenton! Philadelphia!"

The train blasted another warning before the doors were slammed shut and the cars jerked into motion along the track. Abby gripped the armrest near the window, peering out at the Jersey City railroad station. White steam from their locomotive billowed forth as they chugged slowly into the New Jersey countryside.

Daniel had opened his newspaper, but he was apparently unable to concentrate on it. "Is this your first train ride?" he asked.

"At Miss Sheffield's we sometimes went on short excursions." In truth, Abby had very little railroading experience; her parents had rarely taken her along on their travels. Moreover, his tone of voice had implied that she was quite young. She cast a glance at him and found him gazing at her rather tenderly.

She quickly took up the portable drawing case.

"Here, let me assist you," he offered, and there was nothing to do but allow him to set the case across their laps, then for her to extract pencils and sketch pad and thank him.

"My pleasure," he responded, closing the case. He leaned across her to prop it under the window. "You smell of flowers, rather like a spring garden."

"It—it's Fleur-de-lis. My best friend at school gave it to

me for my birthday . . . before I left."

"I'm sorry. Your uncle and I didn't know. Even if we had . . . well, it wasn't a suitable time for birthday festivities, was it?"

"No, I daresay it wasn't."

"How old are you, Abby?"

Oh, why must he ask! she thought. When she was only sixteen, seventeen seemed quite grown-up, but now it didn't sound quite old enough.

He chuckled. "Are you going to inform me again that it's impolite to ask such questions?"

She gave a little smile. "Yes, it's not polite to ask."

He sat back against his seat with an enigmatic smile spreading across his lips. "You are seventeen years old."

"Really, that's unfair! You might at least have guessed eighteen, since most of the girls in my class at school were."

Amusement danced in his eyes. "You are far too beautiful for your own good, Miss Abigail Talbot. But I presume you have often heard that before."

Her heart leapt. "You are the first man who has ever said so."

His blue eyes sparkled. "Well, I am glad of that."

Despite all of his questions and teasing, he did care for her, she thought and turned to the window.

Calming herself, she set about sketching the New Jersey countryside in its spring green while the train rushed by. When she had completed several rough sketches, she noticed that Daniel had finished with the newspaper, and she ventured, "I'm afraid I'm a bit nervous about moving in with Uncle Benjamin and his family. He assures me that I am welcome, but I—I wonder how they will accept me, a complete stranger, particularly since there was trouble between our families."

"You can put any such anxiety to rest," Daniel said. "They will accept you with wide open hearts as they did me." He studied her countenance, then said, "Perhaps you should know how I came to be part of their family. I'm sure that you will eventually find out—not that they would be the ones to tell."

"I only know that they took you in as a child. It didn't seem my place to inquire beyond that."

"Then it is my place to tell you." He gazed past her out the train window. "It began when I was five years old and moving to Missouri with my parents by covered wagon. We had stopped for the night, down by a creek, and I was sent out to find firewood. I looked about for wood for quite some time and, as I returned . . . I saw three Indians approaching the covered wagon. I was so frightened that I hid behind a tree." He drew a regretful breath. "To make a short story of it, the Indians killed my family."

"How terrible! How terrible for anyone . . . and for a small boy—"

"It certainly was." He closed his eyes for a moment. "I saw it. Rather, some of it. I was still shaking in terror behind that tree when they came out into the open carrying my mother's and father's scalps."

"Oh, Daniel!"

"I was shocked, then full of terror and rage and grief. I became filled with a terrible hatred toward all Indians. I might never have come out of it sane if your uncle hadn't found me there trying to bury my parents. I know now that it was not by coincidence that he came. At any rate, he took me in . . . he and your Aunt Elizabeth, who was still alive then, and they raised me as if I were one of their own children."

"I had no idea," Abby said, "but then I know so little

about you . . . or about Uncle Benjamin and his family."

"They were wonderful to me. And now you know why I was so adamant that night about your having to forgive your parents and Roxanna Murray," he continued. "I went through years of agony, nightmares by night and flashes of that memory by day. I finally learned that we must totally forgive others and ourselves, just as God will forgive us if we ask."

She gazed blindly out the window. "You spoke of an uncle in Boston. Why didn't you live with him?"

"At that age, I only knew that my father had an older brother back East. He finally traced me down when I was fourteen, and he had me educated in Boston, with your cousin, Adam, who is my age. Later, I entered the shipping and chandlery firm owned by my uncle, Elisha Wainwright, who is a childless widower. From that beginning grew the firm of Wainwright and Talbot."

Daniel sat back, his brow furrowed. "I rarely tell anyone about that childhood experience, but I wanted you to understand why I spoke so strongly about your forgiveness that night. I don't want you to endure more grief."

"Thank you for your concern," she said and quickly turned to her sketching again. She did not intend to dwell on the scandal; as far as she was concerned, that was over. She intended to forget that she had even heard about—to simply forget it once and for all. True, Daniel had survived a terrible hardship, and it had given him strength, but Abigail Windsor Talbot would survive the hardships of life in her own way.

Daniel dozed from New Brunswick to Trenton, and Abby sketched him, her pencil caressing the soft curls of his hair and beard, his long dark lashes resting against his cheeks. His nose was straight, his forehead high, his neck thick and strong. She quickly drew in his broad shoulders. Now that she knew more about his background she was able to capture not only his aura of strength, but the surprising tenderness about his lips, the fine smile lines near his eyes.

Suddenly his lashes fluttered and he looked up at her. It was an instant before he awakened enough to understand why she was looking at him. He straightened up with a suspicious glance at her. "Are you drawing a portrait of me?"

"Y—yes, I hope you don't mind. I should have asked your permission, but it was such an opportunity. . . ."

He peered at his likeness. "Do I look that . . . boyish when I'm asleep?"

"I thought so. Perhaps I shouldn't have drawn it." She fought the color rising to her cheeks. Didn't he know what a handsome man he was? She withdrew the sketch and closed her sketch pad, hoping that he would not demand the portrait.

"What do you intend to do with it?" he inquired.

"I thought I'd keep it with the others of this journey to share with your family—*Daniel Sleeping Through New Jersey.*"

"Well, I am certain they have seen me looking far worse." He gave a laugh. "It's not everyone who knows what they look like asleep."

"No, I daresay not," she replied, grateful he'd not been angry. As for actually sharing it with his family, she was uncertain now whether she wanted to.

Not caring to examine her feelings, she quickly turned the page in her sketchbook and began a new sketch of the countryside outside the train window. Her life might be in a bad tangle, but at least nature furnished the earth with serene vistas. She supposed that Daniel would say, "God's in His heaven, all's right with the world."

7

It was nearly nightfall when they arrived at Philadelphia's railroad station. A heavy spring rain pounded the roof above the train platform, and beyond the roof, there was nothing except the driving rain. As their porter wheeled their luggage around through the damp station, Abby eyed the dismal weather with disappointment.

Uncle Benjamin said, "I suppose we shall have to take dinner at the hotel and stay in. I had hoped we might stroll around the city, since Abby has never been here."

"I'd hoped so myself," Abby said. Just as sad was the thought of leaving Daniel behind here and not seeing him for months. She'd grown increasingly comfortable in his presence, even though he was a great deal older than she. It heartened her just to see him at her side, strong and handsome in his dark suit, his blue eyes attentive and full of life. He seemed like a stalwart friend.

Surrounded by their fellow travelers, the three of them made their way from the platform toward the exit. As they neared the street, Daniel hurried ahead to hire a carriage. When Abby arrived with her uncle and the porter, she managed to climb into the carriage without getting drenched.

"What was it that Longfellow says about the rain?"

Daniel asked. " 'How beautiful is the rain! After the dust and heat, in the broad and fiery street, and in the narrow lane; how beautiful is the rain!' "

Abby's spirits lifted, and Uncle Benjamin chuckled. "I expect the farmers of Pennsylvania agree," he said. "The train conductor told me they'd had a dry spring so far. And didn't I tell you, Abby, that Daniel has a quote for every occasion and topic imaginable!"

"I am beginning to believe you," she replied with a taunting look at Daniel.

He held up a hand in amused protest. "Not at all."

But it did appear he had a quote for everything; as they rode in their hired carriage to the hotel, he quoted a British writer's description of the major eastern cities. " 'Boston turns up her erudite nose at New York; Philadelphia, in her pride, looks down upon both New York and Boston; while New York, chinking her dollars, swears the Bostonians are a parcel of puritanical prigs, and the Philadelphians a would-be aristocracy.' "

"Precisely," Benjamin Talbot agreed with a chuckle. "Pride makes bigger fools of us than we already are."

As she sat between them in the carriage, Abby was not nearly so interested in civic pride as she was aware of the growing intensity of her feelings for Daniel—and the knowledge that he would remain here.

Minutes later, they arrived at the Philadelphian Hotel, and the doorman helped her in out of the rain. Abby had no idea how the three of them might be accommodated, but the men arranged for a suite with a small sitting room and two bedrooms, one for her, and the other for them.

Once in her room, she removed her bonnet and her damp black traveling dress. It was a relief to wash herself and brush her hair. She swept it up anew, allowing a few blonde tendrils to curl on her forehead and about her ears. Refreshed, she pulled on her more elegant black bombazine frock.

When she returned to the sitting room, Daniel's eyes filled with approval at her appearance, and her heart lifted with happiness. Even her uncle said, "You look lovely, Abby, but then you always do."

Daniel inquired with elaborate courtesy, "May we escort you downstairs now, Miss Talbot?"

"You may, Mr. Wainwright," she returned, taking his proffered arm.

"The Philadelphian is a fine hotel," he said, "but it is not Astor House in New York."

She blushed at the memory of her evening with Cornelius there. "I do believe I prefer the Philadelphian's more subdued atmosphere," she replied, thinking, as well as the company.

"I am glad to hear that," he said.

He looked so pleased that it seemed he'd read her mind, and she was grateful to have to deal with the fullness of her bell skirt as she passed through the sitting room door.

Downstairs, the hotel dining room's lack of opulence seemed insignificant. With Daniel at her side, it mattered little whether the chandeliers were French or the carpeting Persian; nor was it of import to dine upon lobster pie as she had with Cornelius at the Astor House. Here, she was more than content with her roast beef dinner with its spring potatoes, gravy, and fresh peas.

Whenever Daniel caught her eye, she felt a surge of bittersweet joy. They would part in the morning, but she would sketch these precious moments to remember this evening. This painting, however, would not be a scene of sophisticated pretense like *Young Couple Dining at Astor House,* but one that bore a title about contentedness and inner happiness.

After dinner her uncle said, "You two stay for dessert if you like. An old fellow like me has to get his sleep before attempting the portage railroad tomorrow."

Daniel laughed. "It will be a memorable event. I hope Abby will sketch it."

The men had discussed the vagaries of the upcoming crossing of the Allegheny Mountains with amusement, but it sounded precarious to her—boats being dragged from the canal, lifted onto a track and used as a train to get them up and then down the great mountain. "Perhaps I should retire now, too," she said.

Daniel caught her arm as she began to rise. "Won't you have fresh strawberries and cream with me?" he urged.

"Thank you. Perhaps I shall." She settled back, tempted less by the dessert than by his continued presence.

As they spoke, it was as though they were alone in the vast dining room, uninterrupted by their waiter's comings and goings. Their words flowed with ease—where strawberries might come from this time of the year, what a pleasant hotel the Philadelphian was with its subdued chandeliers and fine linen and silver. The words meant nothing; they only bound Abby and Daniel together as the two of them were encircled by this wonderous glow. She did not need décolleté or pretense to interest Daniel, as she did with Cornelius.

After they had finished their dessert and he had signed for their dinner, she was vaguely aware that they were wending their way through the dining room, then seemingly floating up the hotel's staircase to the suite.

In the hallway Daniel unlocked the door, and she stepped into the dimly lit sitting room. He closed the door softly behind them and gazed at her for a long moment. "Abby," he said, "you must not look at a man like that."

Like what? she wanted to ask.

His gaze was so disconcerting that she quickly said, "Thank you for a pleasant evening . . . and, now, if you will excuse me—Good evening." She turned and rushed to her room.

She must not make too much of his words, she reminded herself. Just look at what Cornelius had said to her—not that Daniel was like him. At any rate, Daniel was a far older man.

The next morning, she hurriedly repacked for the trip to Pittsburgh. Daniel was quiet at breakfast. Later, when they arrived at the railroad station, his expression became exceedingly tender. "Good-bye, Abby," he said, his voice making her name beautiful.

My dearest friend, Rose,

I am writing aboard a steamboat, the *Columbia,* which in some aspects is not unlike New York's floating palaces in magnificence. It is new and the finest boat we have seen on the Ohio River. My uncle, Benjamin Talbot, and I embarked in Pittsburgh and have been steaming along for some days. You will be pleased to know that I am sketching the river scenes en route. In the evenings, I add watercolors to the pictures in my stateroom.

Matters did not work out between Cornelius and me, and now that I am on this adventure, I am not too sorry. Daniel Wainwright—the one you thought so romantic with his dark beard and "eyes the color of the sea at Marble- head"—presented me with a portable painting case when we departed from New York, and I have been hard at work at it ever since. And, Rose, I am beginning to think I am smitten by love, too. Unfortunately, I fear he thinks me too young. Worse, I shall not see him for months as he will be in Philadelphia, Boston, and New York.

It took over three days to reach Pittsburgh, where we boarded the *Columbia*. What sights we see as we steam along the Ohio. Last week we noticed a procession of people moving from a village toward the river. At first no one understood their intentions. Finally one of the men left the others standing on the bank and walked into the river with a woman dressed in black. They stood motionless, then suddenly he submerged her backward into the water! A baptism! Can you imagine it! I titled my sketch of the scene *Frontier Baptism*—far too unpoetic. Perhaps Daniel will think of a better title; he understands our divertissement of bestowing titles upon people and scenes as if they were paintings. Sometimes I think he understands everything about me.

A spirit of adventure abounds along the river. Between Cincinnati and Louisville, we saw the mail packet grounded on a sandbank; it had already been there for a day despite their hard work to float it free. Mail, however, can be a minor matter. People tell of a steamboat whose boiler burst and blew her pilot across the river from Ohio to Kentucky! Though that is likely exaggerated, it is no wonder letters to and from the frontier take so long!

Frontier people are a hardy lot. A typical steamboat breakfast includes beefsteak, chicken fricassee, all the griddle cakes one can eat, and for finicky eaters, "Baptized Toast," which we called milk toast at school. The men seem a much rougher lot than those in our circles in New York, but they unfailingly treat me like a lady, perhaps because I wear mourning. The women are abustle with children. Many our age already have two or three!

In St. Louis, I hope to see John Charles Fremont and his famous guide, Kit Carson, who are preparing for another expedition into the Far West. Those aboard discuss the explorations, and the newspapers insist, "Our manifest destiny is to overspread this continent." It sounds exciting, but I cannot reconcile myself to going to California with my uncle's family next year. Oh, dear, I hadn't told you. You must be as shocked as I was to hear about it. I fervently hope something might happen to hold me in Independence or even return me to New York.

How I miss you, my dear friend, and cherish your gift of Fleur-de-lis, knowing how much it meant to you. You must be in the final preparations for your wedding now, and I send my fondest wishes. I am so sorry that I cannot attend. When I am able, I will ship a special wedding gift from the frontier. Now I can only send my love, which I do most heartily.

Your loving friend,

Abby

P.S. Please write me in care of my uncle: Benjamin Talbot, Independence, Missouri. He assures me that it is not necessary to use a street address!

🌟 Benjamin Talbot sat out at a table on the ship's deck. Nearby, Abby sketched yet another river scene, and one of the young men admiring her and her work said, "Wait till you see the great valley of the Mississippi. There are paddle-wheel steamers, keelboats, flatboats, and rafts so thick you won't know what to draw first. They say that Cairo, Illinois, alone is port to thousands of steamships nowadays."

"I look forward to seeing it," Abby replied, continuing to sketch the Ohio River scene before them.

The young man persevered. "Do you know what the Indians thought when they first saw a steamboat?"

"No, I do not," Abby replied.

"They said, 'White man, bad man, keep a great spirit chained and build a fire to make it work a boat.'"

Abby laughed, but did not stop her work.

The young man added, "Indians called it 'a fire boat that walks on the waters.'"

Benjamin smiled. None of the young men who had made overtures to Abby seemed to appeal to her. He suspected, though, that Daniel had. What would come of it? he wondered. Perhaps nothing, with such a vast difference in age.

Drawing a deep breath, he set about writing a letter to him.

Dear Daniel,

I write you from the steamboat, *Columbia,* which is as comfortable as you promised. It was a good plan to take such a luxurious boat to begin, for Abby seems more content than I feared she would be when she first decided to come to Independence. I thank God for inspiring you to give her the painting case, for it has made all of the difference to her. How important it is for all of us to discover our talents and then to be usefully occupied. The only disadvantage to her painting is that it gives all of the young blades aboard an excuse to admire her work—and her. You may be certain that as an experienced father, I am successfully keeping them at bay.

She was uneasy at riding the Allegheny Portage Railroad, but her sketching made it bearable. I expect the sights of a covered-wagon trip to California would make that bearable for her, too, if she decides to go on with us. I am eager to see how many emigrant trains are leaving this year. I am still certain that God means for us to go to California, odd as that seems, not Oregon. Nonetheless, His ways are not our ways, and His thinking is not ours, as you well know.

Thank you again, my dear friend and son, for taking care of the final details of my brother's estate. I pray that something good will come of it all yet, for God so often brings goodness from evil. I pray, too, that all goes well with you.

With Christ's love,

Unable to sign the letter Father to Daniel, whose true father was no longer on earth, Benjamin decided, as usual, to sign the letter Benjamin Talbot.

Abby posted her letter to Rose in St. Louis, which stood at the confluence of the Mississippi and the Missouri Rivers, and was being called the Gateway to the West. The streets of the city bustled with carriages, buggies, drays, ox carts, and covered wagons, and the sidewalks were crowded with a vast array of people: riverboat gamblers, dance hall women, traders readying for the Santa Fe Trail, harried clerks, bull whackers seeking jobs with wagon trains, fur traders from the mountains, merchants loading goods on Missouri riverboats.

Her uncle showed her around the town, then he had to be about his business. At first when she walked out alone with her sketchbook, she felt intimidated by the place, but her mourning attire seemed to keep the rougher elements at bay.

As she gained courage, she sketched scenes of the colorful city market, and, across from it, the broad Mississippi River, which was dotted with steamboats that ranged from the whitest and finest to the unpainted and decrepit, and other riverworthy vessels from keelboats and flatboats to Indian canoes. The picturesque country boats were interesting to sketch: bull boats made of sapling frames covered with buffalo hide, elliptical mackinaws made of wood, pirogues that were two canoes with a platform built between them. Some of the larger vessels carried lumber, corn, tobacco, wheat, and furs downstream to the delta country, and sugar, molasses, cotton, and whiskey upstream. It was no wonder that the Mississippi was being called the national waterway.

More difficult to sketch were the levee scenes, where black roustabouts sang and called out over the tootling and shrill whistles of the boats. Sweat glistened on their muscled bodies as they heaved bales of cotton and wooden crates and barrels into heavy drays. Horses and mules shied in the thick mud, and drivers cursed, fighting for control as they steered their teams up from the wharf to the muddy streets. When a ruffian sidled up to her and said, "Well, ain't ye a beauty! What ye drawin' there?" she scarcely heard and he moved on. Oblivious to everything except her sketching, she even forgot her concerns about what lay ahead in Independence.

Her favorite scenes were of the industrious ferryboats that plied the water between St. Louis and the wooded Illinois shore. She'd quickly sketch their arrivals: a jumble of farm wagons, carts, livestock, and people crowded toward the front, eager to join in the noise and confusion at St. Louis.

Although the sight wasn't as exciting, she made a fast sketch of the gracious two-story brick house that had belonged to William Clark, the famous Northwest explorer, general, and former Indian agent for all tribes west of the Mississippi.

Three days after their arrival, they left on a squat, snub-nosed steamboat with twin smokestacks that rose like rabbit's ears on either side of the wheelhouse, and they began to travel the twisting 250 miles westward on the muddy Missouri River. Their boat carried not only a crowd of passengers, but a heavy cargo of flour, whiskey, sugar, and iron castings. In her filthy cabin, Abby found poor washing facilities, scanty bed sheets, a pillow filled with corn husks, and a leaky roof.

She was tempted to complain, but when she met her uncle out on deck again, he said, "It's a blessing we have cabins. The passengers who sleep on deck say everything is infested with rats and roaches."

"At least the *Columbia* was a fine vessel," she said, "and it took us most of the way."

He nodded with approval. "A good disposition helps a great deal when one travels."

Seconds later, her disposition was not as good when smoke from the smokestacks engulfed them. They hurried away coughing to the other side of the deck. Steamboats might be called "chariots of fire," but this was more a "chariot of smoke."

Once out of the smoke, they stood with the other passengers and stared at the muddy river and its green wooded banks.

"Some boatmen attribute their vigor to drinking the water of the Missouri," her uncle observed with amusement. "They claim it has more nutrients than the clear water of the Ohio."

She had to laugh. "It does look thicker!"

At length she said, "There are no sailboats on the river."

"The Missouri's too shallow for a deep keel," her uncle explained. "It's been said that everything bad about the Mississippi can be doubled for this river. It's crookeder, it's muddier, it's shallower, the current is swifter, it has more snags and bars, and there's a wind that's been known to blow a boat out of the channel. Years ago, herds of buffalo held up the boat traffic for hours while they forded the river. Someone once said, 'Of all the variables in creation, the most uncertain are the action of a jury, the state of a woman's mind, and the condition of the Missouri River!' "

Abby laughed. "No wonder there are mostly canoes!"

He nodded. "Each one made from a single cottonwood. They can carry ten or twelve men and a few tons of goods."

Mackinaws, bull boats, and pirogues moved up and down the river, too, and nearby a rustic flatboat navigated through the brown water with a family aboard, the father poling. "Ofttimes the migrants on them build their houses from the boats' timbers," Uncle Benjamin said.

"Matters could be worse," she replied half aloud. Hopefully they would not be worse in Independence. Her disposition would have to be good there so the family would not resent her presence. Her own parents would not have been very generous natured about taking in an unknown young woman, and the thought of her approaching arrival disquieted her more and more.

There were delays, however. For one, the river was too dangerous to run at night, so they had to tie up for darkness. Even during daylight, it was hard to buck the strong downstream current.

During the three-day trip Abby ate little and made no comment about the coarse meals with salty meats—usually buffalo—and rancid butter. On the third evening she was relieved to see the dock at the wooded Wayne City Landing for Independence.

Uncle Benjamin hired a buggy at the landing and, during the four-mile ride to Independence, Abby's trepidation grew. Upon arrival in the town filled with shanties and log buildings, she saw that it was much smaller than St. Louis, but even noisier, more crowded, and abustle with business. Tawdry signs lined the dirt streets: "Goods for Santa Fe trade! Goods for Oregon and California! All new and cheap!"

Seeing her consternation, Benjamin Talbot assured her, "It's much quieter where we live in the countryside."

Abby's anxieties were only somewhat alleviated. Now she wondered whether his family would expect them this early. Her uncle had sent a message from St. Louis about their arrival, but he'd been uncertain about catching the early boat. What if his family wasn't prepared? And what if they didn't like her?

She must try to remember their names. There was Aunt Jessica—a widow who had run the household since Uncle Benjamin's wife, Elizabeth, had died in childbirth. Cousin Betsy, now ten years old, was the child of that birth. Daniel had assured her that she would love Cousin Rena, who was also seventeen. Jeremy, who ran the farm, was twenty and had married last fall; he and his bride, Jenny, lived in a small house on the other side of the property. Joshua, the family's trader, was now in Boston. The other two children and their families owned houses in Independence so she might not meet them until later.

It was nearly sunset when the hired buggy drove up the wooded drive to the Talbot place on a hill. "Why, it's a log house!" Abby said with delight. After seeing so many frame houses and a few brick buildings, she'd had no reason to expect such a charming place with wild roses and daisies abloom. It was certainly not a mansion like the one in which she had grown up on Union Square, but it looked pleasant and commodious.

"It's old," Uncle Benjamin said, "and we've added rooms unto rooms and wings unto wings. It's a bit of a maze, but we like the place. I suppose we shall miss it in California, but Adam and his family will be moving in so the house and land will remain in the family."

As her uncle helped her down, people hurried from the house. "Rena thought you might be home early!" a girl who must be ten-year-old Betsy called out. "Welcome home, Papa! And, oh, welcome to our house, Cousin Abigail!"

Tears rushed to Abby's eyes as her small cousin with freckles and long auburn braids caught her in a hug.

"I'm Betsy," the girl said, her green eyes twinkling. "And this is Aunt Jessica, and here comes Reenie—I mean Rena . . . and that's Jeremy and his wife, Jenny—"

"Whoa!" Benjamin Talbot laughed. "You'll have Abby's head spinning!"

"Then it's Abby, not Abigail?" Aunt Jessica asked as she gave her niece a warm embrace.

"Yes . . . Abby, please."

Her aunt said, "We are so happy to have you here with us, dear."

"It's kind of you to make me feel so welcome."

The warmth in her aunt's brown eyes was as touching as her words, and she looked just as an Aunt Jessica should, with her gray hair pulled back into a bun and her slight plumpness suggesting she baked pies and cookies.

Behind her aunt stood a beautiful young woman with deep dimples, hair the color of pale moonlight, and disconcerting brown eyes. "Welcome," she said, her voice as soft as the ethereal aura about her. "You do look like an Abby, not an Abigail. I've been eager to meet you for ever so long. I'm Rena. I know we are going to be friends."

Abby did not doubt her words. "Thank you, Rena. I am certain we shall."

Then Abby was shaking hands with Jenny, the shy dark-haired bride, and twenty-year-old Jeremy, whose hair was as auburn as little Betsy's.

At length the luggage from the buggy was carried into the old log house. Inside, a fire danced in the huge rock fireplace in the parlor, its flames imparting a cheerful glow to the chinked log walls of the room. Roughly woven draperies—yes, homespun!—hung at the windows, and the settees and chairs were covered with horsehair; the other pieces were of dark oak. Bouquets of yellow wildflowers brightened the room, as did several oil paintings. Abby's eyes stopped on a painting of Grandmother Talbot—so similar to that which had hung in the New York house—and she flinched at the sight of her wearing the sapphire pendant.

"You're just in time for supper," Aunt Jessica said to her brother. "Your favorite—chicken fricassee."

Benjamin Talbot inquired, "And, pray tell, how were you so sure that we'd come home on an earlier boat?"

Aunt Jessica said, "We hoped so. We've missed you."

But at Abby's side little Betsy shook her head and whispered to Abby, "Rena knew. She talks to God all the time."

Abby's eyes wandered to Rena, who was lighting the candles on the trestle table, her face sweet and dimpled in the candleglow. "She's very beautiful."

"Yes," Betsy agreed, "and she has lots of beaus. They all want to marry her, but she's waiting."

"Waiting?" Abby inquired.

Betsy nodded solemnly, her auburn braids bobbing

against her narrow shoulders. Her green eyes held Abby's. "I thought everyone knew."

Abby shook her head. "No, I must be the exception."

Betsy whispered, "We're not supposed to tell . . . but everyone knows that someday Rena is going to marry Daniel."

8

Benjamin Talbot blinked awake as the first cock crowed. Still gray with sleep, his mind drifted to Peter's words: "Why cannot I follow thee now? I will lay down my life for thy sake."

Christ replied, "Verily, verily, I say unto thee, the cock shall not crow till thou hast denied me thrice."

Benjamin's heart filled with despair. Lord, let me not deny Thee! Let me not deny Thee!

Another cock crowed, and Benjamin opened his eyes to the log walls.

Home. He was home in Independence.

A river of relief surged through him. He had not denied his calling.

He rolled over in bed to the pillow beside his, knowing full well it would be unoccupied as it had been for ten years, yet ofttimes he hoped— If only Elizabeth were still here, if only he could discuss matters with her, for she had been a minister's child too, and she'd had great spiritual insight.

How he yearned for clarity of direction, especially now when the others depended upon him for the same. He closed his eyes and prayed, Who shall go with us to California, Lord?

No answer came.

"Only trust in Him," Elizabeth would have said. "He will tell you in His time." She knew and understood Scripture, ofttimes better than he, even though he'd spent two years in divinity school.

Benjamin reached out to her cool pillow. "I miss you, Elizabeth . . . even after ten years," he thought so strongly that he might as well have spoken the words. She'd not only been his helpmate, but a wife in the fullest sense of the word—a passionate woman, a true friend, and a fine mother to their children.

Guilt struck him. It seemed unnatural to miss a woman after all of these years. Women's health often broke on the frontier, and other widowers usually married again in a year, sometimes even sooner if they had young children who needed a woman's care. Some widowers might have married and buried their second wife and taken yet another by now. At fifty-three he was not too old to wed again, but he had no desire to do so.

At least he didn't berate God for taking Elizabeth home to Him anymore, he consoled himself. In any case, God saw death in a very different light than man did. To God, death was a beginning, not an ending. Benjamin reminded himself, too, it was not good for a man to love his wife more than he loved God.

Rolling over, he glimpsed the colorful plaited rug on the bedroom floor and recalled her working on it years ago. On cold winter evenings, he would read aloud to her and the boys by the kitchen fireplace while she plaited rugs. Remembrance flooded through him of a scene from their early years: young Adam, the eldest, tearing cloth into proper widths; Joshua, a year younger, sorting the scraps of material; and Daniel, whom they'd just taken in that summer, holding the colorful strands as Elizabeth interwove them.

Benjamin smiled at the memory. Others might have considered it unmanly for boys to be pressed into such work, he thought, but the girls hadn't been born yet, and he and Elizabeth had firmly believed that everyone should help. It certainly had not made the boys less manly; if anything, it had caused them to be more thoughtful. "Oh, Elizabeth. . . ."

Almost against his will, he recalled her last hours as he had over and over these past ten years.

It was nigh unheard of for a woman to call her husband into the room during childbirth, but old Mrs. O'Connor, the Irish midwife, had shouted to him, "She sayin' you come! The babe be turned wrong!"

In the bedroom, Elizabeth was straining with all of her might, and he'd nearly fainted at the sight. Finally he gripped the bedpost, praying and half straining himself as though it might help. "Elizabeth, forgive me . . . oh, God, forgive me!" he cried out.

She shook her head as if her travail were unimportant, then she gave one final heave and the babe came, a girl who cried out lustily. They'd already decided that if it were a girl her name would be Elizabeth, too, and they'd call her Betsy.

Elizabeth's face was pale as rice powder, but she smiled weakly at him and whispered, "You must find a wet nurse."

"Elizabeth!" he protested. "You will be fine in no time. You always have been."

She shook her head slowly on the pillow. "No, my love. Not this time."

He should have guessed she could be dying. She'd never been as physically strong as some women, but she'd always had a great spiritual strength, and her blue eyes glowed with it then as never before.

If only he could remember precisely everything that

followed. He recalled the intensity in her eyes and in her voice, which had sounded as strong as an Old Testament prophet's.

"Go to California," she had directed.

Sometimes when he tried to remember, he was no longer certain and it sounded impossible. The babe had even stopped crying. He'd asked, "To California?"

She had nodded.

Because of Elizabeth and the setting, half of his mind had rejected it outright, but the other half said, "So this is why you have always been drawn to matters about California, why you have studied the accounts of Kino, Anza, and Dana, time and again."

Mrs. O'Connor had heard all of it, too, and they'd discussed it several times in the following years before Mrs. O'Connor had died, too. "I heerd it jest like that," she had told him. "I heerd it, so it weren't yer imaginings. As soon as I put the babe down, I crossed meself."

It had all been such a shock then—the childbirth and Elizabeth near death and the prophetic words. In divinity school, he'd received no call to the pastorate, but he'd always known God had a special call on his life. This, then, was it. His call was to go to California. Since then, there'd been dreams of confirmation, including the one that set the year. The more he considered Elizabeth's last words, the more certain he was that it was the Holy Spirit speaking through her. One heard of such things, albeit seldom.

During her final moment, Elizabeth had beamed with such radiance that he knew she saw Christ, and she'd stretched out her arms to embrace Him, her great heavenly love.

The memory of her wondrous smile still before him, Benjamin climbed out of bed and got to his knees on the rug she had made with the children. *Forgive me, Lord, I still miss her,* he prayed. The deeper he delved into prayer, the more deeply the sense of mission surged through his spirit, and a long time later he said, *I am unworthy, Lord, but I am willing. I shall go.*

A strident crowing pierced Abby's sleep. Roosters. Yes, they often heard roosters crowing at daybreak in the village near Miss Sheffield's School. Slowly blinking awake, she glimpsed log walls and realized that she was not at Miss Sheffield's, nor at home in New York, but in Independence, Missouri. What's more, she had spent the night sleeping in Rena's bedroom. Immediately Betsy's words came to her: Everyone knows that someday Rena is going to marry Daniel.

Could it be true? Abby wondered. Betsy was a mere child . . . what would she know?

The fragrance of lilacs drifted around her, but that could only be her imagination, her confusion about being home in New York. Perhaps Betsy's words were only her imagination as well.

Abby closed her eyes and tried to sleep again, but it was useless. At length, she rose up on an elbow and noticed that Rena still slept soundly in the other bed. This log house was not imagined, and—quite likely—neither was what Betsy had told her. Her mind reeled with speculations until she forced them away and examined the room.

Despite the crudely chinked log walls, the place was neat, with its polished plank floors and a great round plaited rug. The logs in the walls looked waxed or oiled, and they held framed pictures of pressed flowers and moss. Unencumbered by her emotional turmoil, she would probably have found them pleasant decorations and this bedroom a pleasant room, different though it was from hers at home.

She slipped out of bed into the morning chill, padding to the window in her blue cotton nightgown to see if there could possibly be lilacs on the frontier.

She pulled aside the homespun draperies. Yes—lilacs. Just below the open window, a bush held the remnants of lavender blooms. She leaned out and reached for a dewy flower, burying her nose in its intoxicating fragrance, reminded of the lilacs at Miss Sheffield's and of those in her garden . . . at home . . . and of Cornelius that moonlit night. But the bittersweet memories must stop. She could not allow her mind to drift to the past.

The glimmering light of dawn revealed more of her surroundings: well-kept herb and vegetable gardens; beyond them, an orchard; in the other direction, a barn and outbuildings. One building was apparently a chicken coop since a rooster crowed from its roof as if he had raised the sun. To her far left was a small log cabin, undoubtedly where Jeremy and Jenny lived. It was probably more pleasant for the newlyweds to live alone, though the main house was sufficiently commodious.

At last night's dinner Aunt Jessica had explained, "I thought you might feel more comfortable sleeping with Rena tonight since the guest rooms are at the far end of the house. Tomorrow you can choose your own room."

Rena had been exceedingly kind when they had retired, but she did want to hear all about their journey—and all about Daniel. If only her beautiful cousin were disagreeable in some way, it might be easier to endure these feelings of jealousy.

"Good morning!" Rena was sitting up in bed with a dimpled smile, clouds of pale hair falling to her pink nightgown. "What are you doing awake so early, Abby? I thought you'd be tired."

"I'm—I'm not accustomed to such wide-awake roosters," Abby responded. "And . . . then I had to see if it was truly lilacs that I smelled."

Rena's lovely face dimpled more deeply. "Not only lilacs, but lilacs from Boston! You'll have to ask Aunt Jessica how they happen to be here in the wilds of Missouri."

"The wilds of Missouri!"

Rena gave a little laugh as she slipped down under her quilt again. "I only thought it must seem rustic here compared to New York. I am so happy to have you here with us! I don't want to hurt your feelings!"

"Thank you. I doubt you'd ever hurt anyone's feelings."

"I do try not to, Abby, but I'm not always successful."

As Abby returned to her bed and slipped in again, she was astonished to hear herself saying, "Daniel said that you are very sweet and good."

"Oh, my! That's not in the least helpful for acquiring the virtue of humility!" Rena protested with amusement. "How did he happen to say that?"

"He told me a bit about everyone in the family. He was probably trying to make it easier for me to become acquainted with all of you."

"What else did he say about us?"

"That you were all more educated than the usual frontier family, thanks to Harvard, the University of Missouri, and Aunt Jessica . . . and that you'd welcome me with open arms, as you did him."

Rena smiled. "Daniel is easy to love."

Abby's spirits sank. "Yes."

"Now that you're certain we have lilacs in Missouri, you must try to sleep again," Rena suggested sweetly. "You've had such a long trip."

"Yes, perhaps I should." She pulled the warm covers up

behind her neck, half wishing that Rena and the rest of her family were not quite so laudable. Last night when they had settled at the supper table, she had expected them to say grace before the meal. Instead, everyone had held hands, both Aunt Jessica and Betsy smiling as they took her hands. Then they had all sung fervently:

"Praise God, from whom all blessings flow
Praise Him, all creatures here below;
Praise Him above, ye heavenly host,
Praise Father, Son, and Holy Ghost."

They had ended with a harmonious "Amen," her own voice absent from the beautiful prayer. No one had mentioned her failure to join in, so perhaps they hadn't noticed.

She snuggled deeper under the covers and decided that she would have to make a great effort to fit into this family, to fit into their kind of life. Anxious over what the morning would bring, what the entire day might bring, she finally drifted off to an uneasy sleep.

At breakfast she was prepared to join hands for prayer and to sing, but this morning they sang a different prayer:

"O for a thousand tongues to sing
My great Redeemer's praise,
The glories of my God and King,
The triumphs of His grace!"

Their eyes were closed and Abby glanced around the dining room table at them: Uncle Benjamin in his black broadcloth suit, Aunt Jessica in a serviceable black dress and white mobcap over her gray hair, Rena in a rose frock that made her pale beauty all the more lovely, and Betsy in a green dress to match her eyes. The plump hired girl, Sarah, had returned to the kitchen. They sang with vigor, joyful smiles lighting their faces as they started the next verse.

"My gracious Master and my God,
Assist me to proclaim,
To spread through all the earth abroad
The honors of Thy name."

While they sang their "Amens," Abby supposed it was not so unusual that the children of a clergyman would sing grace at meals. It was probably more surprising to them that she—that same clergyman's granddaughter—did not even know the words. She glanced around the table, but the others were now occupied with passing the food. She would learn, she vowed. She didn't want to displease any of them.

After they had passed the platters of bacon, eggs, and biscuits around the table, Rena said, "Abby could scarcely believe that we had lilacs here in Missouri, Aunt Jessica. You'll have to tell her how they happen to be here."

"Yes, I would like to know," Abby said, stirring cream into her steaming coffee.

Aunt Jessica spread honey on a biscuit. "You know that I was born in Boston. Well, after I married Noah we moved to a Pennsylvannia farm, and my mother—your Grandmother Talbot—gave me roots from the lilacs and my favorite red rose bush."

Betsy urged, "Tell Abby about the sleigh."

Aunt Jessica smiled in recollection. "Well, it was winter, so we made that first move—and the flowers' first move—by sleigh. It was glorious, dashing over the snow with a pair of fine horses. Hot bricks under our feet kept us warm, and we carried along a big chunk of frozen bean porridge, breaking off pieces to eat. You remember the rhyme: 'Bean porridge hot, bean porridge cold, bean porridge in the pot, nine days old'!"

"I thought it was peas porridge," Abby said.

Uncle Benjamin chuckled. "It's bean porridge when one is born in Boston!"

Everyone laughed, and Betsy said, "Tell the rest, Aunt Jessica."

"Well, Noah was restless, and after some years he felt that there were too many people in Pennsylvania. So we moved to Ohio by covered wagon, taking along the roots of the lilacs and the rosebush, not to mention all of our other belongings. It was wild country, all woods and Indians. But more settlers came, and Noah wanted to move again. We went to Kentucky in an ox cart pulled by four oxen. Sometimes the trail was so narrow that Noah had to chop down trees to get the cart through."

Abby prompted, "And you took your lilac and rose roots?"

Her aunt nodded. "Indeed, I did. I was glad to have them. It was lonely living so close to the forest, especially at night. Wolves howled, and once a bear stole our bacon. Noah overcame his restlessness when he truly found the Lord, and we stayed there until Noah passed on to be with Him."

For a moment she stared into the distance, then she smiled at Abby. "Finally, I traveled here with my lilac and rosebush roots when Benjamin invited me. It seems to me now that the beauty and perfume of their flowers help us sense the Lord's presence. I'm glad that I brought them."

Uncle Benjamin said, "You brought me and seven children a heart full of patience and love. You've been a wonderful aunt to them."

"Now you mustn't flatter me, Benjamin! I'd been praying all of my life to have children, and suddenly my prayers were answered. Seven children! Of course, Adam, Daniel, and Joshua were nearly grown by then."

"Your love still brushed off on them," her brother insisted. "You have a courageous spirit. You're never daunted when duty calls."

"Now if Daniel were here," Aunt Jessica protested, "he would help me by quoting a verse on the evils of flattery!"

"Probably three or four verses!" Rena added to everyone's amusement, and Abby thought as they laughed, *How much better all of them know him than I do.*

Betsy said, "We mustn't forget to take the roots along to California next spring."

Aunt Jessica smiled. "It seems that most of my life has been devoted to carting those roots around this country. Wouldn't it be like me to forget the roots for my last move?"

Benjamin Talbot's brown eyes twinkled. "And what makes you think that traveling to California is your last move?"

His sister said with a flash of humor, "Because I'm not going to have to dig them up and carry them along to Glory!"

Benjamin laughed. "No, that's one place where we won't have to bring anything except our love for the Lord. Wouldn't it be easy to move if that's all we had to carry along!"

Abby felt as uncomfortable when they mentioned next spring's trip to California as she did about their religious remarks. They brought religion into everything, and it made her feel like a outsider.

After breakfast Aunt Jessica showed Abby the guest rooms. "I thought you might like this one with the river view," she suggested. "It's the larger and has north light for painting."

The room itself was much like Rena's with chinked crude log walls and polished plank floors and a great round plaited rug. The logs in the walls shone, and pictures made with dried plants and moss adorned the walls of this bedroom as well. The furniture, equally rustic, included a small oak desk and chair at the window, as well as an oak bureau and four-poster bed.

Aunt Jessica said, "I am sure it is very different from the fine room you must have had in your New York house."

"Yes, it is different," Abby agreed, then hastened to add, "but quite charming in its own way. I didn't know what to expect on the frontier."

Aunt Jessica smiled, her brown eyes full of compassion, then she pulled aside the homespun draperies. "Come look out the window. We used to see occasional wolves and cougars out there, but progress has brought us a different sight, one I am certain you don't see in New York City."

Abby peered out with her.

Just below the property was a dirt road where covered wagons were lined up to leave for the West. It was an interesting scene, albeit an unnerving reminder that next spring she might have to move again. Nevertheless, she would sketch this picture, this westward march of pioneers, as surely as she was watching those below now.

While she and Aunt Jessica stood before the window, the oxen and wagons stirred to a start with a great racket of shouts and whips; it seemed an entire pastureful of cattle were to follow in the dust. "It looks awful, Aunt Jessica. Why do they go?"

"For many reasons, I suppose. Some for cheap land, more than a few to escape the law, others to get away from the fevers that kill entire families."

"Daniel said there are fevers along these rivers."

"Yes. He saw three little Talbot children die of fevers right in this house."

Abby did not care to hear of dying, not with her parents just dead. "There must be other reasons why people go West."

"Some are just plain restless living on farms, and they desperately want to embark on one great adventure in their lives. After all, a good many of their parents moved west at one time or another, even if was just a distance of one or two states. They heard their parents' or grandparents' stories about when they 'moved out west' so often that it seems right to them to go too. When I taught school in Pennsylvania, Ohio, and Kentucky, that's what I heard . . . 'wun Granpappy moved west,' or 'wun Pappy moved to Kentuck,' or 'I hain't stayin' here, I be movin' west, too, wun I'm growed up.' "

Abby smiled at her aunt's imitation of the vernacular that had become increasingly prevalent on the trip to Missouri.

Her aunt added, "Sometimes I think our emigrating to California is no different, though Benjamin and the boys insist it's to expand their trade. And Benjamin has had a call to go as well."

A call? Abby wondered. Of course, manifest destiny. again.

Her aunt was looking at her expectantly, so Abby asked, "What do you think of manifest destiny? It's been in newspapers and on everyone's lips all through our journey here."

Her aunt gazed out at the departing pioneers. "Yes, the westward movement is becoming a crusade—a manifest destiny that we overspread the continent with the blessings of liberty and democracy. I tend to agree, but particularly that we must overspread the earth with God's love."

Abby was not certain that she understood the part about God's love. They moved on to the other guest room that overlooked the orchard—a view so uninspiring that she chose the first bedroom, even if she did have to watch the emigrants' wagon trains departing.

Later in the morning, Betsy was pleased to show her around the small farm with its barn and other outbuildings. There was indeed a dog mill that Uncle Benjamin had built, just as Daniel had claimed. Rusty, their dog, barked at them happily as he ran in place upon a treadmill, his energy causing a rod to turn the churn handle.

Abby laughed, "I can't believe it!"

Betsy grinned. "Papa is always looking for a challenge. He says that life is an adventure, and that we should all be adventurous. Besides, he says he's named after Benjamin Franklin and should be like him."

Abby recalled his interest in the ingenious Allegheny Portage Railroad. "Was he really named after Franklin?"

Betsy giggled. "No. Grandmother Talbot named him for the Benjamin in the Bible."

"I see," Abby replied, though she was unclear about who this Benjamin in the Bible was and a bit embarrassed that ten-year-old Betsy seemed to know.

Near the well house was a jouncing seat that her uncle had built for the children, and, in a shed with the sleigh, there were homemade sleds for each child. How different Uncle Benjamin was from her own father, Abby thought. Her father would never have built anything for anyone, though he had been generous with money . . . generous to a fault!

After lunch Abby arranged her belongings in her log-walled bedroom, setting up the collapsible easel Daniel had given her; she carefully placed on it her sketch of him asleep on the train. Just looking at the picture affected her oddly. Yes, she expected that she was smitten, but if he was going to marry Rena, it was best to forget it.

That evening after supper, Unce Benjamin suggested that Abby share her watercolored sketches of the trip with the family, and Betsy helped fetch them from Abby's bedroom. "Aren't we taking the one of Daniel?" she asked, her green eyes brimming with interest. "I like it best."

Abby flushed. "It—it's not quite finished yet." She quickly removed it from the easel and placed it on her bureau. If any of the others saw the sketch they might deduce that she cared for him.

In the parlor, everyone was delighted at her work. Rena was particularly enthusiastic. "I've always wondered what New York and Pittsburgh and Cincinnati and Louisville and St. Louis looked like—and here they are! It's wonderful, Abby. God has given you a great gift!"

A gift? Abby wondered. She recalled that her art teachers had called her gifted. "Yes, I—I guess so."

Aunt Jessica added, "They are very good, Abby. Do you think you could do a sketch of your grandmother, our first Abigail Talbot? Of all the things we must leave behind when we move to California, I think that I'll miss that portrait of Mother the most. We're afraid to risk it on the trip."

Abby looked up at the familiar oil painting of her grandmother, so similar to the one she'd known in New York. Grandmother Talbot wore her golden hair in a chignon, a cerulean blue gown emphasizing the glow in her sapphire eyes—and the pendant that Abby had sold. "I don't know. I've never sketched from a portrait."

"I hope you'll try," Uncle Benjamin urged. "It would be a great favor to us if we could take a likeness of Mother along. There were no daguerreotypes in her day, of course, and we only have this portrait, which we're leaving here with Adam and his family."

"I'll try," Abby said. Their confidence overwhelmed her,

especially in light of her selling Grandmother Talbot's sapphire pendant, though they did not know that. Perhaps she could redeem herself through her painting; perhaps she could make something of her painting yet.

9

On Sunday morning they brought a vase of wild red roses to the small white church with its simple steeple, and Aunt Jessica reverently arranged them on the altar before other members of the congregation arrived.

Abby sat down in the oak pew between her uncle and Rena, and thought of the elegant New York church she had attended with Uncle Benjamin and Daniel. In this church, however, there were no stained-glass windows, no Gothic towers, no magnificent organ . . . and no Daniel. Here she sat next to Rena, who wore a lavender dress she had made with her own delicate hands. She was surely the most beautiful young woman in Missouri—and she was expected to marry Daniel.

Abby bowed her head, her thoughts so scattered that she was unable to say anything to God. If He did exist, she assuredly should not ask Him to take Daniel away from Rena, for that would be selfish; that much was certain. Finally the service began with the organ wheezing out an anthem, and Abby rose with the small congregation. Rena shared her hymnal, singing out in her melodious contralto:

"Praise ye the Lord, the Almighty,
    the King of creation!

117

O my soul, praise Him,
for He is thy health and salvation!
All ye who hear, Now to His temple draw near;
Join me in glad adoration!"

It was clear what Rena's "gift" was. As if she were not beautiful and sweet enough, she sang like an angel. Abby mouthed the words, knowing she would hit a false note if she attempted to sing.

The young brown-haired minister, Seth Thompson, was rather handsome in his black broadcloth suit. His sermon dealt with forgiveness, reminding Abby of the lecture Daniel had given her about forgiving her parents and Roxanna Murray . . . and Cornelius. She had, after all, led him on, so she couldn't blame him entirely for his ungentlemanly expectations. Moreover, she must write to thank his parents for the reception and let his mother know that she had arrived safely in Independence.

Seth Thompson quoted from the Bible, "And be ye kind one to another, tenderhearted, forgiving one another, even as God for Christ's sake hath forgiven you."

Oddly enough, Abby suddenly felt tenderhearted toward Cornelius. Yes, she thought, I do forgive him.

After church, she was introduced to the Reverend Thompson, who was kind but clearly had a special interest in Rena. Nor was he the only man intrigued by Rena's pale beauty and disconcerting brown eyes. It seemed that every young man in the church stopped by to exchange a hopeful word with Rena Talbot. Rena, in turn, introduced them to her cousin, but in her black crepe dress, Abby felt as plain as a blackbird beside an exotic bird. She must have conveyed her self-consciousness, for the young men almost immediately turned back to Rena.

Later, Seth Thompson joined them at the Talbot house

for a pleasant dinner, after which he and Rena departed for an afternoon stroll.

Abby hopefully asked Aunt Jessica, "Is Rena in love with the minister?"

Her aunt appeared taken aback. "Why, not to my knowledge. Seth is a Christian brother to her. I think he simply wants her suggestions for church music and social events."

Behind them Betsy pronounced, "Reverend Thompson knows that Rena is going to marry Daniel."

Aunt Jessica said firmly, "Now, Betsy, you mustn't meddle," and Abby left the room as soon as it seemed suitable.

Abby sat in her room at the small oak desk, staring out the window for a long time. It would be best to think of other things, so perhaps now was the time to write to Mrs. Adams without saying much about Cornelius. She got out a sheet of writing paper, then took up her quill. It was difficult to know how to begin and how to phrase the letter. Taking pains with her penmanship, she wrote the date, then slowly began.

Independence, Missouri
Dear Mrs. Adams,

Thank you again for your kindness in having the reception after my parents' memorial service. I daresay they would have been pleased to know you cared about them so much. Such a reception must be a difficult social occasion for one to give, but you did it with dignity and graciousness, and I am most grateful.

The trip to Independence was interesting, and I sketched many of the rustic scenes on the way. This is my first week here with my Talbot relations, and they have been kind and welcoming. It is very different here from New York City, but I expect I shall grow accustomed to it.

When I look out of my window, I can see emigrants gather in their covered wagons to go to the Far West. There is an aura of excitement about it, but I fear I should not care to go through the nearby Indian Territory, nor over the chains of mountains. I have been reading about the Lewis and Clark Expedition to the Oregon Territory, and I sketched Clark's house in St. Louis. When I read of their winter quarters at Fort Clatsop and their Indian guide Sacagawea, her baby, and her husband, I don't know how they endured it. Reading about them makes Independence seem far more comfortable.

Again, I thank you for your kindness and the fine reception. Please give my regards to Mrs. Adams, Senior, and to your husband and Cornelius.

Sincerely,

Abigail Talbot

As the days passed, Abby felt more and more at home with her new family. Every morning she toiled with Betsy in the herb and vegetable gardens. She began to feel a pleasure in working the warm crumbly soil with her hands, in the sprouting seeds, and in the sun warming her back as she weeded and hoed. It seemed a time of healing, of drawing beauty from the flowers and joy from the singing of the birds.

One balmy morning when Rena brought them cold buttermilk, Abby said, "I do love the garden, especially the flowers."

Rena smiled. "I think we should consider ourselves to be

like flowers that God created to give off His fragrance of love to others on earth."

How often her cousin spoke like that, Abby thought, yet she was not falsely pious. Rena brimmed with love and laughter and an inner joy. At first Abby resented that Rena did not work in the garden; instead, her cousin sewed, mended, set the table, and did other quiet work. One day Aunt Jessica explained, "Rena is not as strong as the rest of us. Her health is delicate, but we must not seem too aware of it. She likes to do her part."

Abby began to notice that whenever Rena thought herself alone she looked frail, but with others, love transformed her so thoroughly that she seemed strong and enthusiastic, and when she sang solos in church, her melodious contralto voice filled with such power that she seemed to soar.

On another morning when Rena had again carried cold buttermilk out to the garden, Abby suddenly said, "Oh, Rena, I wish you weren't always so good."

"But I'm not good at all!" Rena protested. "I am just like the apostle Paul when he said, 'For the good that I would, I do not, but the evil which I would not, that I do.' "

"You do evil?" Abby protested.

"Oh, yes. I am forever asking God's forgiveness."

"But whatever for?"

Rena's eyes filled with dismay. "I forget to look for the good in others and to love the good in them. I forget to see my unworthiness compared with everyone's worth. And I forget to hush my heart and bid all of my senses be still, so that I might have perfect communion with the Lord. I become too filled with self."

When Rena left, Abby hacked at the dandelions, horseweeds, and cocklebur with mixed emotions.

Another day Rena said, "I think we must love and laugh more, to make the world around us happy. I think that our love and joy are like the ripples when we throw a stone in a pond, spreading out in ever-widening circles, far beyond our knowledge, and that such love and joy are eternal."

It struck Abby as unrealistic. She recalled her father's dabbling in the New England philosphy that said man could achieve perfection on his own. "Can you make yourself perfect?"

"Never!" Rena protested. "Only the Lord, Jesus Christ, is perfect!"

"Is?" Abby asked. "You say is?"

"Yes! He was and is and always will be!"

"I daresay I don't understand."

Rena's eyes glowed. "He came to earth so that we might know God through Him."

"You mean that Christ is the bridge . . . the way to God?"

"Yes! And the way to live forever with love and joy!"

If Abby did not quite understand Rena, she did understand Betsy, who told her everything she knew about herbs, vegetables, and the town of Independence . . . but nothing more about Daniel.

On the first of August, she received a letter from New York. To her amazement, it was from Cornelius.

Dear Abby,

What a pleasure it was for Mother to receive the letter from you. We are all pleased to hear that you arrived and are well. You have no idea how many times I have remembered our last moments together with remorse. The last memory I have of you is your running through the moonlight in your garden and calling out precisely what I was—a cad. I hope with all of my heart that you will forgive me, for I have recognized the error of my ways.

Not only do I recall that last glimpse of you every time I see your old house across Union Park Square, but I recall what a fine friend you were in all of our childhood years. You were kind and thoughtful even then, and not after me for my money as so many young women are now.

The more I recall about our childhood years, the more I realize what a fine person you are. I see, too, how desperate you must have been to avoid going to the frontier, yet you did not allow yourself to be entirely compromised. I admire you, Abby, and hope for your forgiveness and continued friendship.

The only news from New York is that my grandmother has passed on. As you know, she had been in failing health for some time and, to use Mother's words, "It is a blessing that she did not have to suffer longer." Life has changed here since her death. Father has even begun to attend church with Mother, and I sometimes accompany them myself, though not so often as to be thought pious!

The bank sends me about the country on business now, and I hope that someday I might come to Missouri. I am eager to hear if you plan to go on to California next spring.

I hope to hear of your forgiveness and of your news.

Sincerely,
Cornelius

Abby reread the letter several times, remembering the Cornelius she had known as a child. Perhaps he had been an old stick, but he had been kind, too, and she was glad not to have lost his friendship. She would have to write to him in such a way to retain their friendship, but not encourage him, for if there was one thing that was certain, it was that she did not love him. It was more important now, however, to write Rose.

August 1, 1845

My dear friend, Rose,

I have been hoping to hear from you, but you must be busy with your married life. Forgive me for not having sent a wedding gift. There is nothing suitable here unless you would like a buffalo robe, moccasins, or provisions for a covered wagon trip to the Far West. I am exaggerating slightly, but this is not New York!

Independence is a raucous frontier town with log cabins and shanty saddlers' shops, smithies, saloons, carpenter shops, and frontier trading posts lining the dirt street. (Uncle Benjamin and his sons own the largest and most pleasant of the trading posts.) At first I was so appalled at the town that I could not bear it, but now I find it more interesting and have sketched much of it.

Fortunately we live in a large, comfortable log house in the countryside, and my relations have been wonderfully kind to me. I am slowly growing accustomed to the frontier. Now, in August, it is more bearable since there are no settlers moving west in this awful heat, but there are still Indians and drunken river roustabouts.

Much to my surprise, everyone admires my watercolor sketches, and I have even sold some through my uncle's trading post—no doubt because there is so little else to give as gifts! It occurred to me that I could send several pictures as a wedding gift for you and William. I have decided upon two that depict places I have already told you about: *Crossing the Alleghenies,* the portage railroad crossing between Philadelphia and Pittsburgh, and *Frontier Baptism* along the Ohio River. I am also enclosing *Mississippi Madness,* with its river jam of "anything that floats," and *Summer Tranquillity*, a river scene from Independence, where the Kansas and Missouri Rivers flow along together. I hope that my gift will not be too rustic. I visualize you and William amid crystal chandeliers and fine French antiques, but perhaps the pictures will be suitable for your library as studies of the West.

This great undertaking of sending a wedding gift will occur when Cousin Joshua arrives, then departs for Washington in the next few weeks. Daniel is coming with him. It seems years ago, not mere months, that I saw him. But, oh, Rose, it appears that he is to marry my cousin, Rena. I try not to think on it too much. I scarcely know how I will react when he arrives.

I did have an opportunity to wear your precious Fleur-de-lis last week as the schoolmaster, Horace Litmer, took me out walking after church and Sunday dinner. He is about thirty years old and pleasant, but I do not love him. Moreover, I'm sure he loves Cousin Rena. Every man in Independence seems to and one cannot blame them for she must be the most beautiful (and dear) young lady hereabouts.

How happy I am for you—married now to your William. Please convey my best wishes to him.

Affectionately,
Abby
    P.S. I have had a contrite letter from Cornelius! His grandmother has passed on. He may visit Missouri on business for the bank someday!

It was no accident that Abby and Betsy were sketching under a cottonwood tree near the waterfront when the *Liberty* steamed in from St. Louis. Since Betsy appeared to have an artistic bent, they had been sketching scenes all over Independence, albeit near the wharf every afternoon this week. Aunt Jessica did not entirely approve of their proximity to dockworkers and gave in only because shipping activity had quieted for summer. In addition, she insisted that old Asa, a free black worker at Talbot's Trading Post, drive them out in the buggy and stay with them.

"Do you think that's their boat?" Betsy asked over the sound of the rushing river.

"I don't know," Abby replied as calmly as possible as the *Liberty* steamed to the dock. She did have a feeling about the boat, but she had been having "feelings" about every Missouri boat that had docked for the past week.

"Sketch it into your picture, Betsy," she suggested. "A boat coming in always lends a sense of expectancy." She penciled in the sturdy stern-wheeler with its snub-nosed prow and twin smokestacks like rabbit's ears, and her own expectancy colored the scene with excitement. *Daniel's Arrival,* she entitled it to herself hopefully.

"There they are on the deck!" Betsy exclaimed. "It's Daniel and Joshua!"

Abby squinted against the sunshine to the distant boat, disbelieving because she had so fervently wished it to be true all week.

126

"Are you sure?"

One of the men in Eastern dress did remind her of Daniel—his height as he towered over most of the other passengers near the gangplank, his broad shoulders, even his manner and firm stance.

"I'm certain! Come on, let's get Asa to drive the buggy over for them!" Betsy grabbed her sketching supplies and raced toward the buggy, where Asa and the horses drowsed under cottonwood trees in the afternoon heat.

In a daze, Abby attempted to organize her papers and pencils, her eyes scarcely leaving the man who resembled Daniel. To her astonishment, he waved.

"Oh, Daniel!" she exclaimed, though there was no possibility of his hearing over the roustabouts clanking barrows and the letting down of the gangplank. She returned his wave and hurried toward the buggy, where Betsy had already roused Asa.

Abby's heart knocked against her ribs so wildly that she was certain they could hear it. "Daniel and Joshua have arrived," she told the old man.

"Yez'um, Miz Abby," he said, brushing the dust from his clothes before he helped her up into the buggy.

"Please hurry!" she urged Asa.

"Yez'um." He cocked a curious brow at her before ambling around and climbing up onto his seat.

It seemed forever before the horses traversed the short distance on the rutted road, raising a dust cloud at the edge of the dock. Daniel and his companion were already walking down the gangplank.

"Abby! Betsy!" Daniel called out with a great smile.

Abby was out of the buggy before Asa could help her down, then an inexplicable shyness overtook her. "Daniel. . . ."

His blue eyes caught her in their steady gaze, then quite suddenly her hand was in his and he was kissing her fingertips. "You're looking fine now, Abby," he said with a peculiar roughness in his voice.

Behind them Joshua had already hugged Betsy and now he commented dryly, "Aren't you going to introduce me to my cousin, Daniel?"

Daniel's color rose and before he could begin the introduction, Betsy excitedly put in, "Abby, this is my brother, Joshua!"

Joshua nodded slightly. "It is a pleasure to meet you, Abby. Now I see why Daniel wanted to stop in Independence."

Abby fought the blush rising to her cheeks. "I've been looking forward to meeting you," she mustered, barely recovering her wits. This second son of Benjamin Talbot resembled his father only in the squarishness of his chin and the brown of his eyes. Otherwise, there was a toughness in the set of his chin, a daring in his eyes; he was no doubt a good trader for the family's business and he was quite handsome, with a dashing mustache and dark auburn hair.

Betsy said into the silence, "Abby's been teaching me to draw. We have been drawing the wharf all this week."

Daniel glanced at Abby quizzically. "I see."

She managed an innocent smile, and they started toward Asa and the buggy.

Only a few minutes were required for the men to help Asa strap their baggage onto the back of the buggy. Then Daniel helped Abby up into the backseat, his blue eyes and nearness unnerving her so that she almost missed the step. He sat down beside her, and Betsy and Joshua sat on the driver's seat with Asa.

As they rode away toward Independence, Abby nervously

smoothed her black dress, wishing she could think of something to say. She wished, too, that she were no longer in mourning, then felt disloyal to her parents' memory.

"I am delighted to see you are still sketching," Daniel said as they jounced along the rutted road.

"Yes, thanks to your gift of the portable case."

"That was my pleasure. Aunt Jessica wrote that some of your pictures have even been sold at the trading post."

"Yes, five watercolored sketches. But I made copies so you could see the entire trip as if you were with us."

His smile was a brilliant white in the sunshine. "I knew you had talent when I saw your first sketches of the garden and house in New York. You have that rare knack of capturing the spirit of a place. And I knew you had perseverance when you forced yourself to work despite your troubles."

Joshua called over his shoulder, his toughness replaced with amusement. "Sounds mighty serious back there. Just what sort of verse are you already quoting to my pretty cousin?"

Daniel chuckled. "I was circling the topic perseverance."

"I can imagine," Joshua replied dubiously.

As if to prove himself Daniel quoted, "An enterprise, when fairly once begun, should not be left till all that ought is won."

Oddly enough, he directed the words to her.

"Shakespeare, I presume," Joshua said, "but I'll catch you without a quote on something yet!"

Blushing, she asked, "How is it that you can remember so many quotations, Daniel?"

He smiled. "It's very simple. You have a gift for art, and I have a gift for memory."

"My eye!" Joshua put in. "Instead of sleeping nights like

most people, old Daniel stays awake, memorizing those blamed quotations so he can flay us with them all day!"

"Exactly!" Daniel agreed with a laugh. "Moreover, you've given us a fine example of perseverance!"

Even Asa chuckled as he flicked the reins lightly over the horses. "Home, boys," he said. "Home."

If only they didn't have to go home, Abby thought with a rush of trepidation. She could happily ride along in this buggy with Daniel at her side all day.

At length they turned into the drive lined with black walnut trees and oaks. "Well, here we are!" Daniel said.

The buggy stopped at the door of the Talbots' log house, where Rena and Aunt Jessica sat shelling peas for supper.

Rena looked up. Wide-eyed, she rose, unaware that the pan of peas spilled at her feet. "Daniel!" she cried. Such a flash of joy crossed her dimpled face that Abby knew she would remember it forever.

Then Daniel was out of the buggy and her cousin rushed to his open arms. Lifting her from the ground, Rena cried out against his shoulder, "You're home! At long last, you're home!"

Tears swam before Abby's eyes, and she clenched her fists until her fingernails bit into her flesh. Betsy's words that first night were surely true: *Everyone knows that someday Rena is going to marry Daniel.*

Abby turned away angrily.

In the past few months she had already endured her parents' deaths, leaving her friends behind in New York, and moving to the frontier. She would endure this new heartache as well, even if she had to . . . to paint their wedding! She would endure whatever happened to her, and she would do it without any help from their God! She would do it by herself.

10

As the others greeted Joshua and Daniel, Benjamin Talbot surveyed the sunlit scene at his front doorstep with pleasure. Elizabeth's and his sons . . . their tall, strapping sons—one their own, and one grafted into their family as strongly as a branch to a vine. How proud she would be to see the tender bond of love that held all of them together. Gazing at his family in front of the buggy, Benjamin felt that even the turgid air of August seemed less stifling; life was as sweet as the smell of the newly mown hay.

Once Joshua and Daniel had embraced Rena, Betsy, and Aunt Jessica, Benjamin stepped forward. "Welcome home, boys!" he called to them, holding out his arms. "Joshua!" he said, enfolding him first. He clapped him on his heavily muscled shoulder and declared, "You've grown stronger yet!"

Joshua laughed, his brown eyes sparkling with amusement at their old jest. "Almost as strong as you?"

Benjamin chuckled. "Before long, I shall have to quit telling you young fellows 'not yet.' "

"You still feel solid to me," Joshua protested.

"Nicely said!" Benjamin laughed and clapped his son on the shoulder again.

Then Benjamin turned to Daniel, who'd waited with his

usual patience. "Daniel, welcome!" He embraced his adopted son, then clapped his strong back, too.

"It's good to see you again, sir," Daniel said, "and it's good to be home at long last."

As they stepped apart, Benjamin basked in the joy of being with him. Daniel understood him implicitly; he even understood why Joshua must be embraced first. It was a strange matter to feel closer to Daniel than to Joshua, who was his own flesh and blood. Benjamin often thought he'd received Daniel as a special gift from God.

They smiled warmly at each other, Daniel's blue eyes joyous. His adopted son's greater maturity came from his strong faith, Benjamin was certain, although he knew as well as anyone that faith was a gift from God. He'd observed that those who descended to the depths of despair were often rewarded with great faith if they gave their lives to God— and, in that dark night of Daniel's soul after his parents had been killed, he had indeed given his life over to Him.

"Let's help Asa with the luggage," Daniel suggested.

"A good idea," Joshua replied, and they started for the buggy again, Benjamin beside them.

As they unstrapped the baggage from the buggy, Benjamin observed, "With you two here, even such a mundane task as this is a pleasure."

Amused, Joshua returned, "Trying to coerce us to work again, I'll warrant!"

Benjamin chuckled. "It's not such a bad idea. You two have always been good at anything you turned your hands to . . . except perhaps milking cows. I recall Daniel, at a tender age, proclaiming to us one morning that cows kept poor hours."

Daniel grinned. "One thing I haven't changed my mind about!"

Despite the excitement of their reunion, Jessica, as usual, kept her head. Benjamin heard her tell Asa, "Please carry the news of Joshua and Daniel's arrival to Martha's place and invite them here for dinner. And could you stop by to tell Jeremy and Jenny as well?"

"Yez'um," Asa replied. "I do that right now. They shore be happy to see the boys, too. It be a long time since we got both of 'em back heah together."

Once they were inside the front door with the luggage, Benjamin sensed the altered atmosphere of the house. "It feels more complete with the two of you here," he told his sons. "Your mother used to say that a home was a matter of presence, and tonight we'll have everyone still here on earth present. How pleased she would be at that."

He smiled at them as they looked around the familiar chinked log parlor. Daniel had not been back for a year, and Joshua for more than two. "Nothing much changed, except mayhap fresh roses on the tables."

"It looks pleasing to me," Daniel observed, and Joshua nodded his agreement.

"You fellows get yourselves situated in your old room," Benjamin said, "and I'll see if we can't rustle up some cold cider."

Joshua's expression filled with half-amused disbelief. "Don't tell me you're keeping hard cider around here now!"

Benjamin grinned. "Anyone who wants strong drink is going to have to suffer mightily in one of those flea-bitten saloons in town for it."

His young men went off laughing, and Benjamin was glad he'd stuck by his beliefs on the matter of hard liquor all of these years. You couldn't tell a boy over seventeen or eighteen much, but you could set a standard by what you kept in your own house. He was grateful that so far none of his boys had become drunken good-for-nothings.

He noticed Abby watching them. "I believe you have finally met all of this branch of the Talbot family," he told her. "It must be quite different here with a family of seven children and their growing accumulation of spouses and offspring."

She nodded, smiling. "It surely is."

"Rowdier, I expect," he suggested with good humor.

"A bit," she agreed, "but sometimes I rather like that."

"Delighted to hear it." He was becoming more and more fond of her, he realized.

He grinned again. "I presume you womenfolk need someone with muscles to put leaves in the table."

Abby, Betsy, and Rena smiled, and Rena said about the hired girl, "Why, Sarah is as strong as most men!"

Jessica's brown eyes danced with merriment. "I presume you are the one with the greatest muscles in this house now?"

"I doubt that the boys and I will be making any more muscular comparisons," he replied, scarcely hiding his grin. "I don't like them to feel so puny by comparison."

Aunt Jessica laughed. "Benjamin Talbot, you're a braggart, and if our mother could hear you, she'd tell you so herself."

"Guilty," he admitted, "not to mention only half repentant."

He was glad to see Abby laugh with Jessica, Rena, and Betsy at their foolery. Sometimes he suspected his niece tried too diligently to fit into the family, but perhaps she was becoming accustomed to them.

Later, Joshua and Daniel returned to the parlor in their shirtsleeves, and Betsy brought out a tray of frosty glasses filled with cider. "A toast to your homecoming with cider from our own orchard!" Benjamin proposed.

"A toast!" the others called out. "A toast!"

As Benjamin drank down the cider, its full-bodied taste seemed a fitting benediction upon the moment.

When they'd appeased their thirst, he suggested, "Shall we have a stroll around the place? You'll no doubt want to see the crops."

"It would be good to stretch our legs," Joshua said and Daniel agreed.

Outside, they walked from the front yard to the rutted drive that led to the barn, their discussion ranging from the condition of the house and the outbuildings to the crops and the muggy August weather.

"The newly mown hay smells good," Daniel said. "There's such a richness to the earth in August."

Joshua quipped, "And the richness of the manure?"

"A vital part of it all," Benjamin replied. "A vital part of our being stewards of the earth."

After they had inspected the fields and the animals, their talk turned to commercial affairs. Wainwright-Talbot Shipping and Chandlery, according to Joshua and Daniel, was prospering in trade on both land and sea.

"It's far more than we deserve," Benjamin said. He glanced at Daniel. "If it weren't for your uncle, we would still be obscure traders and farmers. To this day, I have difficulty believing our role in the world's shipping trade."

Daniel shrugged. "Uncle Elisha claims if it were not for you and this family, he would be a lonely old man ready to give up the shipping line. He has often said it's providential, our families coming together as they did."

"I think so myself," Benjamin agreed. Still, he preferred not to remember how he and Daniel were first brought together after the massacre of the boy's parents.

Joshua inquired, "How goes the Santa Fe trade?"

"Better this year than ever," Benjamin answered. "We sent twenty additional wagons of supplies to Santa Fe this spring."

"I expect it will continue to grow," Joshua said. "Elisha Wainwright believes the westward movement will become a hundred times greater and swifter in the next few years because of Fremont's expeditions, reports, and maps."

Daniel nodded. "Nothing, not even mountains, can stop emigration if there are rich, free lands over the horizon."

Benjamin added, "More emigrants than ever set off for the Oregon Territory this spring. People spoke of it everywhere on our journey here."

A crow flapped to a nearby copse of trees, and the men stopped to admire the beauty of the August greenery set against a bright blue sky. A soft breeze had come up, fluttering the oak leaves and waving the grasses; birds twittered in the trees near the house. When a breeze came up, Missouri was a most beautiful place.

At length Benjamin turned to Daniel. "I forgot to inquire. How did Abby's family affairs go?"

"As well as could be expected," he replied. "The assets were insufficient to pay off the creditors, most of whom received only a small percentage on the dollar. There is naught left for her."

Benjamin drew a resigned breath. "No surprise there."

A horse whinnied in the pasture, and Joshua said, heading for the fence, "Ah, this year's colts! I want to have a look at them."

After a moment Daniel cast a glance at Joshua and saw that he was too far away to overhear them. "Have you received further direction about your call to California?"

"Only dreams," Benjamin replied.

"What sort of dreams?" Daniel inquired.

Benjamin shrugged uneasily. "A vague impression of white-painted buildings in the countryside . . . accompanied by a great sense of reassurance and peace. Nothing else."

"Can you describe the buildings more fully?" Daniel asked.

"At best I can only guess they might be houses and outbuildings on rolling hillsides . . . but brilliantly white."

"A Spanish rancho, perhaps," Daniel guessed. "They often seem to gleam in the sunlight."

"Perhaps," Benjamin replied. "I am reluctant to speculate, but the sense of my being called grows stronger every day. I can best describe it as how my classmates in divinity school said they felt when they received calls to pastorates. I have perfect peace . . . no doubts about it."

"And are matters falling into place?" Daniel asked.

"As though they were being orchestrated by God. To begin, of course, there is the great number of emigrants setting off this year for the Far West. Every year more. And now neighbors and other folk come to me who wish to join our group. As though that weren't sufficent, last week our young pastor revealed to me that he senses the call to go with us to preach."

Daniel nodded. "I have always wanted to accompany you, and I have a great assurance in my spirit now that I am to go, too."

"Ah, Daniel, I am most pleased!"

Daniel's smile flashed from his dark beard. "In such a raw land, they shall need churches and pastors. I don't feel called to preach, only to be a part of it. Most important, to be certain that God is uplifted in the migration, whether this becomes a new land or a part of our nation."

Benjamin nodded. "Every nation in history, without

exception, has been founded upon some theistic or anti-theistic foundation, from the ancient pagan nations of Egypt, Babylonia, Syria, and Rome, to the modern nations today. And out of those theistic or antitheistic foundations grows a set of ethics or morals from which legislation is enacted. George Washington said it best, that it would be impossible to govern this nation well without God and the Ten Commandments. It is from those roots that our Constitution grew."

"I'm grateful for your willingness to step out in faith," Daniel told him, his blue eyes full of approbation.

"Every great enterprise takes its first forward step in faith," Benjamin replied. "All of us must go in faith."

"Nonetheless, you remind me of Peter walking out onto the water," Daniel said.

Benjamin shook his head in protest. "I am a long way from Peter, but I hope that I . . . that all of us will keep our eyes upon Christ."

"As do I."

Benjamin noticed that Joshua had finished admiring the colts and was on his way across the green summer grasses to rejoin them. He smiled at his own son, the only one of them who still denied Christ. Best to ask Joshua an inoffensive question. "What do you think of the colts?"

"Fine colts," Joshua remarked. "Fine horseflesh."

"Yes," Benjamin agreed, "a year of fine colts and crops. We have surely been blessed."

Joshua asked, "How is Rena? She claims to be fit, but she always puts too good a face on matters."

"She's been well this summer," Benjamin replied. "Better than usual in the heat."

"She looks well," Daniel said. "I was glad to see it."

"If her health holds all year, I think she'll be fine for the wagon trip next spring," Benjamin said hopefully.

Joshua frowned. "Then you still intend to go?"

"Yes, we are going. All of the family who wish to," Benjamin said, then hastened to add, "You are most welcome, of course. It would be a pleasure to have you with us, Joshua."

"Not me!" Joshua objected with a laugh. "I prefer to enjoy adventures in a more civilized way. Riding the Missouri riverboats is sufficient rustification. I am happiest with the refinements of Boston or Baltimore."

"On that particular topic," Daniel put in, "how is Abby faring here among the rustics?"

Benjamin smiled. "She is rusticating well for a Union Park Square young lady. How does she look to you?"

Daniel replied, "Calmer and more rested than when we were in New York, but not quite content."

"She looked content enough sitting with you in the buggy," Joshua said with a grin. "One glimpse of the two of them sitting together, and I couldn't help wondering what had transpired in New York."

Daniel said, scarcely concealing a grin, "I plead innocence. Complete innocence."

"Now I can flay you with a quote myself," Joshua returned. " 'Innocence is but a poor substitute for experience.' Bulwer, I believe."

"So it is," Daniel replied with a wry smile. "And now, if I may flay you with one, 'Innocence is like polished armor; it adorns and defends.' "

"Touché!" Joshua returned, chagrined.

"And now," Benjamin put in with a laugh, "to flay both of you with a quote dear to your Aunt Jessica's heart, 'Boys, don't meddle in each other's affairs!' "

Chuckling together, they headed past the orchard where

peaches hung ripening on the trees, then past the vegetable garden and toward the familiar log house.

When the entire family congregated that evening, Abby was easily able to separate the in-laws from the Talbots, who were all, with the exception of Rena, auburn haired.

She watched the brothers and sisters arrive with baskets and bowls of food as she set the expanded dining room table. They all embraced Daniel and Joshua. "About time you came home!" they said, and, "When are you two going to settle down?"

Daniel and Joshua laughed off their questions.

"Here is what happens if you do," Adam said, proudly showing off his wife, Inga, and their children who ranged in age from one to six. "Five children." At thirty Adam was the eldest, the family's gentle giant, who had attended Harvard with Daniel and Joshua, and, according to Daniel, spent his time there pining for Inga, whom he had promptly married upon his return to Independence. Adam's hair was the reddest, but his eyes were a contented brown. He and Inga would move into the home place with their brood when the others left for California.

Martha Talbot Baker, whose two small sons hid behind her skirt, teased, "Or you could have twins like me!"

Luke, her husband, grinned. "Now, Martha, you're going to scare 'em."

Benjamin Talbot announced, "And here come the newlyweds!"

Jeremy and Jenny smiled shyly, carrying warm peach pies that smelled ambrosial.

At length the women excused themselves to take their dishes to the kitchen. Abby was still setting the table when Rena arrived in the parlor to serve cold buttermilk to the men. Silverware in hand, Abby quailed at the adoring gaze Daniel bestowed upon her cousin. It was true that even Rena's brothers adored her and that she had embraced Joshua with equal enthusiasm upon their arrival—but Daniel was not her brother!

Quickly completing the table settings, Abby hurried through the hustle of the women in the kitchen to set the children's table. After a while she offered, "Perhaps I can sit in the kitchen to help the children, Aunt Jessica. Then all of your family can be together . . . all of the grown-ups."

Aunt Jessica tucked a wisp of gray hair into the bun at the nape of her neck. "That's most generous, Abby, but you are part of our family now, and we can fit twelve at the table."

"There are thirteen of us," Abby objected and ticked off the names on her fingers.

"So there are!" Aunt Jessica replied.

Inga said with her slight German accent, "I sit at the children's table. I am used to five children, and the twins have already eaten."

"I could help," Abby offered.

Aunt Jessica said, "Well, then, if you like. It will give the two of you a chance to become better acquainted."

Abby breathed a sigh of relief at not having to watch Daniel and Rena gaze at each other. She returned to the dining room to remove a place setting and saw them laughing about something together. She quickly finished her task and fled.

Adam and Inga, and Martha and Luke left shortly after supper with their children. Since Sarah, the hired girl, was cleaning up, there was nothing for Abby to do but to join the others in the parlor.

"Ah, there you are, Abby!" Daniel rose from the

horsehair sofa where he had been chatting with Betsy. "Everyone has told me how good your pictures are. I've been looking forward to seeing them."

"I—If you'll excuse me, I shall fetch them," Abby said with a blush and started for her room.

Betsy joined her in the hallway. "Can I help carry them?"

Abby gave one of her small cousin's red braids a playful tug. "May I?" she corrected gently.

"May I help carry them?"

"Yes, you may," Abby replied with a smile.

In her room she quickly assembled the watercolors of her trip west, including the four framed for Rose's wedding gift.

"You never show the one of Daniel sleeping in the train," Betsy said.

Abby faltered. "Oh . . . he's already seen it."

"But Joshua hasn't."

"I'm sure that Joshua has seen enough of Daniel sleeping since they've been traveling together," Abby said, unwilling to share the sketch with the others. She handed several of the pictures to Betsy. "This should be sufficient for tonight."

In the parlor, Daniel moved to the middle of the sofa to make room for her and Betsy on either side.

Abby settled beside him with trepidation. He seemed a different person from the Daniel she had spent time with in New York and Philadelphia, but at that time she hadn't known about Rena.

Betsy said, "I have the pictures of when you left New York. Shall I start?"

"Fine," Abby replied, welcoming time to quiet herself.

"This is first," Betsy explained. "Abby numbered the pictures."

She watched Daniel study the North River scene, the first one she had done when they left New York. It was no longer the black and white picture she had sketched upon their departure; she had painted in the blues of the sky and the river, the whites, silvers, and tans of boats, and the bright dashes of yellows, reds, and greens of the passengers' and roustabouts' clothing.

"It's very good," he said. "I can understand why people wish to buy them."

"Thank you," Abby replied, realizing how important his approval was to her. "I thought perhaps it was because there are no other pictures to buy at the trading post."

"I doubt that," he objected.

"Look at this," Betsy urged, and he continued through the pictures, marveling at how well the scenes had been captured, then passing them on to Joshua, who was equally impressed.

While Daniel studied the pictures, Abby noted the short curly hairs on the backs of his hands and his fingers, as dark as his hair and beard; his hands were broad with long fingers, his fingernails clean and neatly cut. How she would like to touch his hands.

Quite suddenly, as if aware of her scrutiny, he gave her a most peculiar look, and she could do nothing but give him a half-embarrassed smile in return.

After he viewed the pictures Betsy held, Daniel turned to the ones Abby had carried in. She passed him the first sketch of the Mississippi River with its colorful jumble of boats, and their fingers touched. For an instant it felt as though lightning had struck her hand, and she caught her breath at the jolt of astonishment in his blue eyes as they looked into hers.

He returned to the pictures and said somewhat breathlessly, "It's very good, Abby. They're all very good. You surely have found your talent."

She slowly let out her own breath before she could say, "Thank you, Daniel."

Everyone in the parlor must be aware of her attraction to him, she thought, yet when she dared look, it appeared that no one had noticed except perhaps Betsy, whose green eyes were filled with bewilderment.

The next day was Saturday, and Daniel and Joshua accompanied Benjamin Talbot to the trading post to make arrangements for future shipments of merchandise. That evening after supper, the family again took up the matter of their wagon train trek to California, and Abby felt duty-bound to listen to their discussion, if nothing else.

Benjamin Talbot said, "Five thousand people set out for Oregon or California last year by covered wagon, and I think the number will increase. We shall have to beat the crowd so there's ample grass for the oxen near the trail. I'd suggest we depart in early May, no matter how high the rivers are here."

"We don't want to be caught in the California Mountains in an early snow either," Daniel added. "You've no doubt heard that some of the Elisha Stevens party was snowed in last year."

Aunt Jessica shot a suspicious look at her brother. "No, we hadn't heard that."

"Might as well tell them," Benjamin Talbot said. "It's all the more reason for our leaving early."

Daniel drew a deep breath. "It seems that the Stevens party had to split up so the main group could move faster through the California Mountains. Two men and a young fellow, Moses Schallenberger, were left behind to guard the wagons because they contained valuable goods, and the Digger Indians there are unfortunately known for stealing. The two men and Moses built a rough log cabin in a few days, and then it began to snow. The first morning there were three feet of snow, and it didn't melt. It snowed day after day until it reached the cabin's roof." When he had finished telling of their terrible ordeal, everyone was aghast.

"That was just last year?" Aunt Jessica asked.

Benjamin Talbot nodded. "Another reason why we must leave early."

As soon as it was expedient, Abby excused herself. The idea of traveling by covered wagon through prairies, deserts, and over two chains of high western mountains was sufficiently daunting, and hearing about the hardships of other travelers did not help. And then having to endure Rena and Daniel's togetherness!

When she slipped into bed and tried to calm her mind for the night, she half prayed, "If Thou canst hear me, God, I don't wish to go! Please, I don't wish to go!"

11

Before church on Sunday morning, <u>Daniel</u> spoke to <u>Abby</u> as they stepped out the front door. "What are you so concerned about?"

Are my thoughts that evident? she wondered. She hoped he didn't realize how disinclined she was to move to California . . . and that he wasn't aware she was jealous . . . yes, jealous of Rena. She'd tried to fight it ever since he'd come home, but with no success. Worst of all, Rena would sing a solo at church this morning.

<u>Abby</u> temporized, "I have to ask Joshua to deliver the four framed pictures to my friend Rose in Georgetown. She was my roommate at Miss Sheffield's. They're a wedding gift."

"And a fine one," <u>Daniel</u> said, his hand at her elbow to help her down the steps. "I shall discuss it with Joshua for you. Sometimes he enjoys being difficult."

"Thank you." She smiled up at Daniel. He wore his black broadcloth suit and looked terribly handsome. Collecting her wits, she glanced around to see if others were about. "I—I had hoped we could work matters out about the money for my pendant."

He nodded. "I'm glad you've brought it up. We shall

have to bank the remainder of your money in town tomorrow morning."

Panic rose to Abby's throat. "What will Uncle Benjamin say about the pendant money? As it was, I had a difficult time forcing him to accept payment for the trip here."

"I see no reason for you to explain. After all, the pendant belonged to you. I'll borrow Jeremy's buggy, and we can wait until your uncle and Joshua have left for work. If they ask, I shall tell them I have private business to attend to, which is certainly the truth." He added thoughtfully, "You do like to pay your own way, don't you, Abby?"

"Yes. Yes, I do."

His forehead furrowed slightly. "You'll find someday that it's not always possible."

"I'm afraid I don't understand—" she began.

The rest of the family joined them in the shade while Joshua and Jeremy brought around the buggies. Rena's pale hair was swept into a French braid, and she wore a lovely azure frock. She dimpled with joy when Abby and Daniel greeted her.

Uncle Benjamin said to Daniel, "It will be good to have you and Joshua in the family pew again."

"It will be good to be there," Daniel replied.

Later, in the backseat of the buggy as they approached the small white frame church, Daniel spoke to Abby in a serious tone. "Do you know the Lord, Abby?"

His question struck her as peculiar since, after all, she was going to church with him. "I've gone to church every Sunday since I've lived here."

Instead of appearing pleased, Daniel said, "Attending church is not enough, Abby. You must turn your life over to the Lord."

Abby bristled and looked away. After all, she'd been

attending church mainly to please him and his family. Moreover, she was unsure what he meant. Wasn't attending church a sign of being a Christian?

Inside the church, she sat between him and Joshua. She watched Daniel from the corner of her eye as the service progressed, although after a while she decided it was unnecessary to be circumspect. His attention was so concentrated upon the service that he seemed unaware of her or anyone else. She marveled at the joyous dignity in his low voice as he sang out with the congregation:

"When morning gilds the skies,

My heart awaking cries,

May Jesus Christ be praised!"

On the other side of her, Joshua sang with considerably less fervency.

After the Scripture verses and morning prayer, it was time for Rena's solo. She stepped quietly from the front pew to the altar, waiting while the organist played the introduction. Standing there in her blue dress, Rena gazed upward toward the back ceiling, and her voice filled the church like a loving presence.

"Amazing grace! how sweet the sound,

That saved a wretch like me!

I once was lost, but now am found

Was blind, but now I see."

Does Rena think herself a wretch? Abby wondered as the lovely voice soared. She was one of the finest people Abby had ever known.

Abby glanced about and noticed that several women dabbed at their eyes. As for Daniel, the expression on his face betrayed how deeply he was touched. It seemed to Abby that she was either insensitive or on the outer edges of a mystery.

The church picnic that afternoon was a great success, and

neighbors flocked about Daniel, greeting him heartily. "Daniel, are you going to California with us?" they asked, and clapped him on his back when he said yes.

As usual, Abby felt torn about going to California.

Fortuitously, she was never alone with Daniel again until Monday morning and, equally fortuitous, no one else was about when they set out in the buggy for the bank.

Once the Talbot place was behind them, they rode through fields of freshly mown hay toward Independence. To fill the silence she said, "I appreciate your keeping my secret about selling the pendant."

"It caused me no difficulty," he replied. "In any case, I am happy to be of assistance." Most likely he didn't approve, she thought, though he had not said so.

Despite the stifling August mugginess, Abby wore her best black cotton dress for the short ride into town, trying to overcome the foreboding that rose in her like the distant dark clouds. It appeared that another Missouri storm loomed.

"Joshua and I will be leaving tomorrow morning," Daniel remarked offhandedly.

"So soon?" She attempted to hide her disappointment. "I thought you might stay a week."

He kept his eyes on the horses as they trotted into town. "I have numerous matters to conclude back East before the journey to California."

She blurted, "I'm going to—miss you, Daniel."

He frowned, and beneath his beard it was apparent that his jawline hardened. "I am going to miss you, too." He pulled on the reins, directing their team through the horses and wagons and buggies on Independence's main street.

After a lengthy silence, he turned to her. "Abby—?"

"Yes?"

"Nothing," he said.

What was this nothing he'd nearly said? If only he weren't so handsome and . . . so circumspect! And if only she wouldn't continue to hope.

He helped her out of the buggy, and she was heartened to see the tenderness on his face. He did care for her, she thought with a flood of happiness. He did!

As they walked to the bank, the noisy town no longer seemed so ramshackle or raucous; even the deafening racket of the wagonwrights and the clangor of hammers pounding hot iron at the smithies receded. Townsfolk turned to gawk at her and him. With Daniel at her side she paid little heed to her worries or to the dark clouds scudding across the sky toward Independence. Instead, it felt as though she and Daniel moved with the wind.

In the bank, it took no time at all to conclude the business. More time consuming were the conversations as people saw him. "Heard you were back," they said, and, "Good to see you again, Daniel! Heard yer goin' to Californy!" and, then, "Looks like a bad storm comin' on all right."

Finally the last good-byes were pronounced, and Abby and Daniel stepped outside. The wind blew with a vengeance, sending billowing clouds of dust through the town. Horses at the hitching posts whinnied, and the hooves of other horses clopped against the dirt road as people hastily headed their horses, wagons, and buggies home.

"We're in for a fast storm," Daniel said, shielding his eyes against the airborne grit.

Abby clutched her flapping skirt. "Perhaps it will blow over." Storms here often did, though the sky was darkly ominous.

He took her arm, and they struggled against the wind toward the horses and buggy.

With Daniel's assistance, Abby climbed up into the buggy, her black skirt and white petticoats flying. She was grateful for Daniel's strong arm around her shoulders, for the pleasure of his touch and the strength of his presence. Thunder rumbled across the sky as they hurriedly settled themselves in the buggy.

Daniel took up the reins and flicked them against the horses. "Home, boys!" he shouted into the wind. "Home!"

Driving through the whirling grit, they dodged farm wagons and buggies, their occupants intent on beating the storm home. Black clouds obscured the entire sky now, rushing toward them. High above, lightning cracked.

"Hang on!" Daniel warned. "We'll soon be snug at home."

Abby clung to the buggy seat as they raced out of town with the wind. A light drizzle fell, then a driving rain, and, suddenly a downpour that soaked them to the skin. The newly mown hay smelled stronger than ever as Daniel drove the horses through the countryside, then finally past the Talbot house and directly to the barn. "I'll open the doors!" he shouted. "Can you drive them in?"

"Yes!" She took the reins and he jumped down, running through the downpour for the barn doors and pulling them open. She drove the horses in, and Daniel grabbed them by the harness.

At last he was helping her down from the buggy. "You look like a drenched cat," he said with a grin.

"As do you!" she returned. "No, with that beard, more like a drenched bear!"

Suddenly her foot slipped on the wet buggy step. "Oh!" She grabbed for a handhold, but too late.

Daniel caught her and staggered back, regaining his balance and holding her wet body against his. His eyes met hers in astonishment, and he slowly and silently let her down until her feet touched the barn's dirt floor. At length his arms loosened their grip around her back.

Outside, rain pelted the earth, and, inside, the smells of the storm and damp straw flooded Abby's senses. Daniel's shoulders and chest were hard under his soaked clothing; his breath was hot in her hair. Now was the time to back away, she firmly told herself. But, instead of moving away, her hands clutched his shoulders, and she gazed up hopelessly at him.

"Abby . . ." he whispered, his blue eyes full of tumult.

Before she knew what had happened, his lips met hers with hesitation, then with such a mounting passion that she felt lost. *Love me, Daniel!* she wished. *Please love me!*

He kissed her again and again, holding her closer, until she was certain he did love her as much as she loved him. He had once spoken of a love that was like stealing fire from heaven—and this was certainly it!

An eternity seemed to pass before they parted slightly to catch their breath.

Daniel moved away from her, his face a study in stern denial. "No, Abby. No more."

"But, Daniel, I love you!"

He closed his eyes in pain. "You must never say that to a man, Abby."

"But it's true! Moreover, I've never said it to another man, nor do I wish to!"

He shook his head. "You must not say it." His tone was rigid with determination.

Is it wrong to feel so in love? she wondered, backing away from him. Then a flash of remembrance hit her: it was because of Rena . . . always Rena.

The rain had stopped, though the rolls of thunder

boomed through the sky as if from a celestial drum. Outside the open barn doors, the earth steamed. Only a sprawling oak tree shielded them from the view of anyone in the house. Suddenly thunder reverberated again, and a flash of lightning zigzagged down from the sky, splitting the oak tree. She stared at its charred and smoking trunk.

Tears clouded Abby's eyes, and she and Daniel stood as apart as strangers at the barn door while they watched the storm move on, its dark clouds billowing and lit by occasional lightning flashes.

Daniel turned away, his voice harsh and regretful. "I must unharness the horses."

Abby choked at his abrupt coldness and tore herself from his presence, running wildly through the wet grass, as terrified by her passion as she was confused by his vacillation. Inside the house, she ran to her room.

She felt too unwell to join the family for dinner, and Daniel was not there for supper.

He departed at dawn, disappearing like the tumultuous storm that had ignited their passions, leaving only the split oak tree, its branches as charred as her heart felt.

Abby's life seemed suspended as the storms of summer yielded to the fiery foliage of autumn. Fields of goldenrod colored the rolling countryside; sumacs blazed with brilliant reds; there were the yellows, oranges, and reds of the maples; and the yellows and browns of sprawling oaks. Even the split oak near the barn lived on, though it remained blackened where the lightning had struck.

Betsy returned to school, and Abby taught drawing to the two young daughters of one of the prosperous traders, spending her small income on painting supplies and birthday gifts. At home, they finished drying the last of the fall apples, adding them to their store of dried peaches, pears, and summer apples for the trip to California next spring. Horace Litmer, the lantern-jawed, green-eyed schoolmaster, sometimes called upon Abby, but his eyes always drifted toward Rena, who discouraged all beaus now as if she were waiting for Daniel.

Cornelius wrote another letter, but had nothing new to tell, only that he still hoped to visit Missouri on bank matters.

Toward the end of October there was a letter from Rose. Eagerly Abby tore open the envelope.

> My dear friend, Abby,
>
> As you will see by my return address, I am not married.

Shocked, Abby glanced again at the envelope. "Miss Rose Wilmington," it said, and the address was that of her parents' home in Georgetown. Abby returned to the letter and continued to read.

> I have not been able to write because I have been so full of grief. I must tell you quickly and be done with it. William was thrown by a horse just two days before the wedding was to take place. His neck was broken and he was immediately gone. If it were not for my faith—and his—I could not go on with life.
>
> My one pleasure recently has been to see your Daniel when he and Joshua brought your paintings. When I asked Daniel how you were faring, his color deepened so that I nearly laughed for the first time in months. What have you done to the poor man?

Abby swallowed with difficulty. The proper question was: what had he done to her! She read on. Rose was offering to return the paintings, much as she loved to see them.

> They distract me from grief to your great adventure. I have returned all of the other wedding gifts as is proper and will try to find a way to ship the paintings so they will not be damaged.

Abby immediately answered Rose's letter.

> You must keep my poor pictures if they give you pleasure. What gratification it will give me, dear Rose, to do that much for you now!

After she signed her name, she added a postscript.

> As for Daniel, I don't believe that I have had much if any lasting effect upon him. The only help for me is that I try never to think of him.

Autumn's fiery colors faded to a stark landscape that was at last transformed to white beauty by December's first snow. Abby's spirits lifted as she sketched the family's snow-covered log house, their first sleigh ride of the year, and the church shining pristinely under its snow-encrusted roof. Even in winter, there was always enough work in the house to keep everyone occupied until bedtime.

Aunt Jessica and Rena had been teaching Abby to bake and cook, and in the evening by the fire she helped with the sewing, even learning to make sunbonnets. Mainly, they made durable clothing that would last on the trip, much of it of homespun and even of buckskin for the men. In her spare hours, Abby completed the small oil paintings she was copying from the portrait of Grandmother Talbot for Christmas presents.

Two weeks before Christmas, Abby received an odd,

rambling letter from Cornelius. Deciding that he must be lonely, she responded with a note about winter life on the frontier. She tried to strike a cheerful tone, telling him how different life was here; he would be amused that the New Year's Ball would take place at the Independence Courthouse, the most elegant building in town. She thought that Horace Litmer might have invited her to the ball if she were not in mourning, though she did not mention that to Cornelius.

Two days before Christmas, Uncle Benjamin and Jeremy cut a tree in the snowy woods and carried it home by sleigh. Homemade gifts were being readied, and most of the festivities centered around the church. The candlelight Christmas Eve service in the church was so lovely and the carols so heartfelt that Abby held the scene in her memory until she could capture it with her watercolors. And Christmas Day was so heartwarming that she thought if she could erase all thoughts of Daniel and the trip West, she would be forever content.

On New Year's Day there was an announcement. Uncle Benjamin said at the supper table, "I have the great honor of announcing a betrothal."

Abby's heart plummeted. She glanced at Rena with trepidation, but her cousin appeared surprised herself.

Uncle Benjamin said to the hired girl, "Now, Sarah, don't you run off to the kitchen."

Sarah blushed. She was a plump, red-cheeked farm girl whose parents and younger brother had died of cholera the year before, after which the Talbots had hired her, though they treated her as family.

Uncle Benjamin stood and took Sarah's hand happily in his. "It is my pleasure to announce that Samuel Schlatter has asked Sarah to be his bride."

Applause and best wishes followed as the family tried to

hide their astonishment.

"Moreover," Uncle Benjamin continued, "they wish to accompany us to California. They want their own land to farm. Like most of us, they hope to be independent. Seth Thompson will unite them in matrimony next month."

Aunt Jessica beamed. "What a joy it will be to have a wedding in the household again!"

During the next few weeks she helped Sarah make a wedding dress and arranged for a small reception in the house after the wedding. Sarah was overwhelmed and confessed in tears, "Never thought a man'd want one so fat like me . . . 'n then yer better'n my own to me!"

Samuel was dark and raw boned, as thin as Sarah was plump. Despite his taciturnity, he was apparently as in love with her as a man could be. Their wedding was small, but Sarah's gratefulness to be loved made the ceremony especially touching.

In February, the meetings of those traveling to California and Oregon by covered wagon became more frequent, and trip preparations began in earnest. Uncle Benjamin was having six covered wagons built in town; one for him and Daniel; another for Martha, Luke, and the twins; another for Jeremy and Jenny; another for Aunt Jessica and Betsy; another for Rena and Abby; and last, one for Sarah and Samuel, who would cook and drive their wagon. Uncle Benjamin hired five bull whackers to drive the remaining teams of oxen. It seemed uncanny, how matters fell into place for him, Abby thought.

At the emigration meetings, they often read from guidebooks. The Hastings Guide promised, "In California, perpetual summer is in the midst of unceasing winter; perennial spring and never failing autumn stand side by side, and towering snow-clad mountains forever look down upon eternal verdure." One could harvest sixty bushels of corn per acre, it said, and the soil "grows everything—tobacco, rice, cotton, crabapples, plums, strawberries . . . peaches blossoming in January, such grapes as you cannot believe in."

In March, Horace Litmer gave notice to the school board; he, too, was joining the Talbot wagon train to California. He explained to Abby, "I want to be a real part of history instead of merely teaching about it. With Polk as President, 1846 will be a great year of decision. Mark my words, we'll take over the Mexican Territories in Texas and in the Southwest."

"But what will you do there?"

"Teach if I must." He grinned. "But my great ambition is to print a newspaper. How does *The San Francisco Bay News* sound to you?"

"Wonderful. I had no idea—"

He nodded. "We all have our secret ambitions."

At least he was not emigrating because of her, she thought with relief. He had not even asked whether she was going. Apparently he assumed that she would, and she had never refuted the assumption. Possibly she could remain in the house when Inga, Adam, and their five children moved in, but that would be an imposition upon them. It was one thing to live in the household of an elderly aunt and uncle, who were both widowed, and quite another to live with Adam and Inga and their young family.

In early April, spring sprouted across the countryside. One Saturday Abby was reveling in the warmth of the sunshine as she swept the front steps when she became aware of someone's presence. She looked up to find Daniel's blue eyes gazing at her. The broom fell from her hands, clattering against the wooden steps. "Daniel! Where did you come from?"

"A Missouri riverboat, then I borrowed a horse at the trading post," he replied with a laugh. "You look as though I had fallen from the sky." He returned the broom. "Happy springtime, Abby!"

When she did not answer, he added, "Have I been away so long that you don't remember me?"

"I remember," she replied, bittersweet joy returning like the cloudburst on that fateful day in the barn. "It's just that . . . we were not expecting you so soon."

"I hope that I'm welcome."

She stared at him, torn between succumbing to the warmth of his smile or retreating before she could be hurt again. "I am certain you are always welcome here."

"Are you still angry with me, Abby? You have no idea how much I regret—"

To her amazement, she blurted, "The oak tree is still charred!"

"I saw it," he responded, backing away, "but it is alive."

And what does that mean? she wondered as blood surged to her cheeks. "Everyone will want to see you." She hurried up the steps and quickly opened the door. Her voice sounded hollow as she called out, "Daniel's here, everyone! Daniel is home!"

"I am truly very sorry about what took place, Abby," he said before the others came running. "You cannot imagine how often I've—regretted it."

And you cannot imagine how often I've tried to forget! she thought before saying as calmly as possible, "I have regretted it myself."

Rena rushed toward them, beaming with pleasure, and threw herself into his arms. "Oh, Daniel, what a wonderful surprise to have you here early! We've all missed you so much."

Abby turned away in anguish.

The emigrants elected Benjamin Talbot captain of the wagon train and began to meet weekly. Abby took more notice, since her interests were now clearly at stake. One evening the topic turned to the need for an experienced guide. Someone asked, "Do we need one? So many wagons are settin' out this spring that we could follow their trail."

"It'd be a savin'," another man added. "From what I see of it, the Californy Trail is mainly a line o' rivers . . . first, the Platte, then Sweetwater, Little Sandy, Big Sandy, Green, Humboldt, Truckee, and, finally, the Bear."

"That's true," Uncle Benjamin replied, "but there are plenty of miles and days away from the rivers, too. It wouldn't be much of a savings if we followed the wrong trail. Frugality has its place, but not in such a dangerous undertaking. I've been as far as Fort Laramie myself, and I kept a sharp eye out, but nowise would I go without a qualified guide for a wagon train."

He turned to Daniel, who had been sitting back on the sofa and quietly taking it all in. "Daniel here has been all over the world. What's your opinion on this?"

"We need a qualified guide," he replied, "and I think we should discuss the suggested contracts in the guidebooks as well."

Joel Graham asked, "But isn't signing a contract about rules taking matters too far? We've chosen our fellow passengers carefully to avoid the riffraff and desperadoes."

Daniel said, "A community needs rules to live by—"

"But we'll be away from civilization!"

"All the more reason for regulations," Daniel replied. "We will be far more dependent upon each other than people usually are. We'll be a community on wheels. Even the guidebooks suggest contracts."

At breakfast Abby heard that they had voted to have a guide and signed a contract, which included no gambling, no drinking of alcohol, and no traveling on the Sabbath. And they had adopted suggestions from the guidebooks to promote fairness, such as rotating wagons. Every day the lead wagon would move back to the rear of the line so the front oxen would not bear the brunt of breaking trail through brambly country, nor would the same rear wagons forever eat the others' dust.

On Sunday morning, Abby did not attend church. Her heart ached over Rena and Daniel—not that they acted differently, but they were always together. She had just sat down in the kitchen to butter a slice of bread when a knock sounded at the door. Sunday morning visitors?

Opening the door, she was astounded. "Cornelius!"

He doffed his hat and stood smiling at her, his flaxen hair and mustache gleaming in the mid-morning sunshine, his gray suit reflecting the latest in Eastern fashion. "I know it's too early to be calling, but I hoped you would be home. I—I trust that you received my letter of last month."

"Last month?" Abby asked, trying to collect her wits. "No, I have not received one from you recently."

His smile faded. "It should have arrived by now."

"The mail is terribly slow. And one never knows if a letter has disappeared in a steamboat explosion en route."

His gray eyes held hers. "Won't you invite me in?"

"Of course, Cornelius." She opened the door wide. "It's only that I'm so dumbfounded to see you here."

"I thought you might be afraid of me . . . because of that time in your parents' garden. I assure you that I have very thoroughly repented of that evening. I hope you've forgiven me."

"Yes. And I am sorry, too. I shouldn't have led you on like that. It was an intolerable thing to do."

He smiled dolefully. "I didn't require much leading on. However, I've learned that being a roué is not for me."

"I see." She was so unnerved by the direction of their conversation that she scarcely remembered her manners. "Let me take your hat," she finally said and set it on the entry shelf. "Would you like to sit in the parlor?"

"Yes, if we may. Is the family at home?"

"No," she replied.

He smiled at her, then appraised their surroundings. "It is rather rustic with log walls inside a house, too, isn't it?"

She marveled at such an understatement from him. "Yes, rather rustic. But I've become accustomed to it."

"After your elegant life in New York, I thought you might be suffering from cultural deprivation."

A laugh escaped her. "Everything did seem picturesque at first, but the family has been very kind to me, accepting me as if I belong. I've come to feel at home here."

Arriving in the parlor he asked, "Do they often leave you alone?"

"I—I begged off church this morning since I've been a bit unwell. Here, won't you sit on the sofa?" She settled at the far end of it and folded her hands on her black cotton dress with forced calm.

He sat nearer to her than she had anticipated, his gray eyes shining with admiration. "You grow increasingly lovely, Abby. I often recalled how beautiful you were last spring, but either my memory doesn't serve me well or you've become more beautiful still."

"Now, Cornelius—"

He sat back and smiled at her with pleasure, then his long face turned serious. "I do wish you had received the letter. I'd counted upon it to—to break the ice."

"I am afraid I don't understand."

He rearranged his feet on the rug nervously. "The truth is, Abby, that I am not in Independence simply on business. As you know, my grandmother has passed on. . . ." His eyes darted to her hands as if he might like to hold one. "The fact is that you and I have known each other for a long time, and I have become accustomed to being your friend . . . not to mention other facets about you that I discovered last spring."

"Cornelius!"

"I know a gentleman should not bring it up, but I will never forget how desirable you are. I have tried to forget you, but since your departure, I've thought of nothing but you day and night. I can hardly get my work done at the bank!" He stopped and swallowed with apparent difficulty, finally continuing in a calmer tone. "I have discussed my feelings for you with my parents, and they are quite in accord with me—"

"Cornelius, I—"

"Abby, dear, I beg of you to allow me to finish, though this is not coming out at all as I had planned."

She nodded uncertainly.

"The fact is that I can't bear your emigrating to California . . . and my never seeing you again," he said with renewed ardor. "I can't bear for you not to be in New York with me, Abby. What I am trying to say is that I devoutly hope you will marry me, that you will be my dear wife."

Abby's lips parted. "Cornelius—"

"I love you, Abby. I love you so much. I promise I would be a good husband. We can live with my parents in the house on Union Square. My mother is very fond of you, and they are both pleased at the idea. We could be married here immediately and have our honeymoon in New Orleans and then take a coastal steamship back to New York, or we could be married in New York. My parents are agreeable to either. If you like, they would give us a big wedding in New York, although I would prefer to marry you as soon as possible. I know you are in mourning, but I understand that traditions are much more flexible here on the frontier."

She was struck speechless. Cornelius was asking to marry her . . . to take her back with him to New York . . . and she would not have to go on the covered-wagon trip to California . . . nor suffer as she watched Rena and Daniel.

"I—I am deeply moved, Cornelius," she began, "but it is such a surprise to find you here to begin with. I am still unable to take it all in."

He caught her hands in his. "I love you, Abby. Even if you don't love me yet, perhaps in time you will. I've thought of so many wonderful things we could do together."

She heard a sound at the front door, but in her confusion it flew out of mind. Here she was sitting with Cornelius, her hands in his damp, cold grip. "But what of the scandal?"

"I care nothing about it, Abby. I only want to love you and hope you'll love me. I have taken a fine room in Smallwood Nolan's hotel here in hopes—"

Someone cleared his voice loudly behind them, and Abby spun around with Cornelius. "Daniel—"

He glowered at Cornelius. "Either leave this house immediately, Adams, or I shall throw you out!"

"I beg your pardon?" Cornelius replied.

Abby stood up, wide-eyed with disbelief. "Daniel, what are you saying?"

His color deepened. "I heard quite enough to know what he has in mind. Of course, he doesn't care about creating a scandal with an innocent young woman! This—this degenerate would leave town in no time!"

"Degenerate!" Cornelius repeated, his gray eyes wide.

Abby faced Daniel with indignation. "Then you certainly did not hear all of it! Moreover, I can't imagine why you should care! In any event, you have jumped to the wrong conclusion."

The color faded from Daniel's face, but he held firm, unconvinced.

"Come, Cornelius," Abby said, "I think we should go for a walk."

The front door opened, and the others returned from church. Uncle Benjamin, appearing as astounded as she had been, remembered Cornelius from New York, and Abby introduced Cornelius to Aunt Jessica, Rena, and Betsy. If they realized that they'd arrived at an awkward moment, it was not apparent. Indeed, Betsy asked, "Are you one of Abby's beaus from New York?"

"Betsy, what impertinence!" Aunt Jessica admonished, then said to Cornelius. "I do hope you'll have dinner with us. Your family was so gracious to Abby during her difficult time in New York."

"Thank you," he replied, casting a questioning glance at Abby, who nodded imperceptibly. "I am pleased to accept."

Abby said, "And now, if you will excuse me while I get my cloak, we were about to take a stroll."

When as she stepped from her room into the hallway, Daniel awaited her with a stern expression. "I hope I truly did mishear him, Abby."

"You most certainly did!" she retorted.

His countenance softened only slightly. "Then you have my apology and I shall go now to apologize to him."

"Thank you," she said, not entirely relenting.

She started past Daniel, and he caught her arm. "As for your assumption that I would not care, you are mistaken."

She pulled her arm away. "I see no evidence that you care much about me."

He grabbed her shoulders and exclaimed, "I care far too much!" After a paralyzing moment, he unhanded her as if shocked by his own vehemence.

Abby fled down the hallway, the lingering warmth of his touch burning into her flesh, her thoughts roiling. *And what of you and Rena?!* she very nearly flung back at him. *And what of you and Rena?!*

Considering the graveness of the men's misunderstanding, the midday meal and the remainder of the afternoon passed congenially; afterwards, Rena and Daniel departed for a visit with friends.

Before Cornelius left, he said to her at the doorstep, "I shall only be here this week. Please, my dearest Abby, if I may call you that, say you will marry me. I don't even see how I shall manage to do the bank's business here with you constantly on my mind. I must know soon. Otherwise, it is only a matter of weeks before you would leave for California—"

He was so overcome with love and concern that Abby held her hand to his cheek. "My dear friend, Cornelius, I am truly honored. And I will let you know as soon as I can sort out my feelings."

His gray eyes darkened with distress. "Do you love Daniel?"

"Why, what an idea! Everyone has always expected that he and Rena will wed."

"Perhaps," Cornelius replied, "but I can see that he . . . loves you."

"Really, Cornelius!" she objected.

He managed a forlorn smile. "I suppose it is only that I'm

jealous over any man who looks at you."

When he tried to kiss her, Abby ducked her head and his mouth grazed her forehead. "Please," she whispered, "you must not be so—so—"

"I'm sorry. I shall try to contain my feelings," he apologized as he backed away, "but when you're so near, it's nigh impossible."

When she returned into the house, she remembered Daniel's concern for her.

At midweek she had still not given Cornelius his answer, and she knew why: she did not love him.

Finally, she attempted to let Cornelius down as kindly as possible, but he said, "You love Daniel, don't you?"

Full of contrition, she nodded. "Oh, Cornelius, I wish I loved you. Life would be so much easier."

"How I do, too!" At length he asked, "And you will go to California?"

"Yes," she decided, "yes, I will go."

No matter how hopeless her love was, no matter how terribly it hurt to see Rena with Daniel, no matter how awful the covered-wagon trip might be across prairies, deserts, and mountain ranges, she would at least be near Daniel.

By the end of the week, Benjamin Talbot had no doubts as to what had transpired between Abby and Cornelius, for she gave the appearance of dogged determination and he looked heartsick. When Benjamin had a private moment with Abby, he asked, "Do you wish to marry him?"

She shook her head sadly. "No, I—I do not wish to."

Benjamin nodded. "As I thought. It is not the first time a young man has pursued a young woman for naught, though he must care greatly for you to have made such a trip."

"I've told him how sorry I am," she confessed.

"I am sure of that, Abby. I feel sorry for him myself. I understand that he leaves on the Sunday afternoon Missouri riverboat for St. Louis."

"Yes."

Suddenly he understood his own inner urge, that strong spiritual nudging, and he smiled at her. "Perhaps there was a far more important reason than courting or banking for Cornelius to come."

On Saturday afternoon, Benjamin was full of conviction as he left the trading post and headed for Smallwood Nolan's hotel. Upon learning that Cornelius was working at the bank, he proceeded back through town for that establishment.

At the bank, Cornelius was fetched.

Coming around to the front, the young man was amazed to see him. "Mr. Talbot!"

"Sorry to bother you, Cornelius, but I thought I might buy you supper tonight at your hotel. I should not want you to leave Independence and think badly of us."

Cornelius replied stiffly, "Thank you, but I have already accepted another invitation for this evening."

Doubtless the local bankers were entertaining him, Benjamin thought. "Then tomorrow morning, may I take you to church before you leave?"

Cornelius's gray eyes had been wary, but now they glinted with hope. "Yes, thank you. I shall be glad to accompany you to church before I go."

"Fine," Benjamin said and gave the young man's damp hand a hearty shake. "Look for me at eight-thirty."

The next morning, Benjamin drove Jeremy's buggy to pick up Cornelius for church. *Lord, guide me,* he prayed. *Guide me clearly.*

Cornelius stood waiting in front of Smallwood Nolan's hotel and appeared a bit disappointed to see Benjamin alone.

"The others have gone on ahead of us," he explained. "Indeed, I fear we shall be a few minutes late."

When they arrived at the small white church with its plain steeple, Cornelius appeared somewhat taken aback. Inside, the service had begun and the congregation sang out,

"Of the Father's love begotten,
Ere the worlds began to be. . . ."

Benjamin saw that Cornelius had espied Abby up front in the family pew, and he whispered, "We'd best sit in the back pew since we're late."

The young man nodded, hope dying in his eyes.

Cornelius might have been taken aback at the church's modest proportions when they arrived, but when Seth Thompson preached, Benjamin's guest also appeared to be convicted. In any case, while they were all bowed in prayer and Seth asked if there were any who wished to accept Christ, Benjamin felt Cornelius's hand shoot up.

As they all intoned, "Amen," Cornelius wiped his eyes with a fine white handkerchief. He told Benjamin, "When everyone else has left, I should like to speak privately with the pastor for a few minutes."

"Of course."

After the service and Cornelius's talk with Seth Thompson, Benjamin drove his guest to Smallwood Nolan's hotel for dinner, and later to the Wayne City Landing to catch his riverboat to St. Louis.

Before he boarded the squat Missouri steamboat, Cornelius clapped Benjamin on his back. "Thank you for taking me to worship with you this morning. I shall never forget."

"Nor I," Benjamin returned. "It was my great pleasure." When he shook the young man's hand in farewell, Cornelius's firm grip matched his new steadfast expression.

12

The best wagonwright in Independence delivered the Talbots' six covered wagons a week prior to their departure, to everyone's joy and relief, and Abby hurried outside with the rest of the family to inspect them.

Benjamin Talbot said with a glow of pride, "These are the finest wagons made for our purposes anywhere in this country."

Abby already knew that each wagon was solidly built of well-seasoned ash with elm wheel hubs, oak spokes, wrought iron reinforcements around the tongue and hounds, wheel tires of iron, and five hickory bows arching over the wagon bed to support the canvas cover. The fronts and backs of the wagons tipped up so neither babies nor bundles could fall out.

As she and Rena climbed up into their wagon, Abby noted that the white cover drew down tight to the sideboards with a good ridge to keep it from sagging. "Look, there are canvas curtains to put down in front and back," she told Rena.

"They surely are well made," Rena said. "Just the smell of this fresh wood makes it seem exciting! You're going to enjoy the trip, I know!"

"I hope so," Abby replied. She ran her fingertips over the white painted canvas that would be their walls and roof for endless months to come. Inga and Adam had invited her to stay on in the home place with them, but it did not appeal to Abby to remain behind like an old maiden aunt, nor did she relish living near the raucous town of Independence forever. She had insisted upon paying five hundred dollars of her pendant money for provisions, saying it was her personal money. Uncle Benjamin had refused more; he said he would have taken six wagons in any case.

"Why are you so excited about going?" she asked her cousin.

Rena blinked in surprise. "Why, I believe it's God's will for me to go. I am to be part of Manifest Destiny."

And I am going to be near Daniel, Abby thought. She wondered whether the others suspected her motive. Ironically, now that she was to go, Daniel had kept his distance from her.

All week, the sight of the wagons standing between the house and the barn renewed everyone's vigor in their final preparations. There were barrels, some new from the cooper, to fill with flour, salt, bran, cornmeal, water, and molasses, and a new tar bucket hanging on the rear axle of each wagon to grease the wheels and the kingbolt during the trip.

In the house, Aunt Jessica directed the work with a calm that belied the excitement sparkling in her brown eyes. The medicine trunk was stocked with lemon balm for calming nerves and hysteria, citric acid crystals to cure scurvy, hartshorn for snakebites, and, of course, the staples of quinine, blue mass, and laudanum. Matches were stored in tightly capped jars, and hair mattresses were placed on the floors of the wagons to be covered later with featherbeds and quilts.

In the kitchen, Aunt Jessica said, "Store the eggs in the cornmeal barrel against breakage . . . the hams go in the bran where they're safer from the heat." Outside, she wrapped her lilac and rose roots in moist soil and newspapers.

When Abby asked if she might help with the plants, Aunt Jessica thanked her and laughingly said, "It's become a ritual for me. I need to prepare Mother's roses and lilacs myself."

The evening before departure they packed the barrels, sacks, and boxes of provisions in the covered wagons: sugar, coffee, tea, lard, baking powder, dried fruit, sides of bacon, sacks of dried peas and beans, smoked beef, and two hundred pounds of flour per person. It seemed that Uncle Benjamin had emptied his trading post of trinkets to trade with Indians en route: beads, knives, mirrors, fishhooks, and colorful handkerchiefs. Abby hung one of the mirrors from a hickory bow in the wagon for her and Rena's use.

In addition, there were boxes of ribbons, bolts of cloth, and other light goods to begin the Talbot trading enterprise in California. The plan was to carry enough to begin trade near the Bay of San Francisco, then a Wainwright ship full of goods would arrive before Christmas to continue the venture.

They also carried gold. Daniel had accompanied Abby to the bank to change her remaining pendant money into gold, but their outing had been cool in comparison to the previous trip with its stormy passions. Later, she had sewn the gold pieces into her featherbed mattress as Aunt Jessica and the other women had done with their extra funds.

They also carried tools and garden implements, lanterns, canvas tents, rifles, shotguns, and furnishings that ranged from Aunt Jessica's rocking chair to the small paintings of Grandmother Talbot that Abby had copied.

The sun set with streaks of orange brilliance as Abby

attempted to pack the spinning wheel among the boxes and barrels in the wagon she and Rena would share. No question to it, she thought, she had passed the point of no return.

"May I help you with the spinning wheel?"

Abby whirled toward the front of the wagon at the sound of Daniel's deep voice. He wore trail clothing that emphasized his broad shoulders and narrow waist: a coarse hickory shirt and homespun trousers tucked into buckskin boots. He made a handsome frontiersman. "Yes," she said. "I can't seem to wedge it in here."

He climbed up into the wagon and pressed carefully past her. Taking hold of the spinning wheel, he tilted it between the barrels and a leather trunk. "Pack extra blankets around it so it isn't damaged," he suggested.

She nodded. "Yes, thank you, I shall."

He stood gazing at her, and she swallowed hard. After a moment she said, "I don't see how everything will fit."

"I'm sure we shall manage. The thing that surprises me most is your fitting in on this trip."

"What makes you say that?"

"I thought you would succumb to the pleasures of living the Union Square life in New York. From the look of Cornelius, it was not due to his lack of trying, though your uncle assures me that matters turned out for the best."

She very nearly blurted, *You are the one who spoke of love needing to be like stealing fire from heaven!* She had truly tried to love Cornelius, but it had not taken hold. As for matters turning out for the best, she had no idea what Daniel meant. She'd seen Cornelius at church, and he'd bid her a more pleasant farewell than she had expected. Perhaps that was what her uncle meant: matters between them had been concluded without unpleasantness.

When she saw that Daniel awaited her reply she pointed

out rather heatedly, "I don't believe it's your affair."

He chuckled. "That must be one of the set replies taught to the young ladies at Miss Sheffield's."

She raised her chin. "I am sure that I did not learn it there. I have probably forgotten half of what I learned at school already."

"Good," Daniel said with continued amusement.

She hurried along with him to the house in the last rays of the sunset. She did not appreciate his laughing at her, particularly not as they passed the charred oak tree. The tree evoked memories better left behind, and, from the somber expression suddenly crossing Daniel's face, she suspected he shared her vivid remembrance.

In the kitchen, a huge pot of stew simmered, its aroma mingling with that of the apple pies cooling on the table. Aunt Jessica said, "If little old Grandma Graham can be cooking and baking pies to the last minute, so can I!"

Abby smiled at the thought of their energetic but very elderly neighbor going to California. "I have always wondered how she even gets ready for church on Sundays!"

"She's a great one to quote from Isaiah about the Lord being her strength," Aunt Jessica replied. "She has great faith, and she believes that the Lord wants her to go on this journey. For her, it's a kind of pilgrimage."

Manifest Destiny again, Abby thought.

She found Daniel looking at her. He smiled without a trace of embarrassment, and she wondered what he was thinking.

Uncle Benjamin joined them in the kitchen. "The oxen and wagons are ready."

Aunt Jessica removed the stewpot from the fire and set it aside to cool for tomorrow's "nooning"—the name given by guidebooks for the midday meal and rest. "We had better get a good night's sleep. I've already sent Betsy and Rena off to bed."

Despite the early hour, they bid each other good night. She was going to California, she was truly going, Abby told herself, half excited and half numb with dread.

The next morning everyone rose before dawn, and Inga fed them all a huge farewell breakfast. Outside the windows, the bull whackers yoked oxen into teams, hitching three teams to each of the covered wagons.

After breakfast Uncle Benjamin summoned the family into the parlor. "Shall we join hands and pray?" he suggested.

Abby found herself holding hands with Rena and Daniel. There was no time to consider the irony of her position, for Uncle Benjamin immediately began to pray.

"Dear Heavenly Father, we come before Thee with praise and thanksgiving . . . praising Thee for Thy love for each of us . . . thanking Thee for the blessing of sending Thy Son, the Lord, Jesus Christ, here to earth to be our Savior and to show us how to live. We ask that Thou wouldst keep Adam and Inga and their children here in this house in good health and safety. And we ask for Thy guidance and protection on this journey to California. We pray that Thou wouldst not only guide our footsteps and those of the oxen, but that Thou wouldst guide us in our thinking and our speaking so that we might truly be Thy workers in overspreading the continent with Thy Word and Thy love. We pray in the name of Thy blessed Son, the Lord, Jesus Christ. Amen.

"Amen," Daniel and Rena echoed fervently.

Abby added a belated, "Amen."

Outside, heading for the wagons, Betsy said, "Abby, you look so pretty in your new dress!"

Abby blushed with pleasure, noting that Daniel's eyes examined her, too.

"You're not wearing black," he remarked.

"Aunt Jessica thought I might come out of mourning a few weeks early for the trip." She lifted her blue calico dress slightly to avoid the mud caused by last night's rain. The bright color of the dress and her new dark blue cotton cloak had raised her spirits; moreover, she and her aunt had sewn several other colorful dresses for her for the journey.

"Your dress is very nearly as blue as your eyes," Daniel said.

Taken aback, Abby could think of no reply, and she quickly turned so her sunbonnet shielded her face.

She and Rena, who also wore a white sunbonnet, climbed up onto their wagon, and her cousin dimpled in a smile. "It is good to see you out of black at last, and you do look beautiful."

"Thank you," Abby responded, more than a little bewildered by her cousin's generous spirit. Wasn't Rena at all jealous when Daniel took notice of her? Her sweetness seemed unnatural. Abby noted that Rena had placed her Bible near at hand, while her own—the New York family Bible that Uncle Benjamin had insisted she bring for herself—was packed in a box.

Out along the roadside a few other wagons with fellow emigrants awaited them. Uncle Benjamin, Aunt Jessica, Daniel, Martha and Luke and their twins, Jeremy and Jenny, Betsy, Rena, Abby—all of the emigrants—bid a final tearful farewell to Inga, Adam, and their five children.

Inga called out, "We will see you again!"

"Yes!" Abby replied brightly from the seat of the covered wagon. "We shall see you again!" Anguish gnawed at her and she wondered if she'd ever again see them or the comfortable log house that had become a home for her this past year.

Benjamin Talbot raised his bullwhip and snaked it out

into the air with a resounding crack. "Wagons, ho-o!" he bellowed excitedly as he had heard countless others do in the past year's departures from Independence.

The weight of the sturdy Durham oxen's shoulders fell against the yokes, and the wagons creaked and then lurched forward. A cheer rose from all around, but Abby simply waved and tried to smile at Adam's family and the friends and neighbors who had assembled to bid them farewell.

Rena mused, "I wonder whether we shall even see California."

"Rena! What a notion!" Abby said.

"I'm sorry," Rena apologized with a shake of her head. "I can't imagine why I'd say such a thing."

It was odd for Rena to raise such a negative thought, Abby mused.

At length she set it aside to fix the scene before them in mind for sketching: Daniel and the Talbot men riding on horseback leading the way . . . homely oxen pulling the rolling covered wagons . . . hired bull whackers walking beside them, cracking long bullwhips just above the beasts' backs . . . the dogs barking with excitement. . . the log home place disappearing behind them with family and neighbors waving tearfully.

Grieved at leaving and reminded of the dangers ahead, Abby was certain that her sketch would not be dispassionate. *The Ache of Leaving* seemed an appropriate title.

As the Talbot wagons turned onto the muddy side road and passed the other covered wagons waiting to follow them, children and sunbonneted women waved from their seats with excitement. Dogs barked, oxen lowed, and everyone shouted.

Little Grandma Graham called out, "I baked ten pies last night!"

From the wagon in front of them Aunt Jessica replied over the commotion, "You're putting all of us to shame!"

Grandma Graham laughed with delight as did her family. Her son Joel had been one of the first to sign up to go with the Talbot wagon train. He sat on horseback near his family's two wagons, having brought along his wife, Ina, and their seven children, some nearly grown.

Other friends and neighbors in the wagons called out greetings. There was Horace Litmer driving his own oxen like a common bull whacker; he was carrying not only trip essentials, but a newspaper printing press and, of course, his books. He gave Abby and Rena a rare smile as they rode by him.

The Talbot wagons rolled slowly. First, Daniel and Uncle Benjamin's, then Martha's with the twins laughing and waving; then Aunt Jessica and Betsy's, Abby and Rena's, Jeremy and Jenny's, and, last, Sarah and Samuel's, which carried most of the cooking utensils.

Abby and Rena waved at Seth Thompson, whose proposal of marriage Rena had turned down last fall; he drove the oxen and his new bride, Angelica, sat on the wagon seat smiling shyly at them. The Dunlaps and the Williamsons, each with one wagon full of children, were farmers from New Madrid, where the great earthquake of 1811 had hit and was said to have cracked the whole western half of the continent and made the Mississippi River run backwards for days. Abby fervently hoped that New Madrid's former residents did not carry that kind of luck with them. Behind the wagons, three young men herded the loose cattle, spare oxen, and milch cows.

The jumping-off place, where they would meet the remainder of the wagons for the Talbot party, was only a half day west of Independence. The first day's travel was considered a breaking-in time for the long journey ahead.

"Let's name our steeds," Rena suggested, and they laughingly bestowed flowery names upon the slow-moving oxen: Daisy, Petunia, Pansy, Tulip, Lily, and Marigold.

Their bull whacker, Thad Zimmer, was a lean and lanky young man from a nearby farm who wished to seek his fortune in the Far West. He was pleasant, not foul mouthed like most of the bull whackers who'd passed through town. Because Uncle Benjamin lived in Independence, he'd been able to hire better hands than those on wagon trains just passing through; moreover, he knew many of the young men's families and had promised to watch out for their sons.

The morning sun rose higher, its warmth dissipating the early chill. A few of the other families' kin had ridden along to see them off, and they began to turn back home, some vowing, "See ye in California next year!"

As they rolled on, Abby brushed wisps of hair back from her face. All in all, it was a most pleasant morning, even if the seat under her had no springs. After a while she decided to join some of the other women who walked to avoid the wagon's jouncing.

Someone said, "If ye keep yer churn on the seat, ye'll have butter and buttermilk by the time we make camp!"

"All the more reason to walk!" Abby laughed.

The sun shone brightly on the rain washed countryside as the wagons bumped along past outlying farms. Children waved and asked, "Where you headed?"

"Oh, just goin' out fishin'," Thad Zimmer replied, and everyone laughed.

Still smiling, Abby told Rena, "I shall have to do a sketch of that. *Where You Headed?* would be a perfect title."

Rena, who enjoyed the scene-titling pastime, agreed.

The scenery became more beautiful as the wagons rolled

through meadows abloom with wildflowers and past wooded groves thick with oaks, elms, walnuts, and hickories in their new spring greenery.

Hours later they saw the "jumping-off place" in the distance—a meadow with rock outcroppings that was dotted with tents and camps of emigrants waiting for their wagons to be completed in town and for the saddlers to finish harnesses for their teams. Beyond the meadow, valleys lay serenely between deep green wooded ridges.

In the afternoon their wagons joined the ten wagons that awaited them. They drove into a half circle, allowing space for the remainder of the thirty-five wagons that would depart together the next morning, and the herders turned the livestock out to graze. Already minor repairs were required, and several bull whackers returned to Independence on horseback for forgotten items like salt and a powder horn.

"How could anyone forget such important items?" Abby asked.

"I've heard of far worse," Aunt Jessica replied. "Last spring, a family bound for Oregon forgot one of their children. Of course, with fourteen of them, it might be easy for some people to forget one or two!"

Abby, Rena, Betsy, and the twins set out to gather firewood and dry brush and returned with their arms full. Before long Sarah heated up the stew in the cast-iron pot over the camp fire, and everyone took up their eating utensils from the grub boxes. It occurred to Abby that she had never before dined upon tin plates. In this setting, however, it did seem suitable.

Uncle Benjamin brought out ingenious folding camp stools he had devised for the journey, and they all sat down to eat the hearty beef stew and buttered biscuits, followed by apple pie with thick chunks of cheese.

"Isn't this wonderful!" Betsy exclaimed. "I didn't expect the journey would be so much fun!"

Rena gazed across the meadow full of white daisies. "I feel I'm already in an earthly paradise. Just think how much more wonderful the heavenly one will be."

By supper time all of the thirty-five wagons had rolled in and formed a circle in the meadow, and after supper the newcomers ambled about to meet the others. Abby could not help but be curious about her fellow travelers. In addition to farmers, there were saddlers, coopers, and a gunsmith, and even a few foreigners: a French-Canadian couple, the Jacquemans, who kept to themselves; and the Germans, Hans and Freida Schmitt, with their three half-grown children.

After supper most of the settlers gathered in the middle of the camp circle, and Abby sketched the scene. Twenty of the wagons would be heading for Oregon, parting from the California group after crossing the Rockies, and there was much talk about the virtues of each place. "Why, it's so wonderful in California," one of the newcomers said, "they say a sick person is a rare sight." Another claimed, "But Oregon is a vast green land with fine farmland and rivers full of giant salmon."

As the sun set, a fiddler and a banjo player struck up a lively tune and soon everyone in the firelit circle was singing favorites like "On Top of Old Smoky" and "Skip to My Lou" and "Buffalo Gals." Abby sang out the nonsensical words to "Old Dan Tucker":

"Old Dan Tucker was a fine old man,
he washed his face with a frying pan,
he combed his hair with a wagon wheel,
and died with a toothache in his heel . . . .
Old Dan . . . old Dan Tucker. . . ."

And, as Rena put it, they ended with "hymns to sleep on."

They returned to their wagons and tents by the light of stars and low-burning camp fires. As Abby lay down to sleep between her blanket and the featherbed mattress, the words of the second verse of "Fairest Lord Jesus" filled her mind.

Fair are the meadows,
Fairer the woodlands,
Robed in flowers of blooming spring,
Jesus is fairer, Jesus is purer;
He makes our sorrowing spirit sing. . . .

After a while she asked Rena, "How would anyone know that Jesus is fairer than meadows . . . fairer than woodlands robed in spring? And how would He make sorrowing spirits sing?" But Rena had already fallen asleep, and Abby pondered the verse until she drifted off into a sound sleep herself.

13

"W ife, wife! Rise and flutter!"

Abby awakened to the words the next morning with a smile. It was Jeremy calling to Jenny in the wagon in front of them.

Rena laughed from under her covers. "That's how Father used to awaken Mother in fun on those rare occasions when she overslept. It's become a family tradition."

Abby stood up as best she could in the crowded wagon and stretched out her stiffness. How lovely it would be to hear Daniel awakening her with that diverting call!

"What's the weather like?" Rena asked.

Abby peered through the puckering string hole on the back canvas. "It rained in the night, but it's another sunny day."

Soon the entire camp was indeed aflutter for the first full day on the trail, and the smells of camp fires filled the cool air, soon followed by the tantalizing aromas of coffee and frying bacon. Tying on her sunbonnet, Abby stepped out of the wagon into pandemonium. People shouted; cattle bellowed; pots and pans clattered; dogs barked; harnesses jingled. Nearby, Daniel dismounted from his horse. "Sleep well?"

"Yes, I did, thank you." Quite suddenly she realized that she had dreamed of him. Disconcerted and not even remembering what the dream had been, she stammered, "How was your tent?"

"Handy when it rained. But I prefer to look up at the stars."

"I'd like that, too," she said without thinking, then suddenly wondered whether he might misconstrue her meaning. She certainly did not mean that she would like to have looked up at the stars with him last night . . . though perhaps she would have! She noticed that Daniel appeared discomfited, too. She might have blushed if Sarah hadn't called them just then for breakfast. Abby rushed on to cover her embarrassment. "What a luxury it is for us to have hired help."

"It appears we are the only ones who do. We have a great deal for which to give thanks." He noticed Uncle Benjamin getting out the folding camp stools. "Excuse me, I'll go lend a hand."

Before long, they sat down to a breakfast of eggs, bacon, flapjacks, and buttered corn bread, and Abby enjoyed watching Daniel's pleasure more than she did eating. She was glad that Rena did not sit by them.

Horace Litmer, who had been invited to take breakfast with them, extended his thanks to Aunt Jessica. Upon leaving, however, he commented wryly to Abby, "I'll warrant that such feasts won't last the entire trip."

"You may be right." She wished he were not so pessimistic, but she thought he was probably right.

After draining their tin coffee mugs, the Talbot men mounted their horses, and Benjamin Talbot announced, "It's less than a hundred miles from here to the Kansas River ferry, about a week's travel. After we're under way, Daniel and Luke will do the scouting until we meet our guide at the ferry. I'll be busy keeping the wagons rolling. It will be just the bull whackers and you women with the wagons."

Aunt Jessica assured them, "We'll manage fine."

Abby added with nervous abandon, "Just keep us away from wild Indians!" The words had no sooner left her lips than she recalled what had happened to Daniel's parents.

"We plan to," Uncle Benjamin replied evenly. "Most of them won't bother us if we don't provoke them. There's been very little trouble between wagon trains and Indians so far, but I daresay the day will come."

Daniel's eyes met hers as if he could not understand her thoughtless remark. He donned his wide-brimmed hat with a nod and rode off while she gazed after him in remorse. How could she have been so thoughtless?

As the time for departure drew near, eagerness raced through the entire party, and the emigrants called out to each other, giddy with excitement. Finally the snorting oxen were yoked and hitched to the wagons, and everyone awaited Benjamin Talbot's starting shout, for it seemed that now they would be under way in earnest. Daniel, riding by on his mare, called out to Abby and Rena, "Are you lovely ladies ready to go?"

"Ready!" they called out. Caught up in the excitement, they began to laugh exuberantly.

At the head of the wagon train, Benjamin Talbot bellowed, "Wagons, ho-o!" and a tumultuous cheering burst forth across the meadow.

The lead wagon began to roll, then those behind it, their wheels clanking over the dirt road. Thad shouted at their oxen, "Git-yup! Git-yup!" and tugged at the lines. The oxen plodded forward, and the wagon wheels creaked onward, the dogs barking around them.

The sun sent warming shafts of light through the sky, and they rode on across the countryside. All went well during the morning and at their nooning stop, but in the afternoon several oxen still not broken to pull loaded wagons balked and lay down in protest, halting the entire train, while the red-faced bull whackers struggled to get them under way again. Cattle began to stray and had to be brought back, and the hunting party returned with only a few rabbits.

That evening, after they had traveled their allotted miles, everyone was bone-tired. Even the children in their dirtied linsey-woolsey clothing did not romp about the camp as wildly as yesterday. Still, fiddle and banjo music and the singing of folk songs and hymns filled the air before bedtime. Like Daniel, most of the men slept in bedrolls on the ground under the wagons or canvas tents, allowing the women and children to sleep in the wagons. As they turned in, Abby thought again how she would like to look up at the stars with him.

It was turning into a glorious excursion across the rolling countryside, though wagon train life did take getting used to. At first Abby was stunned that they would not take a bit of time to wash clothes, but after several days there was a wagon breakdown and everyone stopped in mid-afternoon to do repairs. Fortunately a creek was nearby.

Aunt Jessica said, "We can't expect Sarah to cook and do the washing, too." She glanced about to be sure that Betsy was out of hearing range. "Sarah looks too tired, and I'm beginning to wonder if she's not with child."

Martha smiled. "If so, she is not the only one."

Rena exclaimed with delight, "Oh, Martha, how wonderful! What if it's twins again?"

Martha shrugged happily. "I don't mind. Now, don't

any of you tell yet."

Jenny smiled oddly.

"You, too?" Martha asked, and when Jenny nodded, she added, "I thought maybe so. You looked peaked for a while."

"I was," Jenny admitted, "but I'm fine now. Jeremy and I can't wait to have our own young'un."

It had never occurred to Abby before how lovely it would be to have a child—especially Daniel's child.

Aunt Jessica questioned the women, and it seemed that Martha's baby was due in September, and Jenny's in August. Both would likely be born on the trail.

Abby, who had never been privy to such talk, was astonished to be asked not to tell. "Oh, no, I wouldn't dream of it!" she replied. She presumed that country women discussed such things more freely; nonetheless it struck her as peculiar and embarrassing to hear such talk.

They trundled the family's dirty laundry to the creek while Aunt Jessica and Betsy cared for the twins. At the creek, they scrubbed and rinsed, and in no time nearby bushes blossomed with Talbot clothing. Abby felt an odd pleasure in washing Daniel's tan shirt and hoped that the other women hadn't noticed her choosing it.

Martha said, "If the water weren't so cold, I'd have an entire bath myself!" She took off her sunbonnet and stripped down to her chemise, then began soaping herself.

The others unashamedly followed suit. After a glance about, Abby pulled down her blue calico dress. Hurriedly soaping herself, she was terrified that the men might arrive. What if Daniel—? What a thing to think of! She rinsed off with the icy water and dried herself, though the front of her chemise was quite damp.

When they returned to the wagons, Daniel and Luke were repairing a wagon wheel, and Luke asked raffishly, "Did you ladies wash more than the clothes?"

"Never mind!" Martha retorted with a smile at her husband.

Daniel's blue eyes searched Abby out, then quickly darted back to his work, causing her to glance down at her dress. The dampness of her chemise had seeped through the bosom of her dress. Blushing deeply, she hurried away.

That evening at the camp fire gathering, she noted that Daniel stayed at Rena's side, though his eyes often turned to her, making her tremble.

The unusually fine May weather held. Although it often rained at night, the days were as lovely as their musical evenings. Even the most skittish oxen settled to their work, and the men learned how to take wagons across streams. It did seem, however, that the fiddling and singing ended earlier, and the travelers tired sooner.

Late Saturday afternoon they arrived at the Kansas River ferry, and Abby shaded her eyes to look far beyond the river at the treeless prairie with its vast expanse of green grass.

Rena said, "It doesn't look so fierce, does it?"

"No. No, it doesn't, but it does look treeless."

They made camp some distance from the other wagon trains awaiting the river ferry since tomorrow was the Sabbath and they would stop. The wagons had no more than formed their circle when the sad news was out: "Grandma Graham died during her nap!"

Aunt Jessica went to Grandma Graham's wagon to help lay out her old friend, and the men set to work building a coffin. That evening after a solemn supper, they held a service under an oak tree for the old lady. Two other graves with wooden headstones lay under the tree. One read, "Elizabeth Sims, December 3, 1797—May 3, 1845. Dead in Christ on the way to Oregon." The other, a fresh grave, was marked, "John Burg, June 7, 1820— May 1, 1846. Jesus is the way, the truth, and the life."

At the open grave, Seth Thompson stood by the simple wooden cross he carted in his wagon. "Let us all say the Twenty-third Psalm."

Abby's voice faltered, and she was certain that she was the only one unsure of the words. The Lord is my shepherd; I shall not want. He maketh me to lie down in green pastures; he leadeth me beside the still waters. . . .

God had led Grandma Graham to the edge of the Kansas River to lie in a lonely grave where wolves howled. Abby wondered whether the Graham family was angry at Him. They appeared saddened, yet accepting in their grief as they stood beside the coffin. She was probably the only grown-up who had not visited the Graham wagon to see the little old lady laid out in her coffin, but she could not bear it. As it was, she could imagine her old body packed in the rough wooden box.

Abby stared at the open grave and the crowd, and suddenly the scene reeled. She could only vaguely hear, Even though I walk through the valley of the shadow of death, I will fear no evil, for thou art with me . . .

Everything around her whirled. She dug her fingernails into her palms to resist the weakness. I will dwell in the house of the Lord forever. . . . It brought back the memory of her parents' memorial service.

As Abby's legs gave way, strong arms closed around her. She was lifted, then carried away from the death words and Grandma Graham packed in the coffin and the open grave.

After they were some distance away from the others, Daniel asked softly, "Are you all right?"

It seemed a long time before she could open her eyes. "I'm sorry," she said weakly, looking up at him. "I'm so sorry.

I couldn't help it. It was the open grave—"

He stood her up on her feet. "I've never seen anyone turn white so fast. You must be terrified of death."

"Why should you say that?"

Daniel held her by the shoulders. "I could see the terror in your eyes. And, then, most people are terrified by what they call the Grim Reaper. What is it that Shakespeare said? 'The weariest and most loathed worldy life that age, ache, penury, and imprisonment can lay on nature is a paradise to what we fear of death.' "

Her arms tightened around his neck.

He patted her back awkwardly. "The apostle Paul spoke of physical death for the believer, the child of God, as being 'absent from the body, and to be present with the Lord.' "

He attempted to step back from her, but she clung to him.

He shook his head at her. "Abby . . . ."

"Oh, Daniel," she said, "you must think I am shameless!"

"No, not shameless, only human . . . all too human, and torn by temptations . . . just as I am."

"You . . . torn by temptations? You always seem in control of yourself."

"Not always," he said huskily, taking her hand from his shoulder.

She felt hurt, rejected. Perhaps he was removing himself because the others were now singing a hymn by the grave site.

"Abby," he said, "I would like to talk to you about the Lord—"

She whirled away. "I don't want to hear anything more of it! I hear enough from all of this family! I am going to the wagon!"

Shaken, she remained in the wagon Sunday morning

and could only hear the hymns from the outdoor service. In the late afternoon, she sat out in the shade of the wagon and sketched the rolling hillsides of Missouri with the wagons in the foreground and the Kansas River across the way. She penciled in a small graveyard under an oak tree and entitled the picture, *Grandma Graham's Graveyard.* She would give it to the Graham family to make up for leaving the memorial service.

Quite suddenly it occurred to her that today . . . today was her eighteenth birthday. Grief caught in her throat. Her eighteenth birthday, and life held no more promise than on her birthday last year when Uncle Benjamin and Daniel had come for her at Miss Sheffield's.

14

Zeke Wilkes, their mountain-man guide, rode in at dawn, his weathered face wrinkled into a squint, his mangy gray beard and long hair blowing in the morning breeze. "Fergit eatin' 'n le's go . . . ain't no Sunday outin'!" he yelled, his voice as ragged as his soiled buckskin outfit. "I held a place fer ye on the ferry, 'n Injuns don' wait! Catch up yer teams 'n le's go!"

Benjamin Talbot mounted his chestnut stallion and cantered out to greet him, noticing that the emigrants had rushed from their wagons, tents, and bedrolls into a flurry of activity.

Zeke Wilkes asked, "You be Ben Talbot?"

"I am Benjamin Talbot. A pleasure to meet you, Mr. Wilkes. I'm told you are a fine guide."

Zeke nodded, apparently not so much in agreement as in approval. "Ye done a better job 'n I 'spected so fer." He glanced out at the camp. "Glad to see ye ain't got horses 'n mules pullin' them wagins. Injuns like 'em. Oxen'll make out on prairie grass whar no horse or mule can, 'n their hooves'll outlast them western prairies. Ye done fine to now."

"Thank you kindly," Benjamin replied. He nudged his horse around slightly upwind of the rank-smelling guide.

" 'Fine to now' is high praise from you."

"Ain't easy to deal with greenhorns, especially flatlanders," Zeke answered.

Benjamin concealed a grin. Daniel, who had hired Zeke, had already reported Zeke's contempt for anyone who didn't live in the mountains, but they knew Zeke was as good a guide as could be had and, just as important, one of the few not bound by drink. Zeke's main drawback, they were told, was he disliked humankind. Judging by the smell of him, the emigrants—and all other humankind, for that matter—would keep their distance.

Benjamin said, "The stock are all sturdy, and Daniel and I inspected the wagons."

Zeke nodded again. "Ye got troublemakers amongst them greenhorns?"

"God-fearing folk, most of them," Benjamin told him. "We don't travel on the Sabbath."

"Hmmmph," Zeke said, shooting a distrustful look at him. "Most of 'em probably ain't niver even seed a real mountain or a desert, let alone felt real hunger or thirst. They got no idee what's ahead for 'em."

"I expect you're right," Benjamin agreed, "though we prepared and studied as much as possible."

Zeke drew a deep breath, then without further ado, yelled again to the company of emigrants, "Le's go!"

"I'll see to them," Benjamin said and rode off.

Before long, the oxen were yoked and hitched to the covered wagons, and Benjamin was aware of his charges as never before: the sunbonneted women and girls, the excited boys ripe for adventure, and the men who entrusted their families to him and Zeke Wilkes.

We truly begin now . . . God help us, Benjamin thought. Then he bellowed himself, "Wagons, ho-o!"

196

Abby felt like grumbling. Even before breakfast the wagons began to roll down toward the Kansas River ferry crossing. She did have to admit that Zeke Wilkes's arrival made everyone bustle. Of course, Uncle Benjamin was still captain of the wagon train, but having a bona fide guide commanded a certain tight-lipped respect from her fellow emigrants.

The wagons rolled into a line facing the river, then awaited their turn to cross. Abby did not like the looks of the dilapidated ferry, nor of the disheveled Shawnee and Delaware Indians who ran it, though in their calico shirts, buckskin trousers, and moccasins they appeared no dirtier or fiercer than those she had seen in Independence. The livestock were already being swum across the rushing river, oxen and cattle bawling, men shouting at them from horseback.

Abby caught her breath as she saw Daniel on horseback leading the livestock across the river. It seemed a precarious undertaking, though no more precarious than the way the dilapidated ferry was carrying the first wagons across. After a while she admitted to Rena, "I don't know how to swim!"

Rena looked up from writing her diary of the journey. "Neither do most of us."

"At Castle Garden in New York City, there were two swimming pools, one for gentlemen and one for ladies, but my parents did not approve—" She stopped. "Oh, Rena! Why am I babbling about New York? You never seem rattled!"

"I often am, but I pray for calm. The Lord makes me peaceful."

"I see," Abby replied, feeling rebuked despite Rena's sweet expression. In any event, she did not care to discuss it. She reached inside the wagon for her sketch pad and settled upon the seat again. After studying the scene, she drew the line of covered wagons waiting to cross the river, capturing her anxiety in the half-terrified expressions of some of the women and children.

Nearby, Hans Schmitt complained, "Ve could have saved money if ve floated ze wagons across behind ze oxen."

Zeke Wilkes returned, "Thet's wut some greenhorns sed las' week 'n ever' last one of 'em drowned. Ye wanna see the graves wun we git over?"

When it was their wagon's turn to cross, Abby was glad that Thad, their bull whacker, was in charge of loading their wagon onto the ferry. Once aboard, she closed her eyes and pretended that she was departing from New York with Daniel on the ferryboat that crossed the North River. She recalled it vividly—his hand at her elbow . . . his tender smile while he presented her sketching case. Then there had been the train ride to Philadelphia at his side and the lovely dinner in the hotel. Despite all of the commotion around her and the rushing sound of the river, Abby focused her mind on the wonderful memories, not opening her eyes again until their covered wagon arrived on the other side of the river.

"We're in Indian Territory now!" Rena said, pleased.

"No need to remind me," Abby replied. It was better not to reflect upon their whereabouts and to simply use the place for drawing. She turned the page of her sketchbook and began to draw the green woodlands: great trees, quivering aspens, hazel bushes, grape vines and other undergrowth. Entering Indian Territory, she'd call it, though it differed little in appearance from the other side of the river.

Uncle Benjamin and Daniel helped Thad rehitch their wet and recalcitrant oxen to the wagon, and Abby and Rena were finally settled with the other covered wagons that had already crossed. The men hurried off to assist the next wagon. It seemed only moments later that Abby heard shouts and a woman's cry from the ferry, "Help him! Help him! He's drowning!"

Rena said, "It sounds like Sarah!"

They craned their heads around the canvas, but saw only people running chaotically near the ferry. After some time the news came up from wagon to wagon. "It's Sarah's husband . . . it's Samuel Schlatter! He slipped, hit his head on the ferry, and fell off into the river! Luke went in after him, but it was too late—"

Abby shivered and remembered Daniel's words: You must be terrified of death. Well, why not! She turned to Rena, who looked as shocked and heartsick as she felt.

"Poor Sarah!" her cousin said.

"What if this is only the beginning of catastrophes?" Abby asked.

"Oh, Abby, you mustn't think that way," Rena replied, wiping the tears from her eyes. "It's true that we should be careful, but we must do the best we can and then turn the rest over to God."

"And where was God when Samuel drowned?" Abby asked angrily. "I remember Sarah's saying she never thought any man would want to marry her, and how . . . happy she was at her wedding. How could God do this to her?"

Rena replied gently, "We can't say God did this, Abby. Besides, I'm sure God sees death very differently than we do. Each of our bodies will someday die. Perhaps in childhood or middle age or when we grow quite old. It seems an ending to us still living on earth, but it is really a glorious beginning with Him."

"And how do you know?" Abby persevered.

"Because the Lord says so." Rena reached back into the wagon for her ever-present Bible and, sitting up again, quickly found her place. "John 5:24. The Lord says, 'He that heareth my word, and believeth on him that sent me, hath everlasting life, and shall not come into condemnation; but is passed from death unto life.' "

Abby blew her nose angrily. Rena's reply did not strike her as any kind of proof. Nothing changed the fact that Sarah's husband was dead.

Samuel was buried near a cluster of graves under one of the great oak trees, and Sarah wept brokenly throughout the service. As the men lowered the rough casket into the ground, she cried, "Lemme die, too! I wanna be with Samuel!" She broke away in an attempt to fling herself atop the coffin. The men grabbed her, wresting her from the grave side.

Aunt Jessica reasoned with her, "Samuel would want you to go on, especially now that you're going to have his baby."

Sarah wailed, "I don't care! I want Samuel!"

"I'll ride with you in your wagon, Sarah," Rena offered. "I'll take care of you."

Sarah flung herself tearfully into Rena's arms, and finally Rena lead her away from the sad little graveyard and shaken mourners.

Abby watched the two of them depart, stunned that Sarah was going to have a baby in the midst of her sorrow. It was obvious that several other women on their wagon train would give birth during the journey—in the Talbot group alone were Martha and Jenny . . . and now poor Sarah.

The men shoveled dirt into the grave, and Uncle Benjamin placed a wooden marker at the head, upon which he had carved Samuel's name, birth and death dates, and a simple cross. Watching him, Abby marveled at his fortitude, for she'd heard him lament before the service, "I should have warned everyone to be more careful."

"Let's be movin' fast now," Zeke Wilkes shouted, "or we'll niver make the Californy Mountains afore snowfall."

Uncle Benjamin called out to them, "No nooning today. We'll drive until dark so we don't lose a day's travel."

They had only eaten cold breakfasts during the grave digging, and they went sadly to their wagons. Before long, they were under way. Daniel and the other scouts had already set out into the prairie on horseback; now Uncle Benjamin and Zeke Wilkes rode just ahead of the wagons, and a few other men rode beside the wagons as flankers. Despite the usual clamor of departure, Abby heard Sarah's wail, "I don't wanna go!"

The trail through the green prairie shifted from west to northwest, and at last it seemed that everything was proceeding properly. Even the weather cooperated, the heavier rains falling at night. Uncle Benjamin constantly pored over guidebooks and notes, and one day he announced, "It's about 220 miles to the Platte River—about two weeks travel from here."

The days began to fall into a pattern.

At daybreak the women built cook fires from the wood gathered by the children the preceding evening, while the men yoked the oxen and readied the herd for travel. Abby liked the morning sounds best: the neighing of horses, the braying of mules, the lowing of cattle, the merry laughter of children, the clatter of cooking utensils, and the exchange of morning salutations. Once they were under way, the mornings were filled with the glorious songs of thousands of birds.

By ten o'clock, the promise of the morning seemed to fade. Instead, the day filled with moving on, moving on. Even the noonings were rushed.

In the evenings, Zeke Wilkes insisted upon tighter night

corrals, claiming, "Ye cain't be too keerful here." Every wagon tongue overlapped the next wagon, and the rear wheel hub of each wagon was chained to the front wheel hub of the wagon behind it. In the enormous corral, the men picketed horses to prevent stealing; outside it, four guards kept watch over the camp and the other livestock in four-hour shifts. "I got a lot to teach you greenhorns," Zeke said. "By the time we get to Californy, yer gonna know everythin' from makin' a good corral to trackin' buffalo."

Most days, Abby and Betsy walked alongside the oxen and wagons, exulting in the beauty of the rolling prairie abloom with wildflowers. In places, scatterings of lupine gave such a blue hue to the prairie's emerald green that, when blown by the wind, it seemed an undulating sea. Among the vast undulations bloomed verbena, indigo, geraniums, wild tulips and larkspur, campanella, sweetbriar, and honeysuckle. At times great fields of clover glimmered with the iridescence of hovering hummingbirds, and occasionally an antelope skimmed over the sea of prairie grasses.

As they crossed through the Indian Territory, the emigrants told tales they had heard about other pioneers. One woman said, "I heard o' settlers who were visited by Indians, and one o' those redskins took a whole platter o' fried eggs for himself! Then, next thing, his friends wanted the same size serving . . . and that woman running low on eggs!"

Someone else spoke of an Indian who ate a whole pot of half-cooked beans and was found dead the next day with his stomach distended. "Can you imagine what his friends might have done to those settlers!" the woman said.

The only Indians they saw came by to trade buffalo robes and moccasins. They were a bedraggled group, their heads shaved except for greased scalp locks and their deerskin garments smelling even more rank than Zeke Wilkes's.

Abby was too unnerved to approach them and asked Horace Litmer, "Would you help me trade for a pair of moccasins?"

"You want moccasins?" he asked, blinking with disbelief.

"Why not? Some of the other women are buying them. These leather boots are too hot here for travel."

He raised his brows and drew a deep breath. "Let the other women do what they wish, but I don't think it's seemly for you, Abby—"

One of the Indians sensed a sale and thrust out a pair of moccasins that looked about her size.

Daniel rode past, then wheeled his horse back toward them. "May I help?"

Abby said, "I—I want to trade for a pair of moccasins. I thought they might take these in exchange." She showed him beads and a pocketknife she'd gotten from her wagon.

"It looks like more than a fair trade," Daniel replied. "Let's see what they think."

To her amazement, he spoke in an Indian dialect to the brave and effected the sale. Despite what had happened to his parents, it seemed that he held no grudge, at least not against this Indian.

"Thank you, Daniel," she said as she took the moccasins.

"My pleasure." Nodding at her and Horace, Daniel rode on.

Horace began to sit with Abby on the folding camp stools during his free evenings. "This is indeed a beautiful sight," he said one evening.

"Yes, the prairie is beautiful," she said as she sketched the scene. "It looks like a vast dome of sky over us stretching from horizon to horizon." She smiled. "No doubt it's always been like that here, but back home it was always broken by trees and houses or a hill or a church steeple."

After a moment she added, "Nobody mentioned how lovely it would be with the wind. It seems to come from somewhere over the edge of the world and stirs the grass like the shimmering waves of the sea. Look how it billows the wagon tops."

He explained rather diffidently, "I meant the sight of you sitting here was beautiful."

"Oh . . . but my skin is so brown and my hair is like straw despite my sunbonnet—" She faltered with consternation. Then she put down her sketch pad and quill. "Worse, I've become so ungracious. I do thank you for the compliment, Horace."

He smiled, and she saw that his green eyes were engrossed with her hands, clasped in the lap of her rose calico dress. She stood up nervously and removed herself from his reach.

Turning at the sound of pounding hooves, she found Daniel riding in for a late supper. If he'd noticed the small drama taking place between her and Horace, he gave no indication. Not that it mattered, she thought as she turned to Horace again. He was a fine man, albeit somewhat humorless and schoolmasterly; moreover, he was within her reach.

Stream and creek crossings, with water high from spring rains, seemed the greatest hazard, though other wagon trains they met mentioned rumors of raiding Pawnees from the north. "Doubt thet," Zeke Wilkes countered, "they ain't got their strength back of the smallpox from ten ye'rs ago, but we'll send more scouts out."

In the late afternoons, they made camp at sites chosen by the scouts for their water and grass. While Abby and the other young women and children gathered brush for the cook fires, the bull whackers looked to their oxen, often cleaning out their sore hooves. Other men were forever repairing wagons and unhooking the tar buckets from beneath the rear axles to grease the wheel spindles. Hunting parties rode out in search of game, often riding back with carcasses of antelopes and rabbits tied on their horses' flanks.

"Sarah's having spells," Aunt Jessica said one evening. "We'll have to take over the cooking."

Abby helped the women make savory stews of antelope or wild turkey for the noonings. For suppers, they ate leftovers with hot biscuits, wild greens, and stewed fruit, then followed with songs until darkness fell. The next morning they would again travel through the great green swells of prairie. Overhead, clouds dappled the blue sky, and the sun blazed so brightly it bleached the canvas coverings of the wagons even whiter.

One afternoon the sky suddenly darkened, followed by three days of lightning, thunder, and rain, reminding Abby of Daniel's passionate kiss, and of the lightning that had split the oak tree. Strange that whenever they had become close, he had afterward scorned her, she thought bitterly.

At length the wagons reached Platte River country, a vast treeless landscape extending to the horizon; only in a few places, along the wide river, cottonwoods and an occasional willow arched over the water's edge. The wagon wheels screeched in protest over the more arid stretches of land, sending up dust all along the column.

For ten days they traveled westward along the south fork of the Platte, seldom far from the shallow brown river. Between the river and low hillsides, the wagons moved on an ample plain. "Yer comin' to the real West," Zeke Wilkes announced. "Afore long ye'll be wishin' fer rain."

Outcroppings of rock rose from the hills and bluffs, and the grasses were no longer a spring green. Here and there, the grass had been grazed by buffalo, which left poor browsing for their oxen and other livestock. Plenty of buffalo "chips" were available to fuel the cook fires, appalling as the thought was. Still, there was no longer wood or brush for firewood, and Abby joined Betsy and the children in gathering the dry chips in her apron and putting them in the "chip" canvas bags tied under the wagons.

Once, when Daniel came riding in from the day's scouting expedition and saw her, he rode over. "I never thought I'd see Miss Abigail Talbot of Miss Sheffield's collecting buffalo chips," he said with a grin as he reined in his horse beside her.

"Nor I," she responded stiffly. She hoped he did not realize how much she still cared for him, and the thought of it piqued perversity in her again. "I find I'm doing a great deal that would have astounded Miss Sheffield."

"Aunt Jessica said you're even helping with the cooking. I'm grateful, Abby. Aunt Jessica is not looking so well lately. I think she is suffering from exhaustion."

"I thought so myself," Abby replied, "but we are all so brown from the sun, it is harder to tell when one is ill." She noted his own brown skin; his dark beard's new reddish-gold glint from the sun; his eyes, bluer than ever. He radiated good health, his body so toughened from constant horseback riding that he seemed solid muscle.

"I hope Sarah will feel well enough to cook soon," he said. He dismounted and accompanied her to the wagons, leading his horse, while Abby carried her apron full of buffalo chips.

She found her resistance to him melting. "What a charming picture this would make."

He chuckled. "I hope you are sketching all along the way."

"As much as possible."

"May I see the sketches after supper?"

She turned away, her sunbonnet shielding her mixed emotions. "If you like." Certainly he would only scorn her again. Still, after supper, she daubed a drop of Fleur-de-lis behind each ear.

At length he appeared at her wagon with Rena and Sarah. "I thought we'd all enjoy seeing your pictures," he said. "I hope you don't mind."

"Of course not." Abby's heart had already sunk at the sight of him with Rena. They were such a striking couple: he, tall and dark, and Rena, small, silvery-blonde, and beautiful. Next to them with their bright smiles, Sarah looked desolate, though thinner since she refused to eat.

Abby brought her sketchbook out of the wagon and handed it to Daniel. "Here they are."

They glanced at the recent pictures of scenes along the Platte and of the prairies, most of which she had already colored in during their noonings and wagon repair stops. At Daniel's nearness and enjoyment of the pictures, all other thoughts fled. Rena admired the sketches with him, but Sarah peered at them vacantly.

He turned the page to *Samuel's Funeral,* and before Abby could think of what to say, Sarah rose up in grief. "Samuel!" she cried out, as if he might hear her from the heavens, then sobbed wildly. "Oh, Samuel . . . Samuel . . . ."

"I'm so sorry! I should have thought!" Abby apologized as Daniel and Rena led the hysterical girl away.

The next morning Aunt Jessica said solemnly, as they cooked breakfast, "Sarah miscarried last night."

Abby felt as if she had been struck. "It's my fault! The picture brought back her grief! Oh, why didn't I think?"

Aunt Jessica shook her head. "You can't take the blame,

Abby. Sarah must choose to become well; that's part of the healing in grief. Some widows are inconsolable forever; others realize they must eventually give it up. Sarah used to be so sound and stable, it's surprising she would be so hard hit."

"She thought no man would ever love her!"

"Yes," Aunt Jessica agreed, her eyes turning to Abby with a curious glint. "Yes, she did."

Abby looked away. "I can understand her heartache." It must be even worse than the anguish she felt about Daniel and Rena, if that were possible.

"We must pray for her recovery," her aunt said, "and we must continue to pray for Sarah's soul, too."

It struck Abby that perhaps they prayed for her soul. In any case, she became more aware of the graves they saw along the trail nearly every day . . . and increasingly aware that Daniel seemed to avoid her now, doubtless because she had caused Sarah's miscarriage. Well, she would avoid him!

Just before their wagon train was to halt late one afternoon, someone shouted, "Buffalo!"

"Buffalo!" the camp echoed excitedly. There they were! Two great old shaggy beasts grazing on the brown grass in the distance.

Zeke Wilkes said, "Old bulls. Let 'em be; the meat's awful. Wait fer fat cows."

The next evening, the hunting party did indeed shoot two fat buffalo cows. The entire camp ate steak, congratulating themselves at having journeyed as far as the land of the buffalo. After dinner, Zeke showed them how to make scaffoldings over the cook fires, and they smoked the leftover meat in long thin strips. "Ye'll be glad fer smoked buff'lo afore long," he warned them. "Smoke plenty o' it."

The ford of the South Fork of the Platte was a fierce sight, the river being over a mile wide. There was no ferry, and earlier travelers had put up makeshift signs of warning at some of the worst places.

Rumor had it that any wagon stalled in the shallow crossing would be quickly swallowed up in quicksand. Unfortunately in the rotation of wagons, Abby's wagon was now in the lead, and Thad would have to take it across. Daniel and Zeke Wilkes made everyone water their horses and oxen well before the crossing so they wouldn't stop to drink in the middle of the river. Now they were in the river on their horses, trying to reassure everyone with the old saw about the Platte, "It's too thick to drink and too thin to plow!"

Zeke shouted at her, "Whar's yer bull whacker?"

Abby looked frantically about for Thad. "I don't know! Thad said he couldn't swim either!"

"No time fer waitin'!" Zeke yelled. "Take 'er across!"

"Me?" Abby cried out fearfully, eyeing the surprisingly strong current.

"I'll guide the oxen," Daniel shouted from his horse. "You just sit tight! It's not deep!"

"Oh, Daniel, I don't know—" She clutched the seat as he led the oxen slowly into the water. Ripples flowed out from around them as they moved along steadily, the water rising higher and higher until the wagon was well into the river. Abby felt as if she were riding into a shallow sea.

"What about quicksand?" she called to him.

He shook his head. "Don't borrow trouble."

The oxen plodded forward in the water until they were a third of the way across, then halfway, then slowly approaching the other shore.

Finally the ordeal was over, and Daniel guided her oxen and wagon ashore, out of the way of the long column of wagons crossing behind them. She climbed down from the wagon and stood by the dripping oxen. "Thank you!"

"You're braver than you think," he replied before riding off to assist the next wagon.

"I'm not brave at all," she replied, but he didn't hear. With her fears she would never be suited to a man with such strength of character, she thought.

Much later, Thad arrived with another wagon, shamefaced and apologetic.

"It's all right, Thad," she said. "You weren't the only one who was scared."

He nodded, abashed, then quickly changed the subject. "The Jacquemans lost their milch cow. She stopped to drink more and sank right in."

They angled over to the North Fork of the river and followed it. It was mid-June, and the country had turned more brown than green, except near the river's edges, but the animals grazed on the dry grass without complaint. "Sioux country," Zeke told them. "Make yer night corrals tight 'n double guards."

Benjamin Talbot called out, "Make the corrals tight and put on double guards!"

A knot of fear constricted in Abby, and she watched for Indians from daybreak until dusk. The Sioux were known as great warriors, still proud and strong. Nights she began to dream of Indian raids and trying to save Daniel from them.

Little by little, the trail began to rise; it became so rough that the wagons bumped and groaned, the earth pounding the wheels mercilessly. Every night wagon wheels had to be mended, and the men hammered in wooden wedges to tighten the iron rims. Two oxen had already died, and their hides were cut into strips to tie up weak wheels.

The days turned blazing hot and the nights cool.

"Mountains!" Betsy called out one afternoon, and Abby saw them showing against the western horizon. The weather grew changeable. One day a sudden storm hit, pelting them with rain that, as the temperature dropped, turned into great hailstones that caused even the oxen to bawl. After it was over, everyone was soaked to the skin and the canvas wagon coverings were torn.

When Daniel rode by to see how they had fared Abby said, "Even the oxen are losing weight. Everyone and everything looks so tired and worn."

"You do, too," he responded. "Take care of yourself."

As he rode on, she wondered whether he had noticed how her body had hardened from the constant walking. She no longer looked like a young lady of New York society. Worse, she always felt bone-tired.

The next afternoon Abby spelled Thad at driving the oxen since he had stood night guard duty. He never complained, but he looked exhausted, and since many now had fevers, it was best for him to sleep in the wagon during the hot afternoons. The oxen were accustomed to following the wagons, and it was usually enough to control them with the reins.

As she walked alongside the oxen, they grew restive, and the dogs began to bark. Abby looked about uneasily, then felt the earth begin to shake under her feet.

"Indians?" she cried to the flanking rider passing by.

The man stopped, his eyes widening, for it sounded as if the ground itself were thundering. "Too loud."

She shaded her eyes against the sun and looked out, seeing nothing but the blue bowl of sky and the undulating land.

"Buffalo!" another flanking rider shouted, struggling to control his whinnying horse. He galloped to a low hill and looked out across the land. "Buffalo coming from the south! Halt the wagons, or they'll pound us into the ground!"

"Buffalo! Halt the wagons!" everyone shouted up and down the line. "Buffalo! Halt the wagons!"

Abby tugged at the reins of the oxen, and in a moment Thad rushed from the wagon to grab the reins from her.

"I'm going to look!" Abby called out. She ran with Betsy and some of the others for a nearby hill. Upon reaching the top, she stood catching her breath while the earth vibrated under her feet. A faraway cloud of dust moved nearer and nearer, and at last she could make out the mass of buffalo, thundering across the land ahead. "What if they veer toward us?" she asked.

"They'll flatten our whole wagon train!" someone replied.

"Get your stock together!" Benjamin Talbot shouted as he rode past the wagons. "Hold your oxen!"

Abby turned again to the huge herd of thundering buffalo. Riders galloped out toward the herd, and she saw Daniel and the other scouts arrive, trying to turn the immense buffalo herd away from the wagon train.

On and on came the great shaggy beasts, the ground shaking under their hooves, the sky above them turning a gritty yellow. Daniel rode forward, and suddenly a huge buffalo at the edge of the herd saw him and halted precipitously. Daniel fired his rifle, and for a perilous moment the buffalo seemed to roar with outrage before rushing at him.

"Please, God," Abby suddenly prayed, "don't let Daniel be hurt or killed! Save him and I promise I—"

For an instant, Daniel's horse stood still and the buffalo was almost upon him.

"Daniel!" she screamed into the thunderous roar.

At the last moment, he whirled his horse aside. The animal ran past him, veering into the herd, starting to turn them before dropping to the ground. A second and third buffalo were shot, and the herd finally turned in a northwesterly direction, their cloud of dust obscuring the afternoon sun, the sound of their thundering hoofbeats slowly quieting as they ran on.

Abby's heart thundered like the buffalo hooves. She had almost tried to bargain with God. What would she have promised Him for Daniel's life? What would she promise Him for Daniel?

She ran down the hill, belatedly aware that their cattle and oxen had stampeded in terror and that everyone was chasing after them.

What next? she wondered. What would happen to them next?

15

For two days the men rode out in search of the runaway livestock, while the women cooked and dried buffalo meat the way Zeke had taught them. Abby helped cut the meat into long thin strips and hung them to dry on a makeshift scaffolding before the fire.

Finally the cry, "Catch up! Catch up!" came again. They made ready to start, albeit with few spare oxen, fewer cattle in the herd, and no milch cows for the Talbots—meaning no more milk, butter, or cream.

As Benjamin Talbot called out, "Wagons, ho-o!" Daniel rode down the line of covered wagons toward Abby. His eyes met hers.

"I'm so glad you weren't harmed by the buffalo!" she found herself saying.

"As am I!" he replied with a brilliant smile, then doffed his hat and galloped away to take up his scouting duties.

She tried to forget his narrow escape and focused her attention on the interesting rock formations to sketch during their stops: Courthouse and Jail Rocks, and then, in sight for a full day's journey, Chimney Rock. While camped at Chimney Rock, the wagon train's first baby was born and named after Aunt Jessica, who aided in the birth.

If the emigrants seemed exhausted after the buffalo scare, by the time they sighted Fort Laramie at the end of June, they were nearly depleted. Fort Laramie was not a military fort, but a fur traders' post where they might buy needed supplies. But when they came in sight of the fort and saw thousands of buffalo-skin tepees all around, they cried, "That many Indians!" and "What if they're gettin' up a war party?" and "They could chew up this whole wagon train before breakfast!"

Daniel and the other scouts rode back to the wagons. "They're Sioux," Daniel told them. "Their warriors are riding ponies and are armed with lances and bows and arrows, but they've got their women and children with them."

Zeke Wilkes advised as the emigrants made camp, "They're tradin', but watch yer belongin's, mos' likely yer firearms. They got diff'rent idees about what we call stealin'. They figure we're on their land."

Indeed the Indians had ponies, moccasins, and skins for trade or sale, and they descended upon the camp for that purpose, though some of them begged for handouts. Two half-naked braves cornered Abby by her wagon the first night, one of them grabbing her shoulder.

"What do you want?" she cried at them.

They grunted, their black eyes taking in everything from her golden hair to her rose calico dress and her moccasins. "Good squaw!"

Abby tried to break free, appalled at their frank stares. "I am not a squaw!"

Horace Litmer hurried toward them, his rifle aimed. "My squaw!" he thundered furiously. "My squaw!"

The brave removed his hand from her shoulder, apparently as astonished as Abby felt. They backed off and nodded reluctantly, bestowing another admiring glance at her. As they departed, Abby became so light headed that she thought she would either swoon or laugh hysterically at Horace's words.

She sat down on a box, trembling at the thought of the Indian men carrying her away. "Thank you for coming to my rescue," she finally gasped.

"I probably seemed a trifle heavy-handed," Horace said with a grin around his lantern jaw. "Nothing else came to mind that they'd understand so clearly. One would think with all of my years of schooling, I could have handled it more intelligently."

Abby summoned a wan smile. "The important thing is that it was successful."

"Yes," he agreed. "It was better than having to shoot them."

"Would you have shot them?"

He nodded. "I would not have liked to, but I would have to save you. I was on the edge of pulling the trigger."

She noticed that Daniel was nearby, no doubt having taken it all in. Why couldn't he have claimed her as "my squaw"?

In camp near the fort, they made wagon repairs. Those who could afford to do so stocked up on overpriced supplies. Uncle Benjamin traded a great deal of merchandise from the wagons, as had been his plan, and he seemed pleased at having planned well what they might purchase. Perhaps most important, the oxen rested and fed on good grass.

The talk at Fort Laramie was about Hasting's Cutoff, a hotly debated route around a great salt lake. Benjamin Talbot said, "This is no time to suddenly change our route," and all of their contingent finally agreed. Fort Laramie marked more than five hundred miles, the end of the first stage of their journey. The wagon train moved on, bound for

Independence Rock. The guidebooks advised arriving no later than the Fourth of July.

The trail grew rougher, and they could no longer follow the river. Ten exhausting days of working up and down hills passed before they arrived at the river again. The upper crossing of the Platte was too deep for fording, and they improvised their own ferry system. During the ferrying, five-year-old Eli Tuttle drowned.

At his funeral, Abby hung back, and some of the other emigrants did not attend at all, among them Sarah, Rena, and Aunt Jessica, who were all too ill.

The company saw the great whale-shaped Independence Rock for hours before they reached it; they were behind schedule by a day, for it was July 5. If their spirits had been flagging, they lifted at the sight of the great, gray mass of rock rising in the wide valley. The guidebooks claimed that mountain men had made a tradition of signing their name upon the rock, but as the emigrants climbed from their wagons, they appeared more worried about the pools of alkali water, one of which Uncle Benjamin said was called "Poison Lake."

"See that the oxen don't drink that water, Thad!" Abby called behind her. "I'm going to climb up Independence Rock." She was tired of rough country, tired of the storms, tired of dried buffalo meat. She would escape to the heights of Independence Rock to sketch. What did it matter that the other women were going to wash clothes? Everything would only be covered with dust again tomorrow!

She hurried away toward the rock, sketchbook in hand. Several minutes later she reached the rugged base of the famous rock, determined to add her name to the signatures and to capture the scene from above. She glanced up at the names etched in the hard surface, then began to climb up the slippery rock, holding her calico dress high enough to avoid stumbling. As her moccasins dug into the cracks and crevices, she glimpsed a white alkali flat in the distance, huge strangely shaped rocks, and a meandering river.

Daniel's low voice said from behind her, "The Sweetwater River."

"Oh!" She staggered in surprise, and he grabbed her arm before she could fall. "I thought I was the first one up—"

His blue eyes held hers, the grip on her arm slackening slightly. "Scouts always have a head start."

Her usual delight at seeing him instantly fled. "If you are implying that's why I'm here, you are badly mistaken. I prefer to avoid you as much as you wish to avoid me!"

Daniel removed his hand from her arm. "Who gave you that idea?"

"Who? You, of course! Who else?"

Daniel looked as if he'd been slapped. "I thought maybe it was Litmer," he replied. "I understand you're his squaw."

"That is detestable, Daniel Wainwright!" she replied, appalled. "I have never heard you say anything so—so ridiculous!"

"I'm sorry. It was a poor jest."

"Never mind! I don't want to hear any more of your apologies!" Turning from him, she climbed on, furious and trembling. He continued up the rock with her. Why did he have to affect her so? And why had she vented her frustrations on him?

Trying to ignore his presence, she attempted to sign her name on the rock with her sketching pencil, which was inadequate for the job.

"Would you like to use my knife?" Daniel offered with a curious glint in his blue eyes.

Her voice quavered. "Yes, thank you." She accepted it,

careful not to touch his broad hand. She turned to the rock and carved her initials: AWT, 1846.

"Abigail Windsor Talbot," he said.

"Yes." Tremulous, she returned the knife, their eyes meeting briefly before he began to carve his own initials: DAW.

Calming herself during the time it took him to carve, she inquired, "What is your middle name?"

"Adam," he replied as he carved the date.

"No doubt as in Adam and Eve."

He gazed into her eyes, causing her to lose her breath. "Yes, as in Adam and Eve . . . in the Garden of Eden."

She saw the flush rise from under his beard, and she remembered the leaf-clad figures in one of her father's books. Blood rushed to her own cheeks, and she was suddenly far too aware of his nearness. "If you will please excuse me," she said, "I would like to be alone to draw now."

He nodded, seeming as unnerved as she. "Yes, of course."

Several minutes passed before she regained control of her emotions and was able to draw the place. At their circle of wagons, smoke rose from cook fires; to the west, the Rocky Mountains were sharp and high; behind them, black mounds appeared to be grazing buffalo; beyond that, another wagon train wound up the trail.

When she finished the sketch, others from her group were signing their names on the famous rock. As she fully expected, Daniel Adam Wainwright was gone.

The next day the emigrants moved on to the valley of the Sweetwater River, deeper into the Rockies. They camped on the banks of the beautiful river, and the women washed clothes and spread them on rocks to dry. The men caught fish for the nooning and again for supper. High peaks and ridges surrounded them, but as they moved on, they found easy grades, fine water and grass, antelope and buffalo, and interesting formations for sketching. Abby kept her mind away from Daniel and on her sketching: Devil's Gate, Split Rock, Ice Slough, Sweetwater Rocks. Daniel seemed to keep his distance from her as well.

They traveled along the Sweetwater for nine days, always resting on the Sabbath. Raiding Crows from the north were now the danger, and Blackfeet and Snake war parties from the west.

"Our prayers keep them away, Abby," Rena said at their camp fire. "Everyone says the wagon trains that observe the Sabbath are the ones that get through most easily." She was peaked despite her browned skin, and Aunt Jessica looked as if she neither rested nor slept.

Abby placed her hand on Rena's forehead. "Why, you're fiery hot! Rena, you must go to bed!"

She settled Rena in Sarah's wagon with fresh water and a cold, wet compress on her forehead, installing Betsy to take care of her. Betsy seemed slightly feverish herself, and Martha and Jenny could scarcely help. In their delicate condition, it was difficult enough for them to endure each day's travel.

As the days passed, Abby found herself not only gathering buffalo chips for the cook fires, but cooking the meals as well. She no longer felt healthy and strong; her constant exhaustion far exceeded any she had ever felt.

One late afternoon after they made camp, she rushed to check on Rena, who still burned with fever. Seeing Sarah sitting in the wagon vacant-eyed, Abby grabbed her hand. "Sarah, we need you to help now. You must eat and get well. We all need your help!" When Sarah continued to stare into the distance, Abby suddenly lost control. "Don't you see, I can't do everything while you sit here in the wagon and stare! I need help!"

Sarah responded by making her way out of the wagon to the camp fire and resuming her old job. "She's mad," Horace Litmer commented. "She might be cooking again, but she's gone mad."

"She's getting well," Abby said. "She must get well. She must feel needed, that's all."

With an undertone of anger, Horace said, "In the event you have not noticed, I would like to feel needed, too!" He turned and headed toward his wagon.

Abby stared after him, stunned. Her treatment of Horace paralleled Daniel's of her, and she hadn't even realized it! She hadn't intended to hurt him. No doubt, Daniel's intentions were the same.

The emigrants began their climb through the Rockies with trepidation, for the great mountains looked formidable and there was neither trail nor track. Meeting great splits in the earth, the company dug up stones and dirt clods to fill the gullies so they could drive the wagons across. In places, rocks from winter storms were so heavily strewn that the men worked for hours to clear them away and make passage. On the days when they had to move one huge boulder after another, it seemed they would never reach the Great Divide, and they all went to sleep more exhausted than ever.

Despite their hardships, Abby thought the country around them beautiful. Wildflowers filled the mountain air with fragrance, and willow groves afforded cooling shade along the riverbanks. Game animals provided plenty of fresh meat.

As they toiled higher up the sides of the mountains, they saw their first fir trees in weeks. The air, redolent with pine, grew so cool at night that the women got out the blankets. Abby felt much better for the cooler air, as did the others. Upon nearing South Pass, they were relieved to see that in the very backbone of the country, the pass was surprisingly like a broad plain, a bumpy opening about twenty miles wide between two solid walls of impassable mountains.

Betsy asked, "Where is the place that water begins to flow to the Pacific Ocean instead of the Atlantic?" but no one could be certain.

At eight thousand feet, they saw snowcapped peaks, and Abby quailed at the thought of more mountains ahead. In the mornings, they found skims of ice in the water buckets.

Often the emigrants would point at a nearby place in the mountains and venture, "That can't be over a mile or two from here," but it would take a long day's travel to reach, for it was difficult to hold back the wagons on steep inclines.

"Look down there," Betsy told Abby, "it's a wagon all smashed to pieces!"

Abby peered down at the remains of a wagon that had gotten away from another party and crashed into the mountain's rock walls.

"What if the people were in it?" Betsy asked in alarm.

Abby swallowed with difficulty, then put on a brave smile. "Likely they decided not to take that wagon through," she equivocated. No one in such a runaway wagon would live to get through the mountains.

Daniel stopped by every morning and night to see Rena. Occasionally Abby came upon him holding Rena's hot hand, the two of them looking happily at each other. The sight of it tore at her heart.

One night she heard Rena say, "I love you so, Daniel," and Daniel reply, "I love you, too."

Abby hurried away in agony.

Several evenings later Daniel caught up with Abby throwing a bucket of dirty wash water on the camp fire. "Abby, you can't do everything," he admonished. "You are driving yourself to exhaustion!"

"I don't care!" she flared, the smoke from the doused fire making her eyes smart. "All I want is to get wherever we're going and be done with it! Three people have died of fever in the past week, and half the others are sick! If I'd had any sense at all, I would have married Cornelius and gone back to New York with him. But, no, I listened to your nonsense about love having to be like stealing fire from heaven—"

"Abby, everyone—"

"I don't care!" she cried on the verge of collapse. "I don't care!"

He held her by the shoulders. "You do care, Abby. You do care, and that's what makes the hurting worse."

"I know it! If only I could be tough and hard and not care about anything or anyone—" She thrust herself away from him. What was she saying?

She turned and ran to her wagon. It was her love for him that was destroying her, she thought. He was destroying her! If it weren't for him, she would never have come!

16

In the grayness before dawn, Benjamin Talbot headed for the cook fire. Sarah was already at work, and the mingling aromas of frying bacon and hot coffee filled the morning air. All around them, emigrants stirred from their wagons and bedrolls, and dogs stretched and scratched at their fleas. Only half awake himself, Benjamin saw Zeke start toward the Talbot cook fire from across the corral.

"Morning, Sarah," Benjamin said.

Receiving no reply he asked, "Coffee ready? It smells exceedingly good. Makes a man feel more like getting up."

Without a glimmer of acknowledgment, she poured him a tin mug of the steaming coffee and handed it to him with downcast eyes. She might be cooking again, he thought, but she performed her duties in a vacant daze.

"Thank you, Sarah." He took a careful sip of the strong brew, nearly burning his lips. "Mighty good coffee," he told her. "You help us get off to a fine start. We appreciate your part in this journey."

Her stolid face still closed up and her broad shoulders hunched, she turned away to stir the thick porridge in the heavy iron pot over the fire.

Benjamin hoped her work and sense of usefulness would

ease her grief over Samuel's death, just as they had helped him when Elizabeth had passed on.

Zeke Wilkes stepped up to them. "Mornin'," he said.

Benjamin returned the greeting and added, "Good coffee as usual when Sarah's making it." He turned to ask her for coffee for Zeke, but she was already pouring him a mugful of the steaming black liquid from the coffeepot.

Accepting it from her with soft-spoken thanks, Zeke took a sip of coffee himself. He took a second sip, then spoke to Benjamin. "If ye think South Pass was easy, ye got a surprise waitin' fer ye. Ternight we make Li'l Sandy Crick . . . nigh on twenty mile."

"Good. Glad to hear it." Benjamin hesitated. "We need to have a private discussion."

Zeke nodded, and they stepped away from the cook fire circle, where other Talbots were beginning to gather.

"I don't like the looks of our company, Mr. Wilkes," Benjamin confided. As usual, he positioned himself upwind of the rank-smelling guide. "Perhaps we should proceed more slowly."

Zeke shook his head. "Ain't no slowin' down now, not unless we leave extra graves."

"We have to consider the womenfolk," Benjamin protested. "My sister Jessica is worn down; and Rena's fever won't break. Even Betsy and Abby are not feeling as well as they should, and a number of the women are . . . in a delicate condition."

"All the more reason to keep goin'," the mountain man replied with conviction.

After a moment Zeke glanced toward Sarah, who was dishing out porridge, and Benjamin saw an opportunity to make his point. "Look at how much weight Sarah has lost."

"She's young," Zeke answered, "'n she's got the look o'

one who outlasts trouble." He turned back to Benjamin and added, abashed, "I know she's a widder woman, 'n mighty grieved . . . 'n like family to ye. In any case, I be askin' fer yer word fer me to court 'er."

"You . . . ? Sarah?" Benjamin asked in amazement.

Zeke nodded, then quickly squinted out toward the first pinkish light glimmering over the horizon. He said into the silence, "I like a woman who knows how to work. I ain't no slacker myself."

"No, from what I've seen of you so far, you're not," Benjamin agreed.

Zeke turned back and allowed a flicker of a smile to cross his weathered face, though his mangy beard hid most of it. "I got me some ranchin' land in Californy. I'd like that Sarah fer a wife, 'n I'd like a passel o' sons."

Benjamin drew a deep breath. Many a man hoped for a strong wife and sons to work their land, but few said as much. If nothing else, Zeke was honest. "I'm honored that you would ask my permission, Mr. Wilkes," he said. "As for courting Sarah, you have my consent if she is willing."

At the gleam in the guide's eyes, he warned, "I expect you to behave toward her like a gentleman." He fought off the sudden temptation to laugh. The whole idea of it—especially telling Zeke, who was near him in age, to behave like a gentleman—struck him as so astonishing that he could scarcely believe their exchange was taking place.

"I reckon I will," Zeke said. He eyed Benjamin. "What'd ye think she'd like o' me?"

The morning light was brighter and, looking at their guide, he saw the face of the problem, so to speak. "Perhaps if you'd wash up a little, get yourself some new buckskins. Sarah is somewhat accustomed to cleanliness."

Zeke raised a shaggy eyebrow. "I'll think on it."

"Now that you have, ah . . . other interests . . . will we be letting up on the pace of the wagon train?"

"No lettin' up," Zeke replied with determination. "I aim to get Sarah to Californy while she got breath in 'er lungs."

Having said that, Zeke turned and bellowed to the emigrants, "Eat up, now! Eat up! Ain't no time to waste!"

"Twenty miles today!" Benjamin added loudly.

As he hurried with Zeke to the cook fire, he thought, Well, I'll be! Several sons and daughters of the emigrants had been courting and keeping anxious parents awake at night, all of which was to be expected. He'd half anticipated sparks between Daniel and Rena, or maybe Abby, too, though nothing had come of it. But he surely had not expected it of Sarah and Zeke. For all of his troubles to keep the wagon train moving, the job had its more humorous aspects. How Elizabeth and he might have laughed at this morning's interchange.

At the cook fire, he told Zeke, "You go first this time."

He watched as Sarah nervously handed the guide a tin plate of porridge topped by thick bacon chunks.

"Thank ye, Sarah," the mountain man said. He stood long enough to make her look up, then caught her gaze with his eyes and, in that instant, something passed between them.

"Yer welcome, Mr. Wilkes," Sarah replied, then abruptly turned to ladling out porridge again.

The first coherent words anyone had heard from her in a long time! Benjamin thought.

By the time he'd thanked her for his porridge, he wondered if she knew Zeke had taken a liking to her, for she said, "Welcome, Mr. Talbot" with some life in her eyes.

Zeke might not be a Bible-toting Jedediah Smith, Benjamin decided as he left the cook fire, but their mountain man guide had possibilities.

In the brighter glimmering of daybreak, Benjamin settled on a folding chair and prayed for Sarah and Zeke, and gave thanks for his food. The porridge was still steaming, so he took the guidebook from his buckskin jacket's pocket and began to read its account for the day.

Three miles to PACIFIC SPRINGS AND CREEK . . . a great abundance of grass, but the ground is in many places miry. Water good.

Four miles north of this place, toward the snowy mountains, is plenty of grass which can be cut (in case you find none rank enough any nearer), and it will be good for all to lay in a few sacks to help the teams on the Great Cutoff, upon which they will enter the Big Sandy River.

CROSSING OF CREEK. Rather bad to cross. After this creek there is no water fit to drink for 23 miles . . . .

He recalled last year in Independence when someone had called the California Trail mainly a route of rivers. So far they'd only put the Platte and the Sweetwater behind them. A lot of rivers and mountains and even deserts lay ahead, and places with worrisome names like Rattlesnake Creek and Rattlesnake Mountains. So far, no one in the party was snakebit—but it seemed that some of them were lovebit.

Abby rushed to her wagon. It'd be best if she tended to Rena, she thought, now that Sarah was cooking and Betsy was caring for Aunt Jessica. Last night Daniel had carried Rena back to the wagon and helped to settle her there.

In the wagon, Abby leaned over Rena who drowsed in her makeshift bed, her face pale. "We're supposed to make twenty miles today, Rena. Isn't that wonderful? You know we've only been averaging fourteen miles a day."

Rena opened her glazed eyes for an instant and smiled, but her dimples were no longer deep in her gaunt face. "Yes, only a few more miles."

Abby placed a hand upon her cousin's brow. It was already hot this early in the morning. She dampened a cloth with water and lay it on Rena's forehead. Her cousin made peculiar comments often now. In the middle of the night, she had laughed happily in her sleep, then uttered, "Oh, yes, Lord! Oh, yes!" It had given Abby such a fright that she had lain listening to Rena's breathing, unable to fall asleep again for a long time.

Outside, Benjamin Talbot was already calling, "Catch up! Catch Up!"

Abby asked Rena, "Is there anything you need before we leave?"

Rena's brown eyes appeared less glazed as she opened them now. "Only for you to love the Lord."

Abby stiffened. If her cousin were not so sweet, she would be furious. After all, she had gone to church with them in Independence and to most of the Sunday meetings on the trail. She was even learning the words to their hymns. No matter what she did, it didn't seem enough to please Rena. "Yes. Well, you concentrate on resting. I'll look in on you often." Trying to soften the harshness in her voice she added, "Daniel stopped to see you before you awakened."

"I thought so," Rena murmured with a blissful smile.

Abby's spirits wavered.

Betsy popped her head in. "Time to depart!"

"I'll be right there," Abby replied.

The girl's green eyes turned with concern to her older sister. "I hope you'll sleep today, Reenie."

"I'll be fine," Rena assured her. "I'm improving all the

time."

Abby did not think so.

Outside, she was glad to hear Benjamin Talbot's call of "Wagons, ho-o!" and to start their descent from the heights of South Pass.

The wagon train set out over rough terrain on the downhill trek, reaching the Little Sandy Creek in good time. Abby could not understand how Rena withstood the terrible bouncing in the wagon. Only the sick and the injured rode in wagons now, not merely to save the oxen, but because it was infinitely more comfortable to walk. At every stop, Abby changed the wet compresses on Rena's fevered brow.

Fortunately the next day was Sunday, and they made camp near the willows of Little Sandy Creek. Clear water rippled over the fine sand and, though the grass had been trampled by recent wagon trains, sufficient grazing remained for the stock. Abby was pleased to see the oxen rest. "I never thought I'd care about such homely beasts," she admitted to Betsy, "but I hold each of them in great affection now!"

Rena and the other invalids were brought out of the wagons for the creekside Sunday services. Abby watched Daniel carry Rena out tenderly and seat her upon a blanket, then settle at her side. Jenny and Martha, who were now great with child, sat on blankets with their husbands in the shade of the willows, trying to quiet the energetic twins. Aunt Jessica sat with Abby, insisting that she was nearly well again, and Betsy joined them.

Together, in front of the cross Seth Thompson had set up for the service, they sang,

"This is the day the Lord hath made;
He calls the hours His own:
Let heaven rejoice, let earth be glad,
And praise surround the throne."

Abby glanced sidelong at Rena as they started the second verse, marveling again at how her cousin seemed to gather strength as she sang. Last night she had washed Rena's hair, and now in the sun-dappled shade of the willows, it shone like silvery silk, and her brown eyes brimmed with faith.

Seth Thompson spoke of the wilderness through which Moses and the children of Israel had wandered, then referred to the wilderness ahead for each of them during this westward trek—and the rest of their lives. "Through all of these wildernesses we must honor God first and foremost," he preached. "We must stand aside, keeping our own sinful natures in abeyance and become holy vessels for God."

Abby did not think herself such a great sinner. She was a good person, she told herself, as good as anyone else.

Toward the end of the service Seth asked Daniel to read a passage from the Book of Deuteronomy.

Daniel might have been Moses giving the commandments as his deep voice proclaimed, "Hear, O Israel: The Lord our God is one Lord: And thou shalt love the Lord thy God with all thine heart, and with all thy soul, and with all thy might."

Then Seth requested, "Now, please, from the New Testament, the Book of Matthew," and he added the chapter and verses.

Daniel turned the pages of his Bible, the soft breeze tousling the curls of his dark hair and beard. Finding his place with assurance he read, "Master, which is the greatest commandment in the law?"

He paused, and Abby could not remove her eyes from his face. An aura of faith seemed to emanate from him.

" 'Jesus said unto him, Thou shalt love the Lord thy God with all thy heart, and with all thy soul, and with all thy mind. This is the first and great commandment. . . And the second is like unto it, Thou shalt love thy neighbour as thyself.' "

Rena's beatific smile wrenched Abby's heart. How well suited her cousin and Daniel were for each other.

The company sang "Amazing Grace," quieting toward the end of the third verse to allow Rena's melodious contralto to rise:

"'Tis grace that brought me safe thus far,

And grace will lead me home."

Abby wiped away a tear with her fingertips. The others' fading voices told her they, too, were touched as Rena sang the fourth verse:

"When we've been there ten thousand years,

Bright shining as the sun,

We've no less days to sing God's praise

Than when we've first begun."

In unison they fervently sang out across the creek banks, filling the camp and the sky: "Praise God, praise God, praise God, praise God. . . ."

The joyous sound of their praise lingered with Abby long after the service, uplifting her heart.

In mid-afternoon Jeremy came running for Aunt Jessica—sick as she was—to hurry to Jenny's wagon. Before long, the word went from wagon to wagon: "The baby's turned wrong."

By sunset, the word went around again, "The baby's lost."

At first Abby's heart constricted, then she was furious. She did not care for this God of theirs! Jenny had wanted this baby! If God existed, He was entirely cruel and unfair!

The next morning, they stopped at the Big Sandy River, where the men cut grass to take along in the wagons, and the women and children filled every possible jug, pan, and keg with water.

As Abby carried the last of the water jugs to their wagon, she looked out at the landscape they would have to cross—a flat, barren tableland, relieved only by occasional clumps of dried sagebrush and rocks. "Never saw anything like it," and "It's sure nothing like home," she heard again and again.

Abby saw her uncle and Zeke Wilkes confer, then the guide warned, "There be no water, no grazin' . . . nothin' till Green River, 'n thet's nigh on forty-five miles."

The wagon train traveled in a straggly column across the desert, through rocky ravines, and past alkali ponds that glistened in the sunshine with a deathly whiteness. The wagon wheels and oxen's hooves sent up fine white dust to fill Abby's eyes, mouth, and nostrils. Sagebrush tore the oxens' undersides and stopped the wagons, and the men hacked at it with axes, gasping in the blazing sun.

Zeke called for two watering stops in addition to the nooning, though there were only a few swallows of water for each of the oxen.

Betsy's green eyes filled with worry, and she told Abby, "The oxen look bonier now."

"Yes, I'm afraid they are, but I'm sure they'll be all right." In truth, she was not at all sure.

The lead oxen, Lily and Tulip, looked the weakest, yet they plodded on. There's no turning back now, Abby reflected, only going forward. Surely California would not be a disappointment after enduring this.

In the afternoon the exhausted oxen pulled the wagons toward the relentless sun. Abby was so blinded that the desert seemed a bright blur. Beside the trail were moldering ox carcasses from recent wagon trains and bones of others long picked clean. Here and there they passed furniture and other goods that earlier wagon trains had thrown out to lighten their loads—heavy blacksmith tools, an old bureau, trunks, even a rocking chair.

The first day in the desert they made eighteen miles. That night there was no firewood for the cook fires, not even buffalo chips. Coughing, Abby helped Sarah build a cook fire with greasy sagebrush. All around them the men worked on the unending wagon repairs; the desert's fierce heat had shrunk wheels, tongues and hounds, and even the hickory bows holding up the canvas.

The next morning they found three oxen dead and two others so weakened that they had to be left behind. "Have to shoot 'em," Zeke Wilkes said and did the job himself.

Abby jerked as each shot filled the air. With her own throat so parched before they even set out, how could the oxen not be suffering? Even the dogs seldom barked now.

At their first water stop, Horace Litmer presented her with a smooth gray pebble.

"What's that for?" she inquired.

"Keep it in your mouth. It helps to make saliva."

"What a sorry pass things have come to," she said. "I can't imagine what Miss Sheffield's reaction to this would be." She immediately regretted her words. "I'm sorry. I seem to think about New York now to avoid dwelling on the dryness and dust."

"I didn't think it would be this bad myself," he said, "and I made a study of it. If only there were shade somewhere. Some of our fellow travelers are slaking their thirst by sucking on rags soaked in vinegar."

Abby said, "I'm not that thirsty . . . not yet."

At mid-afternoon they passed another wagon train that had stopped to bury a woman—sixty years old like Aunt Jessica—who had died from exhaustion. Despair rushed through Abby to see that the body was only wrapped in a sheet and being buried in a shallow grave.

Wolves tracked them now. At night the guards set sagebrush fires around the perimeter of the camp to keep them at bay. Abby lay wide awake, listening to Rena's shallow breathing and the wolves' howls.

On the third morning Tulip was dead, and Uncle Benjamin put Lily out of her agony. At the loud shot, dogs whined and tucked their tails between their legs.

"Oh, Abby!" Betsy cried, burying her face on Abby's shoulder and shaking with sobs.

"It's all right, Betsy," she replied, "It's going to be all right." She felt like crying herself.

Rena's fever burned constantly despite the vinegar-dampened cloths on her forehead. She lay frighteningly still and uncomplaining in the heat, resembling a porcelain doll with a waxen face and bright red cheeks.

Just after high noon Daniel and the other scouts rode back, covered with dust and grit. "The Green River!" they shouted. "Just below those bluffs. There's a ferry and pine forests and good streams and springs!"

No one even had the strength to raise a cheer.

When they finally descended to the swiftly running stream, Abby kicked off her moccasins and waded into the water in her dusty dress. "It's cool!" she called out to Betsy, who joined her.

Many of the emigrants followed suit and, after drinking their fill, even the dogs came in for a swim. Abby noticed that after his swim, Zeke Wilkes trimmed his hair and beard neatly and wore far cleaner buckskins. That night the hunters returned with three antelope, so there would be fresh meat to eat again.

After the awful trek through the desert, the rugged mountainous trail was what Aunt Jessica called "a blessed relief." A week's travel through high ridges and pine forests brought them to the Bear River, from which they swung northward. The great attractions on this dull stretch were soda springs, whose water tasted like sulfur. When they stopped, Abby and Betsy sketched the springs. Surprisingly, Rena felt well enough to sit outside one evening to write in her diary. When Daniel rode in from scouting he ambled over to join them, carrying his tin plate full of antelope stew.

"Look at Steamboat Spring!" Rena called to him over the chugging sounds of the water. "Doesn't the Lord create wonders?"

Daniel beamed. "Yes, He does."

The way he looked at Rena left no question in Abby's mind that he thought Rena one of those wonders. They made a charming picture sitting by the covered wagon and looking out at the spring. Abby did not sketch them into her scene, though she noticed that Betsy did.

It was a dull ten-day pull to Fort Hall, a fur-trading post of the Hudson's Bay Company. They arrived on a Saturday afternoon and settled down to rest, repair wagons, and buy a few supplies while the stock grazed on the green grass.

Benjamin Talbot exulted, "Over halfway to California! We've traveled nearly twelve hundred miles!"

Halfway? It seemed impossible. How could they manage that distance again, with the California Mountains even more rugged than the Rockies?

17

On Saturday night there was music. Abby and the other emigrants sang "Sweet Betsy from Pike" and their other favorites around a camp fire. The evening held a special poignancy since next week over half of the company would split away toward Oregon. Even Aunt Jessica summoned up the energy to join in, a sad-faced Jenny at her side.

Together the group reminisced about their trip—the first days out, fording the rivers, the Indians at Fort Laramie, the buffalo stampede. Zeke Wilkes, sitting near Sarah, was urged to share something from his years of travel and finally gave in.

"Wun I was a boy, we was south o' the Platte wun we had t' corral our wagins t' keep the stock from bein' stampeded by buffalo," he began. "Six days 'n nights forty men kep' killin' buff'lo to keep 'em off the wagons. Nex' day the buff'lo herd spread, givin' us a chance to yoke up 'n cross the Platte. 'N it's a good thing we did!"

"Why is that?" Benjamin Talbot inquired.

"Well," Zeke replied, straight-faced, "we no more 'n hit the other side o' the Platte, 'n here comes the main herd!"

Everyone laughed at his tall tale, even Sarah, and Abby was pleased to see she was no longer so grieved.

Daniel, sitting beside Rena, asked the assemblage, "Did you hear about the emigrant named Harmanius Van Vleck who was crossing the country in a small wagon train?"

No one had, so he continued. "Well, the dangers of the deserts were behind them, and the emigrants were camping near the California Mountains. Suddenly Van Vleck noticed Indian fires and smoke signals up in the hills. He told the other men to guard the camp and he would take care of the dangerous situation himself. Well, he rode up into the hills toward the largest of the signal fires. When he was in an easy distance of it, he straightened up in his saddle, put on a ferocious expression, and galloped at full tilt toward the Indians. When he was in their camp fire's light and the braves' eyes were all fixed upon him, he stuck his hand into his mouth, pulled out his false teeth and flourished them in the faces of the terrified Indians, who promptly fled in all directions."

"Oh, Daniel!" Rena protested and laughed with everyone else.

Zeke chuckled. "Don' be tryin' thet on the Bannocks up in Raft River Country! We'll be in their terr'tory soon."

Abby edged away from the camp fire circle, taking a good look around for Indians beyond their wagon circle in the moonlit night. Stars blanketed the sky all around. Cattle lowed as they settled for the night, guards called to each other around the corral circle, and coyotes howled eerily in the distance. She returned to her wagon while the others sang their "hymns to sleep by."

When Daniel returned Rena to their wagon, Abby still lay awake on her featherbed mattress. She tried not to hear their murmurings. Did he kiss Rena as passionately as he had her that day in the barn? The thought haunted her in and out of sleep all night long.

The next morning during the worship service, special prayers were made by the Oregon contingent for those bound for California, and prayers from the California contingent for those heading toward Oregon.

Forty miles later, the groups parted at the Raft River, their members shaking hands solemnly. Gone was the spirit of audacious adventurers setting out on a lark. As the wagons pulled away, the women rallied slightly, calling out to each other "Now be sure to write so we know how you came out!" and "Maybe we'll see you again!" and "Be sure to come fer a visit!"

Betsy asked, "Do you think we'll ever see them again?"

Abby shook her head sadly. "I don't think it's likely."

"There are only thirteen wagons of us now," Betsy said.

"We'll manage," Abby replied. "We have to."

The California Trail rose southward alongside the Raft River, staying close to a stream, then veered off along another stream. They made camp that night in the City of Rocks, feeling diminished in numbers and by the mountain spires towering over them. After dinner, Abby and Betsy sketched the twin spires high above their small circle of thirteen wagons, naming their sketches *Cathedral Rocks*.

During the next week, the trail dropped into a wide valley, then climbed another great divide and dropped again, this time abruptly to Goose Creek. At night, Indian fires flared on the mountains. The Talbot invalids, who now included Martha, seemed to rally during their next five days' journey toward the southwest. Aunt Jessica said, "It seems to me that the good Lord meant settlers to come this way. Look at how easy South Pass was through the Rockies, and now we have streams all through this dry, rough country. There's water for us and grass for the stock."

"It does seem providential," Benjamin Talbot agreed. "I

pray that He leads us as He did Moses through Egypt and, if there is a Red Sea for us, that He will part it."

It was now, he said, about four hundred miles to the California Mountains, most of it along the Humboldt River. Abby continued to sketch when she could, although for the most part it was uninteresting country: grass along the streams and desertlike uplands with scatterings of dry grass, sagebrush, and prickly pear cactus. Occasionally the hunting parties brought in an antelope, but more often they shot jack rabbits, which Sarah said had to be "stewed to death."

"Watch out fer the Diggers," Zeke warned about the next group of Indians. "They're scavengers, 'n they'll steal the shirt off yer back. Ain't got no horses, 'n they live in the dirt. Worse, they'll eat anythin' they lay a hand on, even grasshoppers 'n rats."

Abby gulped at the thought. "Perhaps they won't notice such a small company of us."

"They know all thet happens here," Zeke said.

Before the day was out, one of the small desert tribes descended upon them, peering from around rocks and clumps of sagebrush. Occasionally Abby caught glimpses of the squalid creatures and shivered. Dirty as she was herself, their filth and half nakedness was appalling. She kept Betsy close to her as they walked alongside Thad and the oxen.

"Pretend they ain't there!" Zeke admonished as he rode his horse along the column of wagons, "but keep yer eyes on 'em, too."

When they made their corral that night, it became obvious that they had not watched closely enough. Two cattle were missing. One of the bull whackers shouted, "We ought to shoot them Diggers . . . teach 'em a good lesson!"

"They have to eat, too," Aunt Jessica replied. "They don't know better, and we have to forgive them."

The river and the days seemed endless as they trudged alongside the wagons. As the week went on, the emigrants became increasingly disenchanted with the Humboldt River, which Horace Litmer renamed the "Humbug." "It doesn't even warrant the appellation river," he said heatedly, "not after one's seen the Ohio or the Mississippi, or even the Missouri. It doesn't run like a river, and no one has seen a single fish in it, nor any other living thing!"

Abby tended to agree. Every day there was less grass for their oxen and the water turned more sulfurous, a sickly white color. Along it, they had come into a vast wasteland, a region of sage, rabbit bush, and scrubby willows along the riverbank.

Uncle Benjamin told them to add a few drops of lemon acid to the water to render it palatable, but Abby could still scarcely swallow it.

As they trekked onward, groups of Diggers continued to dog them. They snatched the emigrants' newly washed clothing from the banks of the Humboldt, and on one dark night, two horses. Several nights later, they stole more cattle. They were difficult to spot, roaming like specters around the edges of the wagon train.

At dawn one day Rena murmured from her bed in the wagon, "I would like to tell those Indians about the Lord . . . about how much He loves them."

"Oh, Rena, they wouldn't understand," Abby responded. She felt her cousin's forehead and drew back in shock. It had never been this hot!

She pulled on her wrapper and rushed outside into the glimmering dawn. Dipping a compress cloth into the water barrel, she was dismayed to find the water lukewarm. She wrung out the cloth and hurried back into the wagon, folding it for Rena's brow. "Let me wash your arms and legs to cool you off, Rena."

"I don't like to be such a bother," Rena murmured.

Abby peered outside at the emigrants sleeping on their bedrolls near the wagons and was grateful that others were beginning to stir. The cattle guards were riding in, and here came Betsy out of the next wagon to sit on one of the folding stools to braid her hair.

"Betsy!" Abby whispered, "please get us a bucket of cold river water. Rena has a fever again!"

Betsy stopped braiding her hair and jumped to her feet, her eyes widening with worry. "I'll hurry!" She grabbed a bucket and ran out toward the river.

Abby changed into her blue calico dress, keeping an eye on Rena. In the light of the rising sun, she saw that her cousin's lovely face was bright red.

Rena opened her eyes, and they were far too bright, too glazed. "Abby, dear," she began in a faraway voice, "if I go on to be with the Lord . . . promise you'll read the last pages of my diary."

Abby caught her breath in despair. "Oh, Rena! What a thing to say! You're not going to—"

"Promise you'll read them," Rena pleaded weakly. Her pale blonde hair spread across the pillow and a tender smile touched her lips. "I love you so much, Abby."

Abby choked back a sob. "I promise. But you aren't— aren't going to—leave." She fell on her knees and placed her face against Rena's flaming hot cheek. "Oh, Rena, I may not have always shown it, but I do love you!"

Rena's eyes glowed. "I know you do."

They gazed at each other for a long moment, and Abby's mouth trembled. "Oh, Rena, please get well!"

Her cousin nodded slighty. "Are the lilac and rose roots still moist?"

Abby blinked at the odd question. "Yes, I'm sure they are again now that we're at the river."

After a long silence Rena murmured, "I'd like to talk with Daniel."

Abby rose to her feet in anguish. She peered out the front of the wagon and spotted him. "Daniel!" she called out, waving frantically for him to come, and noting the instant apprehension on his face.

As he rode up she could scarcely summon the words, "Rena's asked to see you. She's awfully feverish."

"I see."

Dismounting, he quickly tied the horse's reins to the nearby wagon wheel.

Abby clambered down from the wagon. "I sent Betsy for cooler water from the river so I can bathe Rena." It suddenly seemed an indecent thing for her to mention to the man who was going to—marry Rena, and she flushed. "I—I think I'd better get Aunt Jessica to help."

Daniel removed his wide-brimmed hat and climbed up into the wagon. "I'll stay with Rena until you return."

Abby felt uncertain of what people might say of the two of them in the wagon together, but this was no time for niceties. She hurried to the next wagon. "Aunt Jessica?" It was empty. Everyone was beginning to scurry about the camp to get ready for breakfast and the day's trek. She finally spotted her aunt running up from the riverbank with Betsy and Sarah.

"Aunt Jessica!" she called out and ran out to meet them.

"Betsy said that Rena's fever is back," her aunt gasped.

"She's terribly hot!" Abby took the water buckets from her aunt. "I'm sure she's never been this bad before."

"I'll help you bathe her," her aunt said. "Betsy, would you please help Sarah prepare breakfast? And ask your father to stop by Rena's wagon."

"Yes," Betsy replied, her green eyes filling with tears. At the wagon she asked, "Can I see Reenie, too . . . before—before—"

Aunt Jessica gave her a hug. "Just as soon as we get her temperature down. Now, don't you worry, this fever comes and goes with her."

Betsy appeared no more reassured than Abby felt.

Daniel stepped down from the wagon, looking grim. "I'll ask someone else to scout for me today." He unwound his horses' reins from the wagon wheel and led her away, his other hand on Betsy's small back. "Come on, Betsy," he said to her, "give me a hand with my horse first."

Betsy managed a tearful smile up at Daniel, and Abby fought back sobs.

Inside the wagon, she and Aunt Jessica constantly changed the wet compresses on Rena's brow and bathed her face, arms, and legs with the cool water while Rena slipped in and out of consciousness.

Before long Jenny arrived with more compresses and to offer her assistance, and then Martha, whose maternal condition made it difficult for her to walk, let alone climb up into the wagon. Aunt Jessica opened the back canvas flap of the wagon so they might be near Rena. Martha urged, "You have to get over this fever, Rena. You have to help train my new baby."

And Jenny simply whispered, "Oh, please get well. Please, Rena!"

Rena smiled at them with a wondrous love.

After a while Benjamin Talbot came to hold his daughter's hand. His eyes filled with tears. "Now, Rena, you've got to set yourself on getting well."

Her lashes fluttered and she looked up at her father.

"You're such a good and loving father," she whispered.

Benjamin Talbot asked, "How could anyone not love you?"

She closed her eyes in happiness.

"Maybe we shouldn't have come West after all," he said.

Rena shook her head. "No doubts now. We were to come."

Aunt Jessica said, "Please, no more. Rena must rest."

Benjamin nodded and led Martha and Jenny away, while hot tears slipped down Abby's cheeks.

At length Seth Thompson stopped by, Bible in hand. "May I talk to her? Daniel suggested I come."

"Yes, of course, Seth," Aunt Jessica said.

"Rena?" He leaned in from the back of the wagon and took her hot hand in his.

She stirred at his voice, and her eyes fluttered open toward him. "Seth," she whispered, "my dear friend."

He blinked hard and rested his Bible on the wagon gate. "I thought you might like me to read a bit to you."

She closed her eyes and smiled. "Only after . . . I tell you that I knew . . . I knew . . . Daniel did, too."

Knew what? Abby wondered. She quickly looked away from the pastor, who wiped his eyes, too. It was a while before he could continue. "Would you like to hear something from the Psalms?"

"Please . . . John . . . 3."

After a slight hesitation, Seth Thompson found the page, then closed his eyes in prayer before reading. "There was a man of the Pharisees, named Nicodemus, a ruler of the Jews: The same came to Jesus by night, and said unto him, Rabbi, we know that thou art a teacher come from God: for no man can do these miracles that thou doest, except God be with him."

The pastor glanced at Rena thoughtfully, then down at his Bible again. "Jesus answered and said unto him, Verily, verily, I say unto thee, Except a man be born again, he cannot see the kingdom of God."

And what does that mean, to be born again? Abby wondered as she continued to bathe Rena's hot arms.

Seth read, "Nicodemus saith unto him, How can a man be born when he is old? can he enter the second time into his mother's womb, and be born?"

"Jesus answered, Verily, verily, I say unto thee, Except a man be born of water and of the Spirit, he cannot enter into the kingdom of God. That which is born of the flesh is flesh; and that which is born of the Spirit is spirit. Marvel not that I said unto thee, Ye must be born again."

Rena murmured, "Thank you."

Seth nodded, his voice tremulous. "It is my great, great pleasure, my dear Rena. You—you'd better rest now." He turned quickly, his head bowed as he walked away.

Betsy appeared at the back of the wagon. She whispered with a worried glance at Rena's labored breath, "Papa said that I might come now."

Aunt Jessica nodded.

If anything, Rena was even hotter. Abby thought it impossible for a person's body to become so hot.

Betsy's lips trembled. "Oh, Reenie," she whispered, "I love you so."

Rena's lashes fluttered again, her eyes turning to Betsy. Her voice was as soft as the sound of a falling leaf, "I love you, Betsy."

At length Daniel and Jeremy and Luke stopped by, and Rena murmured "I love you" to each of them, to Abby, to Aunt Jessica. She seemed compelled to give out love, and her words touched them like dewy rose petals, even in the

248

morning heat. Suddenly her body shuddered and was still.

Abby felt her eyes widening. "Is she—?"

Her aunt felt Rena's heart and shook her head.

"Not yet," Daniel said wretchedly and turned away. "Not yet."

As wagon train captain, there was nothing for Uncle Benjamin to do but to keep the company moving along, and Zeke Wilkes called them into position for him and bellowed, "Wagons, ho-o!"

Aunt Jessica insisted she remain in the bouncing wagon with Rena, and Abby and Betsy walked disconsolately at its side.

They glanced occasionally toward the Humboldt Mountains, but around them all was desolation—sagebrush and dust.

When they stopped for the nooning, Abby hurried to help Aunt Jessica down from the wagon, for she could not climb down herself. Her wrinkled face was gaunt yet composed, and Abby could not bring herself to inquire.

"How is Reenie?" Betsy asked.

Aunt Jessica's eyes closed. "Rena's spirit has been released from her body to be with the Lord."

"No!" Abby cried, throwing herself into her aunt's arms. A sob escaped as if from the depths of her soul, then another and another until it seemed she might never stop weeping.

She had secretly wished for Rena's death. She had secretly wished it, even though she had never admitted it. She had wished it so she might have Daniel for herself.

"Abby, you mustn't take this so hard," Aunt Jessica said, patting her shoulder. "Rena's spirit is with the Lord. God has promised that to those who believe in His Son as their Savior."

Abby shook her head, feeling as desolate as this hideous

wilderness. As much as she loved Rena, something dark and hateful within her had wanted her to be dead. And now because of that terrible, terrible wish, she could never in good conscience marry Daniel—not that he was asking. Far better if she were dead instead of Rena.

18

Benjamin Talbot stood at the hot desert grave side, hat in hand, head bowed in the sunshine. The entire company stood around the shallow grave, and he tried to listen as Seth Thompson gave the service. He ended with the wondrous words of the Lord. "I am the resurrection, and the life: he that believeth in me, though he were dead, yet shall he live: And whosoever liveth and believeth in me shall never die."

The words brought to mind other times Benjamin had heard them pronounced over the dead: over his mother and father, over Elizabeth and the three little ones who were buried near her. Someday they would be pronounced over him. This time it was for Rena, one of the loveliest daughters who had ever trod the earth. *Lord, was I wrong in allowing her to come on such an arduous journey?* he asked. *Was I wrong?*

Seth had paused for silent prayer, and in the silence the answer came for Benjamin: *Go ye into all the world, and preach the gospel to every creature. He that believeth and is baptized shall be saved; but he that believeth not shall be damned.*

Yes, that was what Rena had wanted, too, to take God's love westward. The pain in Benjamin's heart eased, and his spirit lifted. *Thank You, Lord,* he replied.

Seth spoke to the others. "Rena's father wishes to say a

251

few words now to us. Benjamin?"

Nearby, he heard Abby sob. *Lord,* he prayed, *touch her heart, touch her heart.*

He cleared his throat and began to speak, his voice so strong it seemed to fill the desert air around them. "We only had Rena here on earth for eighteen years," he said to his fellow emigrants, "but she was a blessing every day of those years. She was so like my wife, Elizabeth, in appearance and in spirit that she helped keep her memory alive, for which I am most grateful." He stopped for a moment.

"I am pondering what Rena might have me say here, over her grave." He closed his eyes and recalled his last moments with his daughter. "Tell them I love them . . . yes, I believe that's what she would have me to say . . . tell others how much Christ loves them. He loves you . . . He loves you . . . He wants you to know Him."

He paused, then knew exactly how Rena would have him end her burial service. "My friends, try to remember Rena singing those last verses of 'Amazing Grace.' Close your eyes and try to remember her singing them at church or that Sunday by the creek."

Then he began to speak the words, seeing her in his own mind's eye:

"When we've been there ten thousand years,
Bright shining as the sun,
We've no less days to sing God's praise
Than when we first begun."

"Let us sing the final verse together," he suggested, "just as Rena did."

In unison they sang in broken voices across the desert, "Praise God, praise God, praise God, praise God. . . ."

Tears rolled down his cheeks. It wasn't the first time, nor would it be the last time he'd weep, he thought. Despite the tears and his broken voice, his spirit lifted him beyond grief and he continued to praise his God.

Trembling, Abby stood with the Talbots at Rena's desert grave site while everyone sang. She could not get a word out, not a word or a note. This can't be! she thought, squinting into the blazing sunshine. How can these people sing? And how can Uncle Benjamin endure speaking right over her body, even singing himself?

The open grave alongside the trail was unreal, a nightmare; indeed, everything in the blinding sunshine appeared surrealistic. She sensed that Digger Indians lurked around them, ready to pounce from nearby clumps of sagebrush. We can't leave Rena here! her mind screamed at the men as they placed her cousin's blanket-shrouded body in the dusty grave. We can't leave Rena here! In the monstrousness of it all, the words refused to travel from her mind to her tongue.

Finally she clamped upon Seth Thompson's words: Ashes to ashes, dust to dust. That, at least, was fitting for this dismal place.

As the men did their grim duty, throwing shovelfuls of desert sand into the grave, Abby turned away with great gulping sobs. Aunt Jessica tried to soothe her, but to no avail. When Abby at last caught her breath, she saw that she alone was so overcome by grief. The Talbots looked saddened, but not as heartbroken as she. A memory surfaced of Daniel saying, "You must be terrified of death."

That was not the case here! She was only grieving over Rena. How could the others already be so composed? Perhaps they had not loved Rena so deeply.

Betsy turned to Abby. "We can't have a headstone for Reenie."

"And why is that?" Abby asked so sharply that her small cousin drew back.

"It's the Diggers . . . they dig up bodies for clothes."

Abby shuddered, imagining them digging up Rena's body. "And Rena wanted to tell those creatures how much God loved them!"

"She was always full of love," Betsy responded.

"And look at how she was repaid!"

When the grave was filled, Daniel, Luke, and Jeremy planted sagebrush over it and scattered sand around until the ground appeared as undisturbed as the surrounding desert.

Abby returned to camp, unable to endure another instant at the grave site.

At last Zeke summoned the wagons into position for Benjamin Talbot again, then bellowed the familiar "Wagons, ho-o!"

Walking alongside the oxen, Abby stared out at the landscape. This entire desolate landscape along the Humboldt with its sagebrush, patchy grass, and dust was Rena's grave. This is what she would remember when she thought of Rena—a beautiful young woman who had been killed by this loathsome land and this senseless trek west. If only the sun would obliterate her memory of this place.

That night Martha gave birth to a daughter and named her Rena. The tiny baby, with its thick black hair, bore no resemblance to the Rena everyone had loved.

For days they crossed the strange terrain, and the thought constantly crossed Abby's mind that death awaited all of them in unseen dangers at every bend of the trail. Sometimes the river snaked off into impassable canyons, and the trail swung over sage-covered bluffs for miles before they could return to the poor excuse of a river. High water forced them to take further detours. Often they had to cross the river to trek for a few miles, and then ford back again.

A week after Rena's funeral, Abby was washing clothes in the river water when Daniel appeared nearby. She bristled at the sight of him, turning her back. *Stay away from me,* she thought, *I will not be hurt again!*

"It's dangerous for you to be alone here with the Diggers always about," he said.

"Jenny was washing clothes with me just minutes ago."

"She told me you wanted to be here alone," he replied. "You know it's not safe."

Abby shrugged with attempted indifference.

"I know you miss Rena, too," he said, "but something else must be wrong. What's happened to make you so unhappy, Abby?"

She no longer cared how beautiful her name sounded from his lips; she no longer cared about anything. "All of you who wanted to come on this trip are insane!" she flung at him, half believing it.

"Perhaps you're right, in a sense," he replied.

She wrung the alkaline water from her yellow calico dress and decided not to respond. Casting a sidelong glance, she saw he had found a comfortable place to sit on the bank and watch her. If she didn't have to finish her washing, she would depart with dispatch.

"It's this desert wilderness that makes everyone seem mad," he said, then gave a small smile. "Maybe it's not all bad either. Dryden said, 'Great wits are sure to madness near allied . . . and thin partitions do their bounds divide.' "

Abby retorted, "Great wits have nothing to do with it. I am talking about out-and-out insanity."

Daniel did not reply.

"Surely with your vast store of quotations you must have something else to say."

He looked out across the river. "I was thinking that the difference between an insane man and a fool is said to be that the fool draws a wrong conclusion from a right principle, while an insane person draws a just inference from a false principle."

Perhaps that explained why Christians seemed so different, Abby mused. They drew their conclusions from a different set of principles.

The river meandered sluggishly past them, its stench putrid. After a while Daniel spoke into the silence, "What are you thinking about so seriously?"

She scrubbed at the dirtied hem of her dress. "Aunt Jessica told me when I first moved to Independence how delicate Rena's health was. It only seems inevitable that she would die on a trip like this."

"Rena came for a cause far greater than herself."

"For God?" Abby asked angrily.

"Yes, in most part for God."

You are insane, every one of you! she thought again, furiously wringing out the dress. She tossed it into the basket on top of the rest of her washing.

Daniel rose. "Here, let me help you."

Abby grabbed the basket and jerked it from him. "You are all mad!" she cried as she hurried away. "And I am equally so to have traveled with you!"

After that encounter, Daniel appeared to avoid her as determinedly as she attempted to avoid him. Yet when she remembered how rudely she had treated him, her eyes filled with tears of regret. Fortunately in the awful August heat, tears dried immediately. In any event, too many barriers stood between them now—Rena, Daniel's faith. . . . Just recently Seth Thompson had preached that Christians should not be yoked in marriage to unbelievers, and it seemed to

Abby that he had been speaking to Daniel and her. Well, Seth Thompson could save his breath as far as she was concerned!

The Humboldt River's water deteriorated with every mile, becoming increasingly tepid and alkaline. The water's color changed from milky-white to yellowish-green as it seeped into marshes and finally into the evil-smelling sink. To Abby's mind, each of them had deteriorated just as badly, barely struggling along, hunger their constant companion.

After their two-day rest at the sink, they trekked through a dry stretch of fifteen miles to camp by a pond of brackish water. "This be the last grass 'n water 'til we pull through Forty-Mile Desert," Zeke Wilkes warned. "Fill yer water barrels 'n cut all the grass ye can fer the stock."

They are all mad, Abby thought again, *and I am going mad, too.* Not that madness here was unique. The captain of a wagon train they had passed told of several of his people who had gone insane. "An' if they ain't all crazy now, they will be in Forty-Mile Desert!"

If the Humboldt Sink was terrible, the Forty-Mile Desert was hideous. Leveling out in all directions and encrusted with white alkaline, the earth was baked hard. Each step seared their feet, and every parched day stretched out to an unbearable eternity. A saliva pebble under Abby's tongue scarcely helped. When she attempted to look at the dazzling horizon, her eyes swam and dots danced across the burning landscape. No living thing showed itself, neither lizard nor Digger Indian.

Daniel appeared before her out of the burning sunset one evening with a diffident nod of greeting. "Abby, I fear that Marigold and Daisy are too weakened—"

"Then shoot them!" she replied coldly.

He frowned. "I am going to have to."

"Then be done with it! It does not surprise me at all!"

This time when the shots rang out, she scarcely flinched.

Walking alongside the oxen one scorching afternoon, her thoughts turned for relief to memories of New York and then to Miss Sheffield's School and to Rose. She envisioned again their last evening together when they were to practice for the musicale in the ballroom. How beautiful all of the girls had looked in their colorful gowns. What a carefree existence they'd enjoyed until Daniel and Uncle Benjamin arrived and her fine life had been ruined. What was it Rose had said that night in their room? "Place it in God's hands. . . ."

Rose reminded her of Rena with her faith. What if she could be so certain of God? Abby wondered. She peered out into the glaring light. "Where are You, God?" she cried. "Where are You?"

Thad turned back from driving the oxen and shot a peculiar look at her, but she simply returned his stare. Who cared what he and the others thought!

Not long afterward, Betsy joined her again, probably sent by Aunt Jessica. They walked along together, saying little, simply enduring.

One afternoon Betsy cried, "Look . . . a lake! Look at the trees and the blue water!"

Abby said wearily, "Close your eyes and then open them again."

Betsy reluctantly obeyed. "It's gone. . . ."

"Another mirage. Like so much in life."

Abby noted the dejection on Betsy's face. She was no longer the bright, cheery girl who had met her with such enthusiasm that first night in Independence—and just as well. Now she would not become disappointed in what life had to offer.

When they reached the hot springs gushing into the air, Horace shouted wild-eyed, "I'm turning back! No one will read my newspaper in such a god-forsaken place!"

"Educated people live in Buena Vista," Daniel assured him. "It is not like this at all. It's on the Bay of San Francisco, with cool ocean breezes."

"I don't believe you!" Horace replied as he stared at the boiling geysers. "No one told us how terrible this trip would be . . . about this desert . . . water boiling from the earth! Nobody warned us . . . ."

"None of us has ever been in this desert before except Zeke," Daniel explained.

"I'm turning back . . . turning back!" Horace cried.

At last Benjamin Talbot convinced him to bear up one more day and continued to persuade him, day after day.

Abby carried Horace's supper to him one evening. His lantern jaw hung slack, and his green eyes vacillated from vacant to wild. His breakdown was her fault in part, too, she told herself. He had been attracted to her, and she had rebuffed him. Love again. Love brought nothing but woe. How much better to remain cold and sealed off, drawing deep into the recesses of one's self.

The next day they traveled in silence across a sandy ridge, the sand becoming deeper and deeper until Sarah's two lead oxen sank knee deep. They struggled in the hot sand, bellowing hideously, their legs broken.

Zeke's rifle shots sounded again.

Sarah's wagon had sunk to the axle, which snapped. "It's past fixin'," Zeke decided and helped Sarah unload her belongings into Abby's wagon. Her two remaining oxen were joined with Abby's, and they left the wagon behind. As they moved on, Abby glanced back at it. The party had lost three other oxen, too, and the hulks of five dead oxen and Sarah's wagon lay half sunken in the desert graveyard.

"Don't matter anyhow," Sarah said as she plodded along

beside her.

Travel was easier on the sagebrush-covered downgrade, and finally Abby caught sight of cottonwoods along a river. Another mirage, she warned herself morosely, but it was real. The Truckee River . . . California! Or at least it was nearby since no one knew precisely where the territory began.

Abby's spirits lifted, along with those of her traveling companions. When the oxen scented the river, there was no stopping them as they rushed for the water.

The emigrants rested and repaired the wagons all day Friday while the oxen grazed. That evening after their rabbit stew, Seth Thompson announced, "We will be having our first wedding tomorrow evening. Sarah and Zeke will marry. They invite you to attend the ceremony."

Some of them raised a feeble but surprised cheer, and the women took stock of provisions they could pool for the wedding supper. There was no sugar, and only the Schmitts had flour, a small amount. "Might be deer hereabouts," one of the men said, and they formed a hunting party.

Abby pondered Sarah's decision. Why would she marry the old guide? The rest of them had become gaunt, but once-massive Sarah looked rather pretty now. Abby's curiosity must have been apparent for Sarah confided, "Ain't no good bein' alone at night, 'n Zeke wants to settle. He's got a ranch in California fer runnin' cattle."

The wedding ceremony took place alongside the swift Truckee River. Benjamin Talbot gave Sarah away again, and Betsy held the gold ring—the very wedding ring that Samuel had given to Sarah in January. Zeke had trimmed his gray beard and hair again and wore his cleanest buckskin outfit. Sarah wore her old white wedding dress, the seams taken in considerably; her sun-bleached hair was coiled in her usual bun at the nape of her neck. She looked so lovely that Zeke seemed dazzled. Standing at his side, Sarah repeated the vows. "I, Sarah, take thee, Ezekiel, to be my wedded husband. . . ."

Abby felt Daniel's eyes upon her and ignored him. There was nothing for them now. Nothing.

She turned her attention to the Talbot family, all with clean hair and wearing clean clothing again. How they had changed since Sarah's first wedding. Aunt Jessica's gaunt face was deeply lined; Uncle Benjamin's hair nearly white; Betsy had grown taller, thin, and serious; Jenny and Jeremy appeared saddened; Martha held her new baby while Luke held the hands of the twins, quieter now. The most dire change, of course, was Rena's absence.

Seth Thompson pronounced the familiar words: "Forasmuch as Ezekiel and Sarah have consented together in holy wedlock, and have witnessed the same before God and this company, and hereto have pledged their faith each to the other. . . ."

After the final prayer, Zeke kissed his bride with unabashed pleasure. The hunters had brought down a deer, and for the wedding supper there were roasted venison, beans, wild greens, and ten small biscuits. Afterwards they sang, and Andre Jacqueman played his fiddle.

Sarah moved to Zeke's tent, and Abby thought again of the hired girl's words, "Ain't no good bein' alone nights." What would it be like to be held in Daniel's arms? she reflected for an instant, then turned away the torturous thought.

19

They toiled into the California Mountains along the Truckee River for over a week. It was steady uphill work all the way, though there were water and grass again for the stock. The scenery changed from sagebrush and scrubby pines to patches of forest as they crossed and recrossed the boulder-strewn river, shivering in the icy water, fighting its swift current. They climbed higher and higher into the mountains. At nine thousand feet, they labored for breath and tired quickly. The route was the most precipitous they had traveled, and the men and oxen strained in their efforts to lift the wagons up the nearly vertical mountain walls. High above them snowcapped peaks rose, even now in early September.

Finally they eased the wagons down into Bear Valley by snubbing ropes around the trees. Progress was slow. Each day they met harrowing obstacles. The California Mountains were beautiful with their sheer passes and gleaming crags above, but Abby no longer cared for their beauty, nor for anything else.

When the sun began to set at their camp in Emigrant Gap, she sat on her wagon seat, lonely and exhausted. She had never in all of her life felt so wrenchingly alone. Life offered nothing. It seemed senseless to carry on at all. Beyond tears, her despair drew her down into darkness, a vast black wilderness that entangled her mind and her soul.

From the depths of despondency something within her recalled Rose's words: "Place it in God's hands. . . ."

And then Rena—What was it that Rena had asked Seth to read from his Bible? She reached for Rena's Bible and reluctantly opened it to the ribbon marker. Yes, here it was, underlined. She read in the light of the sunset. "There was a man of the Pharisees, named Nicodemus, a ruler of the Jews: The same came to Jesus by night, and said unto him, Rabbi, we know that thou art a teacher come from God; for no man can do these miracles that thou doest, except God be with him. Jesus answered and said unto him, Verily, verily, I say unto thee, Except a man be born again, he cannot see the kingdom of God. "

Abby thumbed through the pages, reading Rena's underlined words. "For God so loved the world, that he gave his only begotten Son, that whosoever believeth in him should not perish, but have everlasting life."

The words seemed alive, and she read on, page after page, drawn along by she knew not what, only that it seemed possible she might discover wisdom in these pages . . . that she might even discover the purpose of her life. "Jesus saith unto him, I am the way, the truth, and the life; no man cometh unto the Father, but by me."

She was weary of resentments, despair, and fear. She had struggled and debated and doubted for so long now, and suddenly she simply wanted to see if God were real, if the Gospel were true. Now is the time, a small still voice within her seemed to say. Now is the time.

She recalled Seth Thompson's preaching that the Holy Spirit would not strive forever with one to come to God.

No! You must not give in to this, the familiar voice of despair within her protested.

Now is the time, the softer, loving voice urged.

She remembered Daniel's words when she first heard of the family scandal. "You must forgive them . . . your father, your mother, the woman. You must forgive them."

And the loving voice within her echoed his words: *You must forgive them if you want to know God.*

The strident voice protested, *It's entirely irrational!*

She ignored it. "I want to forgive them," she declared. Then by an act of will she added, "I do forgive them."

A tear slid down her cheek, and her resistance began to crumble. Her lips trembled as she gazed out toward the sunset and said, "Oh, Lord Jesus, I do repent of my sins—my pride, my dark wishes and jealousy about Rena. I want this new birth. I want to believe. I give my life to Thee . . . make of me what Thou wilt."

She caught a deep breath and let the air out slowly, then awaited an answer—a great voice from the clouds lying across the sunset . . . lightning striking a nearby pine tree . . . .

For a long time there was only the chirping of birds in the pines, then slowly, slowly she felt peace flow into her heart, peace as she had never known it, peace that surpassed understanding. As she stood there, the trees became greener and the mountains became beautiful beyond belief. The very air glistened, and she felt compelled to fall to her knees. Thanksgiving welled up within her and flowed from her heart. "Thank Thee! Oh, thank Thee!" she prayed, her arms upraised to God as if in an ancient rite.

Sudden joy burst through her like a golden radiance, and she glowed with His love, feeling at one with the glorious sunset, at one with the universe. She wished that she might go on with Him like this forever, that her spirit might always be with Him. She realized that this was the fulfillment she had always yearned for—knowing Him. The emptiness within her was at last overflowing with joy. She was scarcely aware that darkness fell, and that night in her wagon she was so pervaded with His love that she fell asleep murmuring her Savior's name.

The next morning Abby awakened with the first light of dawn. Peering out the puckering-string hole at the back of the wagon, she marveled at the mountains and the sky's magnificence. She felt wonderfully refreshed and overflowing with joy. It was Sunday and, though she had always appreciated the day for its rest, she had never looked forward this eagerly to their morning services. Now expectation beamed around her like the sun's morning rays. Rough travel and the unknown still lay ahead, but now the prospect—the entire prospect of life—promised excitement and adventure.

She slipped into her favorite blue calico dress and swept back her hair into a chignon. Peering into her small mirror, she saw that her eyes were no longer dull, but lively with anticipation.

She stepped out of the wagon. The mountainsides of Emigrant Gap surrounded her, lush and green with tall ponderosa and juniper and sugar pine, their fragrance filling the air. Around them were great boulders, some larger than her family's old mansion on Union Square. She hurried to the stream and washed her face in the cool, clear water, then set out to climb a boulder for the sheer pleasure of it.

Later, as she helped Sarah get breakfast, Betsy asked, "What's happened to you?"

Abby's joy bubbled out in laughter. "Something wonderful!" She realized that Daniel had taken note of it, too, and she smiled at the bewilderment on his face.

After breakfast she returned to her wagon and recalled Rena's final request: to read the last few pages of her diary. It wasn't that she'd forgotten. She'd picked it up earlier and, overcome by grief and anger, had put it away without reading. It would just be more of Rena's "preaching" anyway, she'd thought, and she didn't want to hear another word about God.

Now Abby opened Rena's trunk and took out the diary from her cousin's belongings. On the last pages of the bound book, she saw that Rena had written a letter to her. To think that she'd been foremost in Rena's thoughts just before her death . . . to think that Rena had cared for her this much! Tears of gratitude stung her eyes, and she had to calm herself to read.

Along the Humboldt River
Dearest Abby,

I love you so very much, and I know your feelings about me must be very confused, for I realize that you are deeply in love with Daniel. As you have probably guessed, everyone has always thought that he and I would someday marry. The peculiar thing is that I have always known I would never marry at all. I am certain Daniel knows it, too, for he has never proposed or even hinted about marriage. We love each other dearly, but it is simply a great Christian love between a brother and sister who love the Lord.

I shall try to explain. When I was a sickly and difficult child, it was Daniel who told me about Christ's dying upon the cross for our sins so that He might lead us back to our heavenly Father. Although my parents were devout believers, it was Daniel who showed me the way, the truth, and the life eternal. This is our great bond.

267

I know Daniel loves you, but he knows—as Seth preached last Sunday—that believers should not be yoked to unbelievers. And so I pray for your salvation every day. When you have found the Lord—for I know in my spirit that you will—you must never allow my memory to stand between the two of you.

In this past year, I have known I would not live much longer. Now it appears I will not finish this journey, though I did so want to help carry God's love westward. Do not grieve for me, my dear cousin, for I rejoice at being with the Lord in glory.

With His love,

Rena

Abby reread the letter, tears streaming down her cheeks. Rena had indeed carried God's love westward to the very last moment. In retrospect, it was Rena's final request for Seth to read about being born again that especially touched Abby's heart, for she knew now that Rena had done it for her.

Oh, Lord, Abby prayed, *help me to carry Thy banner in Rena's place. Help me to carry it to the very last instant of my life on earth, too!*

As for Daniel, having him love her no longer seemed of such overwhelming importance. *I place that in Thy hands, Lord,* it occurred to her to pray. *I place that in Thy hands.*

On the way to the wooded site Seth had chosen for their Sunday morning service, Abby gathered up wildflowers. She arrived long before the others and arranged the flowers reverently at the base of the cross, praising God for His love. The fragrance of pines drifted on the soft morning breeze, and birds sang from all around the wooded glen. After a while she became aware of someone's presence, and she knew in her spirit who it was. She turned.

Daniel beamed, approaching her with wonder. "You've found Him . . . you've found the Lord, haven't you?"

"Yes. How did you know?"

"I saw the joy and love all around you this morning . . . and when I arrived here to pray just minutes ago, there you were on your knees arranging flowers by the cross. I presume only those who love Him would do that."

As she looked at Daniel, at this good, godly man, it seemed that God was smiling upon them in the shafts of sunshine streaming through the pine trees.

"I've prayed for you every day, sometimes every hour," Daniel said. "I've never prayed so much for anyone . . . since the moment I met you in Miss Sheffield's sitting room and saw your life breaking up before you. I know now that I already loved you—" He faltered, coloring from the edges of his beard to his forehead.

"You loved me then?"

He nodded. "When we drove up to Miss Sheffield's, I had a premonition . . . and then when I saw you coming down the stairway at Miss Sheffield's, it seemed that God was saying 'This is the one, this is the one I have chosen for you!' "

"Oh, Daniel, you told me I must never say this to a man, but I love you, too! I love you!"

He caught her in his arms and for a long moment they simply gazed at each other. "God is so good, so wonderful. His timing is so perfect," Daniel exulted. "I couldn't be patient much longer! Will you marry me now, Abby . . . now . . . today . . . as soon as possible? I don't have a ring yet, but I do have a special gift for you." He took a soft leather pouch from his shirt pocket. From the pouch, he withdrew something wrapped in white silk.

As he removed the silk, Abby could scarcely believe her

eyes. Her grandmother's sapphire pendant glowed in the morning sunlight.

He said simply, "I always knew that someday I would return it to you."

"You purchased it, Daniel. You saved it for me."

"Yes." He smiled ironically. "And now I'm trying to tempt you into marrying me for it."

"Oh, Daniel! Oh, yes! But I would have accepted without anything."

He drew her into his arms again, and their lips met with sweet yearning and tenderness. In the fragrance of pines and the choir of bird song, it felt as though God had filled and surrounded them with His joy and love.

Benjamin Talbot announced the news after the morning worship service. "We have a special celebration tonight, a fitting conclusion to this last part of our trek. It gives me great pleasure to invite all of you to another wedding." He beamed. "It's Abby and Daniel!"

The Talbots cheered and hugged the two of them—the women "having guessed it all along" and the men stunned.

The emigrants threw themselves into wedding preparations with joyous abandon. Even Horace Litmer managed to congratulate the couple.

Later, Abby stood in Sarah's white wedding gown while Aunt Jessica delightedly pinned in the seams. Abby confided, "I can scarcely believe this is happening to me. It seems unreal . . . as unreal as our being only a week's travel from Sutter's Fort."

"I don't think any of us can believe that yet!" her aunt agreed. "Only one week and all downhill!"

After a moment Abby said, "I'm grateful that Horace's enthusiasm for printing a newspaper is returning."

Her aunt nodded as she fitted a side seam. Removing the pin from between her lips she said, "I've prayed for him for a long time."

"You must have been praying for me, too," Abby said. "You and Daniel and Rena and . . . who knows who else!"

"Only the entire family!"

Tremulous, Abby turned for her aunt to pin the other side seam. "I can never thank you enough."

"But you can. You can thank us by praying for others all of your life."

"I will. I promise I will."

Aunt Jessica added, "And you and the other girls could keep my roses and lilacs blooming wherever you go."

"We will! Oh, we surely will! And they'll always be known as Aunt Jessica's roses and Aunt Jessica's lilacs." Ignoring the pins in the wedding dress, she caught her aunt in a hug. "I promise for all of us."

When they returned to the fitting Abby said, "I'm going to miss everyone from the train." Sarah and Zeke would head south to his ranch; the Jacquemans, to the coast to plant vineyards; the Schmitts, north to farming land. The rest of them would settle near Sutter's Fort.

"We'll all miss each other after enduring this trek together." Aunt Jessica remarked, then smiled. "But let's set our minds on this wonderful wedding. Daniel told Benjamin that he doesn't have a ring, and I thought you might like to borrow mine until he can buy one. I'm finally thin enough to be able to take it off again, and it would give me such pleasure to see Daniel place it on your finger." She removed the gold ring and proffered it.

"Don't you think lending it will bring bad luck?"

Aunt Jessica laughed. "I don't believe in luck, Abby. I believe in the Lord. Here, my dear, why don't you try it on?"

That evening Abby stood with Benjamin Talbot on the edge of the piney glade, listening to Andre Jacqueman play the wedding prelude on his fiddle. She wore the refitted white gown, a splash of Fleur-de-lis in remembrance of Rose, and Grandmother Talbot's beautiful sapphire pendant. Her hand went to the pendant, and her heart filled with happiness again at Daniel's keeping it all of this time for her.

Uncle Benjamin whispered just above the music, "You do look like your Grandmother Talbot."

Abby remembered the lovely woman in the portrait, her eyes aglow with faith. "Do you think that she knows I have accepted the Lord as my Savior?"

"The Bible says 'there is joy in the presence of the angels of God over one sinner that repenteth.' I wouldn't be surprised if angels tell our loved ones."

The prelude came to its concluding notes, and her uncle gallantly offered his arm to escort her into the glade. "Ready now, Abby?"

"Oh, yes!" Her bouquet of wildflowers trembled slightly when the company began to sing the song she had requested, the words filling the air in the first rays of the sunset:

"Amazing grace! How sweet the sound,
That saved a wretch like me!
I once was lost, but now am found,
Was blind, but now I see."

As she and Uncle Benjamin made their way through the emigrants, she stored the beauty of the scene in her memory so that she might paint it someday—*Marrying Daniel*.

Standing at the front of the glade, he wore the handsome black suit she first saw him wearing that evening at Miss Sheffield's door; now he proudly awaited her beside the cross.

272

His blue eyes held hers as they both sang with the others:

" 'Twas grace that taught my heart to fear,
And grace my fears relieved;
How precious did that grace appear
The hour I first believed!"

Tears welled in Abby's eyes as she remembered Rena's melodious contralto rising through the others during the fourth verse, and it seemed that somehow she was among them again singing,

"When we've been there ten thousand years,
Bright shining as the sun,
We've no less days to sing God's praise
Than when we've first begun."

Seth Thompson began the service. "Dearly beloved, we are gathered together here in the sight of God, and in the presence of these witnesses, to join together this man and this woman in holy matrimony, which is an honorable estate, signifying unto us the mystical union which exists between Christ and His church—"

Abby and Daniel listened to the words as one. " . . . the union of husband and wife in heart, body, and mind . . . ."

Then Seth was saying to Uncle Benjamin, "Who giveth this woman to be married to this man?"

Benjamin Talbot replied with love, "I do."

Daniel repeated the familiar vows, his eyes overflowing with love. "I, Daniel, take thee, Abigail, to be my wedded wife, to have and to hold, from this day forward, for better, for worse, for richer, for poorer, in sickness and in health, to love and to cherish, as long as we both shall live."

And then she spoke, "I, Abigail, take thee, Daniel, to be my wedded husband, to have and to hold from this day forward. . . ."

It seemed only moments before Daniel placed Aunt

Jessica's gold wedding ring on Abby's finger.

"Those whom God hath joined together, let not man put asunder," Seth pronounced. He blessed them and looked at Daniel. "You may now kiss the bride."

Betsy beamed as she accepted the bouquet of wildflowers, and Abby turned to Daniel.

His strong arms encircled her, and his lips touched hers softly for an instant, then with such mounting and joyous passion that it did feel as though they were stealing fire from heaven. Surrounded and filled with love, they scarcely even heard the emigrants cheer.

ABOUT THE AUTHOR

Elaine Schulte is a wife, mother of two sons, and a writer whose short stories, articles, and novels have been widely published. She says, "I identify strongly with our pioneers, whether they were moving here from other countries or from New York or Missouri to new lands and new hopes. I can't imagine a more courageous, more adventurous people.

"In 1846, Walter Colton, the navy chaplain in California, said, 'The American people love valor, but they love religion also. They will confer their highest honors only on him who combines them both.'

"Many of the pioneers who traveled by covered wagon were valorous men and women of God. They spoke eloquently of their faith—and of their trials—in their diaries and autobiographies. I hope that my writing about them will help to counteract today's stories about the pioneers that dwell mainly on the sordid and ignore those people who were worthy of honor."

The Journey West is Schulte's first book in The California Pioneer Series about the Talbot family and their covered wagon journey to California in 1846.

The second book is *Golden Dreams*, which brings Abby's best friend, Rose Wilmington, around Cape Horn by clipper ship into the beginnings of California's gold rush.

The third novel is *Eternal Passage*, in which cousin Louisa Talbot Setter flees an abusive past in Virginia in 1849, enduring the dangers of sailing by gold ship and trekking through the jungle of Panama. Finally she sails by coastal steamer to California, only to learn that she cannot outrun her past.

Betsy Talbot is the heroine of the fourth novel, *With Wings as Eagles*, which takes place in the gold rush town of Oak Hill in 1854.